Host Government Agreements and the Law in the Energy Sector

The energy industry is a key source of growth stimulation for developing states. Understandably, developing states are eager to enter into petroleum investment contracts with international investors, with the expectation that this will benefit their countries. The domestic law of some developing states provides a welcoming investment environment in the form of guarantees and stability, while other states provide these opportunities by agreeing to investment contracts or treaties drafted by international organisations established to facilitate such agreements.

This book identifies the political risks, particularly of indirect expropriation, that arise from the unilateral actions of host governments during the lifespan of energy investment projects. Focusing on stabilisation clauses as a political risk management tool, this research-based study draws on comparative empirical evidence from Turkey and Azerbaijan to determine what influences host states to consent to the insertion of stabilisation clauses in long-term host government agreements. Proposing a framework for the role to be played by both internal forces and external forces, it examines political regimes and state guarantees to foreign investors in Azerbaijan and Turkey from a comparative perspective, assessing how effective internal factors in Azerbaijan and Turkey are in facilitating contractual stability in their energy investment projects.

Providing a comprehensive analysis of stabilisation clauses and the internal and external factors that compel host states to commit to them, this book will appeal to practitioners, students and scholars in international investment law and energy law.

Hakan Şahin is an Assistant Professor in Private International Law at Maltepe University, Istanbul. He regularly advises state entities as well as private clients on a range of issues, including international energy law, international arbitration and international investment law.

Routledge Research in Energy Law and Regulation

Regulation in the European Electricity Sector
Maciej M. Sokolowski

Law and Green Energy Policies
Roy Partain

Nuclear Energy Regulation, Risk and The Environment
Abdullah Al Faruque

Local Content Oil and Gas Law in Africa
Lessons from Nigeria and Beyond
Pereowei Subai

Host Government Agreements and the Law in the Energy Sector
The case of Azerbaijan and Turkey
Hakan Şahin

Host Government Agreements and the Law in the Energy Sector

The case of Azerbaijan and Turkey

Hakan Şahin

Routledge
Taylor & Francis Group
LONDON AND NEW YORK

First published 2019
by Routledge
2 Park Square, Milton Park, Abingdon, Oxon OX14 4RN

and by Routledge
605 Third Avenue, New York, NY 10017

First issued in paperback 2021

Routledge is an imprint of the Taylor & Francis Group, an informa business

Publisher's Note
The publisher has gone to great lengths to ensure the quality of this reprint but points out that some imperfections in the original copies may be apparent.

British Library Cataloguing-in-Publication Data
A catalogue record for this book is available from the British Library

Library of Congress Cataloging-in-Publication Data
Names: Sahin, Hakan, 1979- author.
Title: Host government agreements and the law in the energy sector : the case of Azerbaijan and Turkey / Hakan Sahin.
Description: Abingdon, Oxon; New York, NY : Routledge, 2019. | Based on author's thesis (doctoral - Anglia Ruskin University, England, 2013) issued under title: Host country contracts in the energy sector : Azerbaijan-Turkey case study. | Includes bibliographical references and index.
Identifiers: LCCN 2018036530 | ISBN 9781138591332 (hbk)
Subjects: LCSH: Investments, Foreign--Law and legislation--Turkey. | Investments, Foreign--Law and legislation--Azerbaijan. | Petroleum pipelines--Law and legislation--Turkey. | Petroleum pipelines--Law and legislation--Azerbaijan.
Classification: LCC K3830 .S234 2019 | DDC 346.4754/092--dc23
LC record available at https://lccn.loc.gov/2018036530

Typeset in Galliard
by Taylor & Francis Books

ISBN 13: 978-1-03-224172-2 (pbk)
ISBN 13: 978-1-138-59133-2 (hbk)

DOI: 10.4324/9780429955037

This work is dedicated to my family

Contents

Acknowledgements

This book is a culmination of many years of work and is derived from my doctoral thesis at Anglia Ruskin University, Cambridge, UK. I would like to express my gratitude to all those who supported and assisted me in completing this book.

First of all, I am deeply indebted to my supervisors, Professor Robert Home and Dr Teng Guan Khoo, for their help, stimulating suggestions and encouragement over the course of my PhD research.

During the transformation of this work from a doctoral thesis into a book, I have been mentored and inspired by Professor Ilias Bantekas. Therefore, I would also like to express my sincere and special thanks to him. He is both a valued colleague and a great friend of mine. Without his untiring support, it could not have been what it is today. I would also like to express my sincere and special thanks to Professor Yusuf Aksar. He has been another key influence in my academic career and I am grateful for his support and encouragement in building my portfolio of publications, particularly at an international level. I would also like to thank my colleague Dr Hulusi Alphan Dinckol for helping me to resolve technical issues in the writing stage of this work.

I am pleased that Routledge has agreed to make my work available to a wider audience. I would like to thank Commissioning Editor for Energy Law Siobhán Poole, Editorial Assistant Nicola Sharpe, Production Editor Jashnie Jabson, and all the other staff at Routledge who have contributed to the publication of this book.

A big special thanks to my partner, Rachael Claire Gibbon, and her family. Rachael, your patient love has enabled me to complete this work. I will never forget the time you spent on my draft chapters. Thank you so much again and again for helpful insights, advice and comments. I am also thankful to Beverley Gibbon, Chris Gibbon and Andrew Gibbon who have encouraged me through some stressful times. Their constant support added greatly to my confidence and belief in the possibility of publishing this work.

Finally, I would like to give my special thanks to my father, Dr Vahap Şahin, my mother, Gulsum Gonenc, my sisters Canan Şahin and Fatmanur Şahin, my brother Omercan Şahin and my step-mother, Yasemin Şahin, who supported and encouraged me from the beginning to the end of this work. I owe you a lot! Your existence means a lot to me!

Hakan Şahin
Istanbul, Turkey 2018

Abbreviations

ACG	Azeri–Chirag–Gunashli
AfDB	African Development Bank
ADB	Asian Development Bank
AMINOIL	American Independent Oil Company
BIT	Bilateral Investment Treaty
BP	British Petroleum
BTC	Baku–Tbilisi–Ceyhan
CERDS	Charter of Economic Rights and Duties of States
CIS	Commonwealth of Independent States
EBRD	European Bank for Reconstruction and Development
ECA	Export Credit Agency
ECHR	European Court of Human Rights
ECT	Energy Charter Treaty
EIB	European Investment Bank
Eps	Ecuador Principles
EU	European Union
FDI	Foreign Direct Investment
HGA	Host Government Agreement
HGC	Host Government Contract
HSE	Health, Safety and Environment
IBRD	International Bank for Reconstruction and Development
ICJ	International Court of Justice
ICSID	International Centre for Settlement of Investment Disputes
IDA	International Development Association/Agency
IFC	International Finance Corporation
IGA	Intergovernmental Agreement
IIA	Investment Insurance Agency
IMF	International Monetary Fund
IOC	International Oil Company
JDP	Justice and Development Party
LSTA	Lump Sum Turnkey Agreement
LIAMCO	Libyan American Oil Company
MDB	Multilateral Development Banks

MIGA	Multinational Investment Guarantee Agency
MIT	Multilateral Investment Treaties
NAFTA	North American Free Trade Agreement
NGO	Non-Governmental Organisation
NOC	National Oil Company
OECD	Organisation for Economic Cooperation and Development
OPEC	Organisation of Petroleum Exporting Countries
OPIC	Overseas Private Investment Corporation
PCA	Permanent Court of Arbitration
PSA	Product Sharing Agreement
PSC	Product Sharing Contract
SOCAR	State Oil Company of Azerbaijan
SPV	Special Purpose Vehicle
S&P	Standard & Poor
TANAP	Trans-Anatolian Natural Gas Pipeline
TPAO	Türkiye Petrolleri Anonim Ortakliği
UN	United Nations
UNCTAD	United Nations Conference on Trade and Development
UNGAR	United Nations General Assembly Resolutions
WTO	World Trade Organisation

Part I

Political risks in the energy sector

1 Introduction and framework of the research

Introduction

Petroleum[1] is one of the most crucial natural resources for modern civilisation and has long been a key element in the economic development of a state. For this reason, energy investment is a crucial component of the global economy. In a broad sense, foreign direct investment (FDI) between a host government and an investor in the energy sector may encompass a range of energy sources and related activities, such as oil and mineral exploitation or other types of natural resources. The energy industry as a whole is a key source of growth stimulation for developing states. This is true not only in terms of economic growth, but also in the transfer of knowledge and skills as well as in the provision of employment opportunities. Understandably, developing states are well disposed towards international investors, and are eager to enter into petroleum investment contracts with the expectation that these will bring the aforementioned benefits to their countries, particularly where the host state is less able to act as a provider of such resources autonomously. The domestic law of some developing states provides a welcoming investment environment in the form of guarantees and stability, while other states provide these opportunities by agreeing to investment contracts or treaties drafted by international organisations established to facilitate such agreements.

On a global scale, regardless of their type, all investments face risks and these risks are changing in nature and reach as the world economy globalises. It is, of course, true that political risk phenomena *per se* are potentially destructive to all industries. However, it is fair to say that, due to its high stakes, the energy industry is more acutely exposed and subject to political risk than most sectors. Therefore, the energy sector and its long-term projects require more guarantees of stability than other industries.

Specifically, 'the capital-intensive nature of the industry, market price volatility, geographic scope of assets and operations, the high risk nature of exploration and

1 In this book, the term 'petroleum' refers to gas and oil. The term 'energy' will also be used with reference to gas and oil as fuel types.

exploitation of natural resources, technology and requirements, environmental concern, downstream brand promotion and protection issues, political sensitivities, scale and diversity of employee base, etc.'[2] are contributing factors to the political risks international investors face. If these risks are 'known quantities', how is it that the industry so frequently finds itself the target of political risk phenomena and why are energy investment projects so frequently a target? Thomas W. Waelde answers these questions as follows:

> Political risk reflects the exposure of the technical and business approach to the industry to the often much more volatile, less forecastable, and less manageable events in the 'political' sphere – as contrasted to the supposedly more 'rational' sphere of commercial decision-making. Politics sometimes specifically targets and hits the petroleum industry not only due to its strategic character, large capital investment, and public visibility, but also because the industry's global nature, imbued with 'foreign' elements resented in nation states, makes it a very suitable target. But politics can also hit the petroleum industry rather accidentally, in particular when this industry is in the way of conflicts between states, between conflicting ideologies, or within a country, between ethnic groups or classes that hate each other.[3]

In other words, a number of reasons can be listed as to why petroleum projects are vulnerable.[4] First, some developing countries' economies depend on oil, gas or other types of natural resources. As a result of being dependent on oil and gas, the expectation of politicians in petroleum-producing and exporting developing countries is extremely high.[5] If a country obtains more rent or royalties from energy investment projects, this will mean that the citizens of the developing state can enjoy increased earning power, and be provided with 'more schools, more employment and general wellbeing'.[6] Second, decisions taken by governments play a significant role in the energy sector. In other words, the politically aware citizens of developing states will lobby for more transparent policy and the consideration of public interest by their governments, with the consequence that

2 Lovells International Law Firm/Association of Corporate Counsel, 'Sino-Foreign Oil and Gas Industry: Legal Risk Comparative Analysis' (November 2005) 2, available at <www.acc.com/vl/public/Article/loader.cfm?csModule=security/getfile&pageid=16024>

3 T. W. Waelde, 'Managing the Risk of Sanctions in the Global Oil & Gas Industry: Corporate Response Under Political, Legal and Commercial Pressures', *Texas International Law Journal*, Vol. 36 (2001) 183–4.

4 M. Erkan, *International Energy Investment Law: Stability through Contractual Clauses* Energy and Environmental Law and Policy Series, (Alphen aan den Rijn: Kluwer Law International, 2011) 27.

5 Ibid.

6 J. L. Valera, 'Political Risks for International Oil Companies Investing in Latin America', *OGEL, Journal of Oil, Gas and Energy Law Intelligence* 4 (2006) 1available at <www.ogel.org>

voters will use the ballot box to express any dissatisfaction with government policy in this regard at the next elections. For this reason, 'governments are likely to play a prominent role in regulating entry, of prices, of quality of services, and of other aspects of investor behaviour'.[7] Third, energy investment projects are lengthy and perhaps risks are inevitable in a relationship that entails such a long-term commitment. According to Valera, 'the political risk facing international oil companies is directly related to the behaviour of political players in the policy-making process within the host country'.[8] It would not be unreasonable to assert that international politics play as important a role as the internal policy-making process.[9] Evidently, over the course of a project, contractual terms and conditions may be breached as a result of government change or changes in the political system.[10] The new government and/or political system may not welcome investors or respect previously agreed terms. Finally, as mentioned above, some developing states suffer from political[11] and economic instability. This destabilising influence renders the energy sector vulnerable.

This study aims to analyse the political risks, particularly indirect expropriation in host governmental long-term energy investment contracts, focusing on stabilisation clauses, and examines which driving forces influence host states to agree stability in their long-term host governmental contracts. It goes on to propose a framework for the role to be played by internal and external forces, namely: political regimes, domestic laws (FDI, petroleum and energy law) (internal); rating agencies, public or private insurers and project finance lenders (external). The secondary aim of this work is to examine political regimes and state guarantees to foreign investors in Azerbaijan and Turkey from a comparative perspective. The work dedicates particular attention to how effective internal factors in Azerbaijan and Turkey are in facilitating contractual stability in their energy investment projects.

Political risk defined

The era of modern economic understanding was ushered in by Adam Smith with the publication of *The Wealth of Nations* in 1776. Following his research into the political economy approach, he acknowledged that politics and economics are interrelated and indivisible.[12] The nexus between political risk and investment

7 T. H. Moran, 'Political and Regulation Risk in Infrastructure Investment in Developing Countries: Introduction and an Overview', *CEPMLP*, Vol 5–6 (1999) 4

8 Valera (n. 6 above) 3.

9 Erkan (n. 4 above) 28.

10 M. Sornarajah, *The International Law on Foreign Investment*, 2nd edn (Cambridge: Cambridge University Press, 2010) 69.

11 S. C. Wallace, 'Symposium: Energy and International Law: Development, Litigation and Regulation', *Texas International Law Journal*, Vol. 36 (2001) 54, available at <www.tilj.org>

12 H. L. Lax, *Political Risk in the International Oil and Gas Industry* (Boston, MA: International Human Resources Development Corporation, 1983) 8.

would seem to exemplify Smith's conclusion, as all types of foreign investments and capital come with risks.[13] Since risks are unavoidably attached to any investment, foreign investors, especially in the energy sector, are inevitably faced with a myriad of political risks as part and parcel of an investment scenario. At a global scale, numerous energy projects have been made and are currently being committed to by international investors. Energy projects, such as oil and gas exploration and their transportation through pipelines, can encounter unpredictable economic and political risks.

Norton defines risk as 'the possibility that something may or may not happen'.[14] Kolo and Lax seek to provide a sense of the unpredictability of risks in energy investment projects. According to Kolo, such risks may not only occur in the commencement of an energy investment, but can emerge at any stage of an investment project.[15] Lax argues that risk is a dynamic concept that centres on the probability of change.[16] He qualifies what constitutes a risk by asserting that investment conditions present from the outset cannot be deemed risks in themselves; rather, risk arises from changes in those conditions.[17] Lax asserts that the risks affecting an investment form the parameters at the time an investment decision is made. Risks can also be a future incidence that may change the rules.[18] As is the case with all key terminologies in the field of social sciences, attempts have been made to provide an accurate definition of political risk phenomena by numerous scholars as well as organisations such as the Organisation for Economic Cooperation and Development (OECD) and the Multinational Investment Guarantee Agency (MIGA). The OECD describes political risk as follows:

> The risk of non-payment on an export contract or project due to action taken by the importer's host government. Such action may include intervention to prevent transfer of payments, cancellation of a license, or events such as war, civil strife, revolution, and other disturbances that prevent the exporter from performing under the supply contract or the buyer from making payment. Sometimes physical disasters such as cyclones, floods, and earthquakes come under this heading.[19]

It is apparent that the OECD's definition is broad and comprehensive, as it encompasses all types of investment. Although some risks are outlined in this

13 K. M. Quinley, 'Managing Political Risks', *The Risk Report*, Vol. 24, No. 7 (March 2002) 1.

14 S. D. Norton, 'The Natural Environment as a Salient Stakeholder: Non-Anthropocentrism, Ecosystem Stability and the Financial Markets', *Business Ethics: A European Review*, Vol. 16, No. 4 (2007) 390.

15 A. Kolo, 'Managing Political Risk in Transnational Investment Contracts', Centre for Petroleum and Mineral Law Policy (CPMLP), Professional Paper No. PP11 (1994) 2.

16 Lax (n. 12 above) 8.

17 Ibid.

18 Quinley (n. 13 above) 1.

19 OECD, 'Glossary of Statistical Terms', available at <http://stats.oecd.org/glossary/detail.asp?ID=5990>

definition, they are not directly related to any specific sector. It is possible that the OECD has erred on the side of caution in defining political risks by covering all investment areas. MIGA's definition is also broad but still more specific than that of the OECD. According to MIGA, political risk can be defined as a breach of contract by a host government; adverse regulatory changes by host states; restriction on currency transfer and convertibility; expropriation; political violence (war, terrorism, sabotage, and civil disturbances such as revolution) and the non-honouring of sovereign guarantees.[20]

In doctrine, several definitions of political risks have been provided by scholars such as Comeaux and Kinsella and Boulos. Comeaux and Kinsella present the following scenario as an illustration of risk: 'the laws of a country will unexpectedly change to the investor's detriment after the investor has invested capital in the country, thereby reducing the value of the individual's investment'.[21] Boulos's definition is narrower than Comeaux and Kinsella's, but more appropriate to this study, as it focuses on the energy sector. According to Boulos, 'political risk in any oil and gas investment will be expropriated, nationalised or otherwise unilaterally changed by the foreign government to the detriment of the oil company'.[22] After providing a broad definition of what political risk is, it is also crucial to apply this to a tangible framework. Political risk is categorised in academic literature and assessed by several scholars. The following section explores the categorisation of political risk.

Classification of political risks

Political risk phenomena have been classified by various authors in the field of international business. Wagner's classification separates political risks into two categories. According to this author, the first distinction must be between firm-specific political risk and country-specific political risk.[23] The author states that firm-specific political risks target a specific company. However, country-specific political risks are countrywide and may have an influence on a company's physical activities, although they do not necessarily hold such an intention.[24]

Another categorisation is provided by Yescombe. According to this author, political risks can be divided into three categories: the first category is investment; the

20 World Bank Group, *World Investment and Political Risk Report (2010): Investing in a Low Carbon Economy* (New York and Geneva, 2010) 19, available at: <www.miga.org/documents/WIPR10ebook.pdf>

21 P. E. Comeaux & N. S. Kinsella, 'Reducing Political Risk in Developing Countries: Bilateral Investment Treaties, Stabilisation Clauses, and MIGA & OPIC Investment Insurance', *New York Law School Journal of International and Comparative Law*, Vol. 15 (1994) 4.

22 A. J. Boulos, 'Assessing Political Risk', available at <www.ipaa.org/wp-content/uploads/2017/01/PoliticalRisk.pdf>

23 D. Wagner, 'Defining Political Risks', October 2000, available at <www.irmi.com/expert/articles/2000/wagner10.aspx>

24 Ibid.

second is change of law; and the third is quasi-political risk.[25] Other analysts, such as the HIS Energy Group, prefer a more detailed approach, HIS sub-divides political risk phenomena into a further three categories. The first is political risk, which comprises war, political unrest, violence and instability. The second category is social-economic risk, which consists of economic, energy, environmental and ethnic factors. The third and final category is commercial risk regarding investment, repatriation and fiscal terms.[26] While all of these definitions and categorisations of political risk are valid, in the interests of having a clearly delineated frame of reference most appropriate to this study, the author will focus only on the following phenomena: expropriation, nationalisation and specifically the most prolific and controversial risk of late: indirect expropriation. The terminological identification of expropriation and indirect expropriation is significant, as one of the central arguments in this subject area surrounds the identification and application of appropriate terminology.

Host government agreements defined

A host government agreement[27] in the energy sector can also be regarded as a state contract. In other words, a host government energy investment contract is an agreement created between an investor and the host state (or state-owned agencies) for the purpose of operating a particular investment project in the host country. The term 'host government contract' (HGC) includes the full variety of host government contracts between international investors and the host country, usually represented by a state-owned company. HGCs can be found most frequently in less-developed regions.[28] The fundamental principle that underpins a HGC is to permit, within established boundaries, a foreign investor to explore and exploit the natural resources of that state. While the host country permits a foreign investor to operate in its territory, it also provides a guarantee to that investor that the operation will not be disturbed by state intervention. Notably, HGCs are defined either by administrative law or public law contracts.[29]

25 E. R. Yescombe, *Principles of Project Finance* (San Diego, CA: Academic Press, 2002) 204–5.
26 L. Bossley (HIS Energy Group), 'Political Risk: A Hedge Too Far', *Petroleum Economist* (October 2002) 33.
27 Notably, the following terms are used in the literature: host government contract, host government agreement, long-term investment contracts, investment agreements, petroleum contracts, oil contracts, state contracts, economic development agreements, foreign investment contracts, international investment agreement, energy investment contracts and so on. In this study the term 'host government agreement' will be used.
28 G. Goolsby & M. Rowley, 'Building a Cross-Border Pipeline: For Multi-National Projects, Host Government Agreements Can Reduce Risk and Create a Stable Investment Environment', available at <www.bakerbotts.com/~/media/files/ideas/publications/2007/03/building-a-crossborder-pipeline/files/goolsby-rowley-pgt-march-2007/fileattachment/goolsby-rowley-pgt-march-2007.pdf>
29 K. Talus, S. Looper & S. Otillar, 'Lex Petrolea and Internationalization of Petroleum Agreements: Focus on Host Government Contracts', *Journal of World Energy Law Business*, Vol. 5, No. 3 (2012) 183.

Expropriation or nationalisation?

The term 'expropriate' means 'to exercise eminent domain over; to take, by legal action, private land for public purpose'.[30] What can be understood from this definition is that expropriation is the exercise of governmental executive power to rescind an individual's property rights. As an individual's property rights are 'taken' by the host government, an important question arises regarding whether this 'taking' is legal or not. International customary law does not prevent a host state from expropriating a private asset unless the host governments meet certain conditions. These conditions: the taking should be for a public purpose, as provided by law, and should be in a non-discriminatory manner and with compensation.[31] Furthermore, expropriation itself can take different forms: it could be direct, where an investment is nationalised by a host government, or indirectly expropriated.[32] Systematic taking of a foreign investor's property 'within one or more specific sectors of a nation's economy within the framework of socio-economic or political reform is often referred to as nationalisation. The difference between expropriation and nationalisation is one of scope and extent rather than of legal nature'.[33]

Indirect expropriation

Indirect expropriation is one of the most egregious political risks that a foreign investor may confront when seeking to invest in a host country. It can be described as a measure or measures taken by a state that have a similar or, indeed, worse effect than direct expropriation, although the property is not seized and the legal title to property is not affected.[34] The United Nations Conference on Trade and Development (UNCTAD) has described indirect expropriation as 'where a measure that does not directly take property has the same impact by depriving the owner of the substantial benefits of the property'.[35] In the light of the above definition, Erkan argues that direct expropriation includes the physical takeover of property by the host government or government authority. There are four crucial components for indirect expropriation. According to the author, there ought to be

30 B. A. Garner, *Garner's Dictionary of Legal Usage*, 3rd edn (Oxford: Oxford University Press, 2011) 72.
31 UNCTAD, 'Taking of Property', UNCTAD Series on Issues in International Investment Agreements (2000) 12–13.
32 OECD, 'International Investment Law: A Changing Landscape', OECD Working Paper (2005), 45.
33 K. Hober, *Investment Arbitration in Eastern Europe: In Search of a Definition of Expropriation* (New York: Juris Publishing, 2007) 1.
34 OECD, 'Indirect Expropriation and Right to Regulate in International Investment Law', OECD Working Papers on International Investment Law (2004) 3–4.
35 UNCTAD, *Investor State Disputes Arising from Investment Treaties: 'A Review'* (New York and Geneva: UNCTAD Series on International Investment Policies for Development, 2005) 41 (hereinafter 'UNCTAD 2005'), available at <http://unctad.org/en/docs/iteiit20054_en.pdf>

a measure, a state measure or a regulatory measure, as a private asset should not be seized directly; the action or inaction of the state should have the same effect as direct taking; and this action's result should deprive the owners of the substantial benefit of the profit.[36] He goes further to state that the UNCTAD's definition covers all the probabilities that may interfere with an investor's property rights accruing from the investment.[37] This could be any legislation or administrative action or omission in which a host state interferes with the investment in a way that makes it impossible to operate.[38] Indirect expropriation can take two different forms.

Creeping expropriation

Creeping expropriation is used to refer to indirect expropriation that arises as a result of a series of state measures either introduced gradually or made to come about at one time. According to Hoffman, creeping expropriation is the most dreaded and, indeed, most potentially destructive risk, in which the host government utilises a combination of taxes, fees and other charges and devices to increase its share of the project's profits.[39] The tribunal in *Generation Ukraine* defined creeping expropriation as 'a form of indirect expropriation with a distinctive temporal quality in the sense that it encapsulates the situation whereby a series of acts attributable to the state over a period of time culminate in the expropriatory taking of such property'.[40] UNCTAD defines creeping expropriation as 'the use of a series of measures in order to achieve a deprivation of the economic value of the investment. In this case, no individual measure in itself would amount to an expropriation.'[41]

Regulatory expropriation

The definition of regulatory expropriation is: regulatory measures which are generally made in the name of public purpose but deprive the foreign investor of the commercial value of the asset owned to a degree sufficient to be considered expropriation.[42] In this scenario, the commercial value of an investor's property or assets is reduced by the introduction of new rules or the adaptation of current laws in the areas of taxation, environment, health and human rights. Energy investment projects require stability, on account of their nature and characteristic features. These projects are vulnerable and need to be based on the development of a long-

36 Erkan (n. 4 above) 64.
37 Ibid.
38 Ibid.
39 S. L. Hoffman, *The Law and Business of International Project Finance*, 3rd edn (Cambridge: Cambridge University Press, 2008) 69.
40 *Generation Ukraine, Inc. v Ukraine*, ICSID Case No ARB/00/9, Award of 16 September 2003, 44 ILM 404(2005) para 20–22.
41 UNCTAD 2005 (n. 35 above) 42.
42 Ibid.

term relationship of mutual trust and accountability between an international investor and a host state for the lifespan of the project. If a host state has a negative impact on its investors' assets directly or indirectly or makes unilateral changes to the contractual terms, this long-term relationship could come to a calamitous and costly end. Although political risks cannot be avoided, they can be mitigated or managed.[43] There are various ways to minimise or manage the political risks inherent in energy investment projects, the first of which is by drafting a fair and flexible contract[44] which makes reference to national law[45] and international law,[46] as well as inserting contractual clauses[47] such as arbitration clauses, stabilisation clauses, renegotiation clauses, choice of law clauses. Another means of damage limitation to mitigate political risks is to insure the energy investment through public or private investment insurance mechanisms.[48]

Why are stabilisation clauses a controversial issue?

A contractual guarantee in the form of a stabilisation clause is widely considered to be an effective immunisation against political risk.[49] These contractual mechanisms are inserted by international investors in an investment contract to ensure that the contract shall not be unilaterally altered or terminated by a host government's legislative or administrative activities. During the lifespan of the contract, the laws and regulations applicable to it may change. It may be the case that some of the changes will have an impact on the economic outcomes or expected profit of the project. Therefore, in order to mitigate such risk, investors require host governments to agree stabilisation clauses in host governmental agreements or international investment agreements. The potential benefit of this clause from the perspective of investors is that a stabilisation clause aims to safeguard the foreign investment contract from a variety of issues, such as taxation, environmental controls and other regulations, as well as to deter the destruction of the investment contract itself before its scheduled termination.[50]

In literature, scholars argue vehemently about whether stabilisation clauses are employed by investors as a legitimate means of safeguarding an investment, or whether, in conflict with their intended role of providing mutually beneficial protection, the main effect they have is of disenfranchising a host state of its sovereign rights. The dominant view is that inserting stabilisation clauses does not hinder a

43 Kolo (n. 15 above) 3.
44 Ibid.
45 Energy Law, Foreign Direct Investment Law, Petroleum Law.
46 This could be multilateral and bilateral treaties.
47 T. W. Waelde & G. Ndi, 'Stabilizing International Investment Commitments: International Law versus Contract Interpretation', *Texas International Law Journal*, Vol. 31, No. 2 (1996) 216.
48 For instance, Lloyds, AIG, etc. or through national or multilateral government insurance programmes; OPIC or MIGA.
49 D. Johnston, *International Petroleum Fiscal Systems and Production Sharing Contracts* (Tulsa, OK: PennWell Books, 1994) 171.
50 Sornarajah (n. 10 above) 282.

host state from enjoying the full use of its sovereign rights to change or create new domestic laws.[51] This view is defended on the grounds that stabilisation clauses cannot restrict or overrule a state's rights and legislative power. Nevertheless, when the impact they have on environmental protection, health and human rights is assessed by non-governmental organisations (NGOs), stabilisation clauses are often the subject of criticism. The reason why such clauses often come under fire is that they diminish or reduce the reach of state power in terms of legislative power, judicial decision-making and administrative activity to such an extent that it becomes very challenging for the host government to regulate in the public interest.[52]

From the perspective of investors and practitioners, inserting such clauses can only be seen as beneficial to a potential investment. From the perspective of governments, agreeing such clauses in a host governmental contract or adopting stability in domestic laws is a way of welcoming investors with a view to fostering the flow of capital, the transfer of knowledge and so on. However, cash flow and knowhow seem insufficient returns when some of the more negative by-products of stabilisation clauses are offset against them. With this in mind, this study will focus on a central question: what driving forces influence host states to agree stability in their long-term host governmental contracts?

Host government agreements

There are three main types of host government agreements between host governments and investors, the first two of which are much more common: royalty and tax contracts (sometimes called oil and gas modern concession contracts); product sharing contracts (PSCs), as well as agreements specifically contemplating a multistate investment (such as a cross-border pipeline development); and service agreements. Royalty and tax contracts (concessions) are contracts whereby the host government grants the investor the right to explore and exploit natural sources or run utilities or other public services in an area defined by that government during a specific period of time.[53] PSCs are the most common genre of agreement between investors and host states or, more commonly, a state-owned national oil company in the petroleum industry.[54] In this type of contract, although the investors are granted the right to explore and develop a petroleum

51 K. Hober, 'Ownership of the Oil and Gas Resources in the Caspian Sea: Problems and Solutions– International Arbitration and Contractual Clauses', Stockholm Arbitration Report 1 (2004) 14.

52 A. F. M. Maniruzzaman, 'The Pursuit of Stability in International Energy Investment Contracts: A Critical Appraisal of emerging Trends', *Journal of World Energy and Business*, Vol. 1. No. 2 (2008) 154.

53 L. Cotula, 'Investment contracts and sustainable development: How to make contracts for fairer and more sustainable natural resource investments', Natural Resource Issues No. 20. *IIED* (2010) 24.

54 P. D Cameron, *International Energy Investment Law: The Pursuit of Stability* (Oxford: Oxford University Press, 2010) 37.

field, they are also responsible for covering all exploration costs and investment risks. While the investor explores, develops and produces the petroleum, the exploration and production costs will be divided between the host state and the investor as follows: the investor receives a share of oil to recover costs ('cost oil') and make a profit ('profit oil').[55] The host country obtains a share of the profit oil.[56]

The final type of HGCs are service contracts. The commonly applied condition underpinning this contract type is that the host country hires the services of the international oil company (IOC) as a 'contractor'.[57] All of the extraction and production rights are retained by the host country,[58] while all the risks in the areas of finance, exploration and development are shouldered by the investor. In this way, 'commercial production becomes possible from the contract area, the contractor is reimbursed for its costs and investments and paid a fee for its services from the sale of the oil produced'.[59] Compared with other types of contracts such as concession and product sharing agreements (PSAs), service contracts are held to be the type of arrangement whereby the host government exercises the greatest amount of control over a project.[60]

The concept of a service contract is primarily based upon a simple formula: the contractor is paid a cash fee by the investor for performing the service of producing petroleum resources.[61] Under a service contract, the ownership of the mineral resources remain with the host state at all times, including after production.[62] Service contracts, in the main, can be divided into two types: *risk service contract* and *pure service contract*. In *risk service* contracts, the foreign investor bears all the exploration risk and the government compensates the foreign investor's services through payments that are dependent on and limited by the amount of proceeds from hydrocarbons produced within the area defined by the agreement.[63] The downside of this type of contract is that if stores of hydrocarbon are not found in the contract area, then the company is left out of pocket.[64] Risk service contracts have traditionally been used in states such as Iraq and, more recently, in Mexico.[65] The use of risk service contracts seems to be on the

55 K. Bindemann, 'Product Sharing Agreements: An Economic Analysis', *Oxford Institute for Energy Studies*, WPM25, October (1999) 1.
56 Ibid.
57 E. E. Smith, *International Petroleum Transactions*, 2nd edn (Denver, CO: Rocky Mountain Mineral Law Foundation, 2000) 480–93.
58 Ibid.
59 Ibid.
60 M. Likosky. 'Contracting, Regulatory Issues in the Oil and Gas and the Metallic Mineral Industries', *Transnational Corporations*, Vol. 18, No. 1 (2009) 14.
61 D. Johnston, *International Exploration Economics, Risk and Contracts Analysis*, (Tulsa, OK: PennWell Books, 2003) 41.
62 Talus, Looper & Otillar (n. 29 above) 188.
63 Ibid.
64 J. S. C. Neto, 'Risk-bearing Service Contracts in Brazil', *Journal of Energy and Natural Resources Law*, Vol. 3 (1985) 114, cited in Likosky (n. 60 above).
65 Talus, Looper & Otillar (n. 29 above) 188.

increase, particularly in situations 'where the technology is high demand, but the exploration risk is relatively low'.[66] The second form of service contracts are *pure service contracts*. In this form, the foreign investor carries out exploration and development work on behalf of the host state for a set fee. Unlike risk service contracts, the host country bears all the risk. These types of contracts are most common in the Middle East, where the host state often has substantial capital reserves but is nonetheless lacking in the required expertise.[67]

Host government agreements in cross-border pipeline projects

Cross-border petroleum pipelines can be regarded as the blood vessels of the global economy, the sustainable growth of which is increasingly dependent on international investment in energy products and materials.[68] The term 'cross-border pipeline' refers to a pipeline that has its origin in one sovereign country and traverses one or more other states along its route.[69] While these projects are significant for the nations involved for a number of reasons, legal jurisdictional issues are the source of most of the complications they typically encounter. Owing to the fact that such projects become subject to the domestic laws of the states in question, operating cross-border petroleum projects across two different jurisdictions is a complex undertaking. Therefore, with a view to achieving a fully integrated international pipeline project, and to give the project a firm legislative basis, the investors of the project and project sponsors make additional contractual support with the power to exercise a binding effect on the host government a *sine qua non* requirement. This support can be built in via intergovernmental agreements (IGAs) and host government agreements (HGAs). It is apparent that the requirement of the project sponsors is to rule a cross-border project in a 'blending of local law and international law'.[70]

Furthermore, the applicability of HGAs and IGAs in tandem in cross-border projects is endorsed by the Energy Charter Treaty (ECT). Notably, in 2003, the Energy Charter Conference confirmed the first addition of model agreements (IGA and HGA) in cross-border pipeline projects.[71] In this respect, the Baku–Tbilisi–Ceyhan (BTC) Petroleum Pipeline project between Azerbaijan, Georgia and Turkey with the BTC Co. can be cited as the best example of model agreements approved in the Energy Charter Conference. The said treaty is a

66 Ibid.

67 Iran, Saudi Arabia, the Philippines and Kuwait are examples of countries where *pure service* contracts are used; see M. Mazeel, *Petroleum Fiscal System and Contracts* (Hamburg: Diplomica Verlag, 2010) 27.

68 S. V. Vinogradov, 'Cross-border Oil and Gas Pipelines: Legal and Regulatory Regimes', Association of International Petroleum Negotiators (AIPN) (2001) 7.

69 M. Dulaney & R. Merrick, 'Legal Issues in Cross-Border Oil and Gas Pipelines', *Journal of Energy and Natural Resources Law*, Vol. 23 (2005) 247.

70 Ibid.

71 For more information about the Model Agreements, see the website of International Energy Charter, available at <www.encharter.org>

multinational agreement that has the explicit purpose of managing the transit of energy products and minerals and the goal of increasing the promotion of long-term international cooperation in the energy sector between its member states. To date, 53 signatory states have become members of the Charter.[72]

Following this brief mention of the ECT, the main features of HGAs in cross-border petroleum pipeline projects should also be delineated. An HGA (or HGC) is a legal contract between the state and affiliates of project sponsors that identifies both contracting parties' rights and contractual obligations to ensure the success of the proposed investment project.[73] As a contract, an HGA lists and describes the specific grants, rights, privileges, exemptions and obligations that the host government propose to the project sponsors and investors. The contract also outlines the host country's expectations from the agreement in financial and non-financial areas. Tax, duties and fees constitute the expected economic return of the agreement. The recruitment of employees for the project is an example of a non-financial area. As the legal status of an IGA is that of a treaty, it will prevail over the legal systems of each host state. For this reason, most project sponsors and investors seek to attach HGAs to an IGA in order to elevate it to international status. By internationalising the agreement, a favourable position is granted to investors with additional support against the legislative activities of sovereign states.

Objectives and scope of the research

The objective of this book is to identify the political risks, particularly from indirect expropriation, that arise from the unilateral actions of host governments during the lifespan of energy investment projects and to examine what driving forces influence host states to consent to the insertion of stabilisation clauses in long-term HGCs.

The book places comparative evidence in the context of the existing literature on this subject to provide its findings with a theoretical basis and situate them in the broader context of the practice of and discourse on international private investment law. In order to understand how effective internal factors in Azerbaijan and Turkey are in facilitating contractual stability in their energy investment projects, the political regimes and state guarantees to foreign investors in Azerbaijan and Turkey are examined from a comparative perspective. In the interests of accomplishing the above-mentioned objectives, the author has intentionally constrained the scope of the book. This work does not seek to address all types of

72 The government of Afghanistan informed the Energy Secretariat on 19 February 2013 that the country's domestic procedures for ratifying the ECT were successfully completed. The Treaty will enter into force in Afghanistan and the country will be the 54th member state of the ECT. For further information, see the ECT's official website: ECT (n. 71 above).

73 A. Dufey & R. Kazimova, Baku–Tbilisi–Ceyhan Project: Implications of Project Finance', Chapter 12 in S. Leader & D. Ong, *Global Project Finance, Human Rights and Sustainable Development* (Cambridge: Cambridge University Press, 2011) 381.

political risk, energy investment contracts and all manner of contractual mechanisms that are used in the management of political risks.

This book focuses on upstream oil and gas contracts and pipeline projects within the petroleum sector. The upstream petroleum sector is engaged in the quest to find potential underground or underwater crude oil and natural gas fields. The activities employed in the upstream sectors are known as exploration and production. The study excludes electricity contracts, power contracts and gas and oil sale contracts. Furthermore, it should also be noted that, for the purposes of this research, there will only be a brief examination of purely indirect expropriation over other forms of political risk. Nor does the study attempt to provide a detailed legal commentary on the laws of Azerbaijan and Turkey: specific focus is given to political regimes, FDI law, constitutional promises and the BTC agreement.

International energy investors, to mitigate political risk for the duration of the projects in which they have invested, negotiate with host governments the insertion of one or more of the following contractual clauses in their agreements: stabilisation clauses, renegotiation clauses, choice of law and alternative dispute resolution clauses. Alternatively, they may seek to benefit from the power of bilateral or multilateral agreements which provide full protection to investors for the duration of energy investment projects. It is to be noted that, rather than examining all the contractual mechanisms and tools available to reduce political risk, this work concentrates on the insertion of stabilisation clauses in petroleum projects and attempts to find out why host governments assent to the inclusion of this type of clause.

This book has the following objectives:

- To furnish a theoretical understanding of the major political risks of direct and, more particularly, indirect expropriation in the context of energy investment contracts.
- To identify the strengths and weaknesses of stabilisation clauses inserted in host government contracts and determine whether, in contradiction of their intended guardianship purpose, they instead disenfranchise the sovereign rights of the host state.
- To analyse, from a comparative perspective, Azerbaijan and Turkey's political regimes, foreign investment laws, constitutional promises and policies, with particular focus on the BTC agreements.
- To analyse, through theoretical investigation, the influence of lenders, credit rating agencies and political risk insurers on the relationship between the host state and the investor.

The gap in conventional literature

Extensive literature on stabilisation clauses as a political risk device can easily be found. However, much of what is known about stabilisation clauses concerns their role as a political risk management tool, their importance in terms of FDI flow in host states, the protection and exemption they grant to foreign investors in energy investment contracts and their potential impact on human rights. Previous studies on stabilisation clauses in petroleum-producing countries have tended to concentrate on the political, economic[74] and regulatory aspects of this device, as well as the relationship between FDI and democracy.[75] Several studies, to date, have attempted to examine their function, validity and effectiveness, and how and why they are used in petroleum contracts.

The possible reasons why so many developing countries agree to insert stabilisation clauses in the investment contracts they are party to have been attributed to economic pressures. Al-Faruque posits that an economically weak bargaining position at the initial phase of the negotiations may pressurise host states to agree to accept stabilisation clauses with the prospect of being able to better exploit their resources, and in so doing accelerate economic development and improve general standards of living.[76]

In 2008, the International Finance Corporation (IFC) sponsored an empirical study on stabilisation clauses in HGCs. The research was led by the United Nations (UN) Special Representative of the Secretary General for Business and Human Rights, Professor John Ruggie, and authored by Andrea Shemberg.[77] This constituted the first study based on empirical research into modern stabilisation practice, including a number of industries and regions of the world. Andrea Shemberg, in cooperation with the IFC and UN Special Representative, obtained 76 current investment contracts and 12 model contracts from various sectors.

The research found that contracts from non-OECD countries are much more likely than those from OECD countries to insulate the investor from new social and environmental laws, or to provide compensation to the investors for compliance with new social and environmental laws in host governmental agreements.[78] In contrast to the contracts forged with non-member states, the research also found that contracts and models made with OECD member states contained stabilisation clauses that protected investors only against new laws that were arbitrary or discriminatory.[79] The research went on to identify two factors which might provide evidence for the apparent disparity between OECD and non-OECD country practice. In the first instance, it was suggested that the practice of including more extensive stabilisation commitments in non-OECD

74 A. Al-Faruque, 'Validity and Efficacy of Stabilisation Clauses, Legal Protection vs. Functional Value', *Journal of International Arbitration*, Vol. 23, No. 4) (2006) 317–36.

75 O. Bayulgen, *Foreign Direct Investment, Oil Curse and Democratization: A Comparison of Azerbaijan and Russia, Business and Politics.* (Cambridge: Cambridge University Press, 2010).

76 Al-Faruque (n. 74 above) 335–6.

77 The UN–IFC Report was authored by (and research for the report was conducted by) Andrea Shemberg, a legal advisor to Professor John Ruggie.

78 A. Shemberg, 'Stabilisation Clause and Human Rights: A Research Project Conducted for IFC and the United Nations Special Representative to the Secretary General on Business and Human Rights', IFC/SRSG Research Paper, 11 May (2009) ix.

79 Ibid.

contracts was related to the perception of investment risk.[80] Second, the report asserted that lawyers surveyed during research for the UN–IFC Report had expressed the view that freezing clauses were unlikely to be enforceable under the laws of many developed states.[81] Nevertheless, the research did not explicitly address the question: what are the driving forces that persuade host states to contain stabilisation clauses in host governmental energy investment contracts? It is also worth mentioning that the research did not cite any evidence that investors or multinational companies have used stabilisation clauses deliberately to discourage the adoption of environmental or human rights laws in a host state.

There is a discernible gap in the literature of an exhaustive inquiry into the reasons why host governments agree to clauses that are of no obvious benefit to them, and that are often appreciably to their detriment. In this regard, it is more usually the case that the literature presently available oversimplifies why a host state gives consent to stabilisation clauses – for example, the prospect of economic gain. However, HGCs are not merely two-sided relationships. As well as the investor and the host country, there is a third group of external players, consisting of rating agencies, project finance lenders and political risk insurers, all of which may have an influence on the terms and conditions of the agreement. The extent of influence exerted by each of these parties varies from project to project. This research not only takes into account the internal reasons that may compel host states to agree to stabilisation clauses under their host governmental contracts, but also takes stock of the external factors and their role in advancing the inclusion of such clauses, thereby providing a rounded and fully comprehensive analysis of these contractual scenarios.

Consequently, the research aims to contribute to the literature in two ways. First, this study provides, for the first time, an empirical and comparative work on the internal and external reasons that compel host states to commit to stability clauses. Second, it reassesses the issues that have arisen from the BTC agreement and the impact on Azerbaijani and Turkish domestic laws of the terms prescribed by this agreement. Through analysis of the countries' political regime, FDI laws and constitutional promises, and an assessment of their investment environments, it provides invaluable recommendations to both the governments of these countries and foreign investors about to enter into contractual agreements or do business in the aforementioned countries. What differentiates this study from other works is that it compares one specific OECD member country with another non-member state and attempts to answer questions that research to date has not addressed, as well as exploring the internal and external motivations and consequent behaviours of the selected countries and other stakeholders in energy investment agreements.

80 Ibid.
81 Ibid.

Research questions

The main research question posed in this book is: which driving forces influence host states to commit to stabilisation clauses in their long-term host governmental contracts? In order to answer the main question, the research also addresses the following series of sub-questions:

- What constitutes indirect expropriation and what mechanisms can be deployed by foreign investors to mitigate such risk?
- To what extent are stabilisation clauses effective in protecting investments; or, conversely, in contradiction of their intended guardianship purpose, do they instead disenfranchise the sovereign rights of the host states?
- Do stabilisation provisions constitute a threat for environmental and human rights issues?
- Do rating agencies, project finance lenders and political risk insurers play an active role in lobbying for the inclusion of stabilisation clauses in host governmental contracts?
- How effective are different political regimes in promoting FDI and giving consent to stabilisation clauses in Azerbaijani and Turkish HGCs?
- What reason have caused Azerbaijan and Turkey to agree to contractual stability in the BTC host governmental agreements?

Methodology

This book applies comparative legal research and is based on exploratory and descriptive research of internal and external factors that are proposed in this study by providing fieldwork in 2012 and 2013 in Azerbaijan, Turkey and the United Kingdom. Comparative legal methodology is used to inquire into foreign legal systems in order to seek solutions to the issues of a particular legal system, or to improve the combination of law between national legal systems.[82] In this context, it is therefore important to recognise that comparative law presupposes the existence of multiplicity of legal regulations and institutions and examines to what extent they are alike and divergent.[83]The role of comparative methodology in this book is to facilitate a comparative analysis of the divergent political regimes and foreign investment laws and policies of Azerbaijan and Turkey.

This research engages with the following materials: comprehensive literature, host government agreements, arbitral decisions and the ongoing review of laws and petroleum legislation. These constitute the primary sources of this work. Notably, a major hurdle in this study has been the review of energy investment contracts, as they are, by nature, confidential. This project also utilises secondary materials and data has been gathered from books, journal articles, reports,

82 L. Bickman & D. J. Rog, *Handbook of Applied Social Research Methods* (London: Sage Publications, 1998) 15.

83 R Sacco, 'Legal Formants: A Dynamic Approach to Comparative Law', *American Journal of Comparative Law*, Vol. 39, No. 1 (1991) 5.

conference papers, newspapers and statistics. In order to broaden the scope of the information gathered, and to exploit the research tools of our digital age, several online discussion groups have also been monitored.

Why was the BTC project selected as a case study in this work and why was comparative approach was adopted for Azerbaijan and Turkey?

One of the principal reasons why the BTC project was chosen as a case study was the availability of information about it. A major hurdle in energy-related studies is the restricted availability of information on contractual arrangements between parties. In this book, the BTC project was selected as a case study because project backgrounds, issues arising from the BTC project, intergovernmental agreements between Azerbaijan, Georgia and Turkey, and host governmental agreements of these states with the project consortium are made publicly available. In addition, there is also a significant number of legal documents produced by NGOs, financial institutions and project sponsors involved with the BTC project that are also publicly accessible.

Azerbaijan and Turkey have been selected for the purposes of this study to examine whether their respective political regimes and legal and regulatory structure foster the inclusion of stabilisation clauses in the agreements made for energy investment projects to be undertaken on their territory (whether intentionally or through a lack of proper checks and controls). If this proves to be the case, this prompts the question: what are the other reasons these two countries agreed to contractual stability in the BTC host governmental agreement? There is no doubt that there are considerable differences between these two countries in terms of energy reserves, size and other economic factors, yet Azerbaijan and Turkey are both Turkic countries party to a number of significant international energy investment projects, and share much common ground in terms of language, religion and history.

The reason for choosing these two countries for comparison is twofold: the first relates to the organisation and structure of their political institutions and the second to their involvement in the BTC agreement.

The legal regime of Azerbaijan is a presidential system; however, Turkey is ruled by a hybrid parliamentary regime. In literature, discussion can be found regarding the influence of legal regimes on FDI and on their perceived attractiveness to foreign investors. Analysis of these two divergent regimes, and their political and democratic institutions, laws and foreign investment policy, may provide an insight into these states' internal motivations for conceding to stabilisation clauses in their host governmental contracts.

Both Turkic states (along with Georgia) are party to the BTC agreement. This agreement is arguably the most debated petroleum pipeline project in the energy field, chiefly because it contains provisions that place heavy burdens on its host governments. This study explores the issues that arise from the BTC agreement and measures how this agreement and its host governmental contracts have impacted on Azerbaijani and Turkish domestic law.

It is also pertinent to justify why Georgia was not selected, even though the country is also party to the BTC project. It was in the interests of the study to select two countries with key differences in terms of political regime and role in the agreement. Georgia and Turkey share the commonalities of having a hybrid political regime and being transit countries under the BTC agreement, whereas Azerbaijan, as a petroleum-producing country with an authoritarian political regime, provided the best contrast.

Overview of Azerbaijan and Turkey

The Republic of Azerbaijan is located in the south-east of the Caucasus, and shares borders with Russia, Georgia, Iran and Armenia. The country gained independence in 1991, after the collapse of the Soviet Union. The political system of Azerbaijan is based on the principle of the separation of powers. With regard to this principle, the constitution determines that executive power is in the hands of the president of the Republic of Azerbaijan, legislative power is the domain of the parliament of the Republic of Azerbaijan, while judicial power is held by the independent courts of Azerbaijan, the Constitutional Court being the highest of these courts. The political regime in Azerbaijan is assessed by scholars in the literature; however, there is little agreement on which categorisation should be assigned to it.[84] The categories suggested range from neo-patrimonial dictatorship, sultanistic, authoritarian, to decaying semi-authoritarian, sultanistic semi-authoritarian, hybrid and partially democratic.[85]

Another Turkic country, Turkey is located in Western Asia, and has been a republic since 1923. More specifically, Turkey is a secular parliamentary republic established on the principle of the separation of powers into legislative, executive and judiciary. The constitution is the supreme law and the Constitutional Court is the highest court in the country. The executive branch is dual-headed in Turkey. The president is the head of the state and the prime minister is the head of the Council of Ministers. As determined by the 1982 Constitution, the country's legislative organ rests in the National Grand Assembly (Turkiye Buyuk Millet Meclisi) unicameral parliament which is located in Ankara. Furthermore, the 1982 Turkish Constitution decrees that national courts and judges in Turkey are independent. Turkey is often classed as a hybrid regime. It should be highlighted that following the outcome of a referendum held in 2017, constitutional amendments that will transform Turkey's current parliament system to an executive presidency system are to take effect. Under the new system, the president will have enhanced executive powers and the office of prime minister will be eliminated. The new system will be implemented following the 2018 presidential election.

The Economist Intelligence Unit published a report entitled 'The Democracy Index' in 2017. The set of values it proposes can be used to place states within one of four typologies of regime: namely, full democracies, flowed democracies,

84 Bayulgen (n. 75 above) 97.
85 Ibid.

hybrid regimes and authoritarian regimes. A country to be classified a hybrid regime scores between 4 and 5.9, while those deemed to be authoritarian regimes score below 4. According to this matrix the political regime of Azerbaijan is classified as an authoritarian regime and Turkey ranks as a hybrid regime.[86]

The Republic of Azerbaijan is a dynamic emerging economy with a skilled workforce and the benefit of rich natural energy resources. The energy sector is the backbone of the Azerbaijani economy. Azerbaijan is richly endowed with natural resources and has a long history of oil and gas exploration. According to the BP Statistical Review of World Energy, Azerbaijan's confirmed crude oil reserves were estimated at 7 billion barrels at the end of 2016.[87] The oil sector is not a new industry for Azerbaijan. The country is the one of the longest-established oil-producing countries in the world, and experienced an oil boom at the beginning of the twentieth century and thereafter served as one of the main refining centres within the former Soviet Union. The involvement of international oil companies in petroleum projects in Azerbaijan commenced with the activities of the Nobel brothers in the early 1870s.[88] 'By 1897, the oil fields in Baku delivered more than 45% of the world's crude oil. And a few years later, by the end of the century, these Russian-run wells accounted for more than half the total world output.'[89] In the context of Azerbaijan's more recent history, the oil sector has played a key role in the economic and political development of the country, strengthening the country's independence, protecting its territorial position and stimulating economic growth by attracting international energy investors.

While it is the case that most former Soviet states have been endeavouring to become a part of the global economy as new independent states, Azerbaijan distinguishes itself from its peers through the sheer extent of its success in adapting to the global economy and attracting foreign investors. In UNCTAD's inward FDI index, Azerbaijan ranked the third highest among 140 countries in the years between 1994 and 1996, and eighth highest from 1998 to 2000.[90] The Azerbaijani government boasts a successful record for oil and gas policy-making, signing the 'Contract of the Century' in 1994 regarding the Azeri–Chirag–Gunashli fields (ACG), swiftly followed by the Shah Deniz gas field in 1996, which led to a huge boost in international investment in the petroleum sector. Moreover, another crucial project emerged in 2006 on the signing of the great Baku–Tbilisi–Ceyhan

86 Economist Intelligence Unit, 'Democracy Index 2017: Free Speech Under Attack', available at <http://pages.eiu.com/rs/753-RIQ-438/images/Democracy_Index_2017.pdf>

87 G. Camal, 'BP Keeps Unchanged Azerbaijan's Proved Oil Reserve Estimates', available at <www.azernews.az/oil_and_gas/114751.html>

88 G. Askerov, 'Oil and Gas Pipeline Strategy of a Landlocked Countries: Case of Azerbaijan', *Khazar Journal of Humanities and Social Sciences*, Vol. 3, No. 4 (2000) 5.

89 R. Ebel, *Caspian Energy Resources: Implication for the Arab Gulf, Emirates Centre for Strategic Studies and Research*, (Lebanon: Ithaca Press, 2000) 2, cited in Askerov (n. 88 above) 5.

90 UNCTAD, 'World Investment Report 2002: Benchmarking FDI Performance and Potential' (2002) 26–31, available at <www.unctad.org/en/docs/wir2002p1ch2_en.pdf>

(BTC) pipeline project. The economic goal of this project is to transport oil from Baku to Western markets via the cities of Tbilisi and Ceyhan. The political objective is, technically, to end the Russian monopoly of transportation of energy resources from the Caspian Sea.

The Baku–Tbilisi–Erzurum gas pipeline and the Baku–Tbilisi–Kars railroad projects are significant international infrastructure projects designed to enable the country to transport its energy resources. However, Azerbaijan's landlocked location in the Caspian region and unresolved conflict with Armenia, which occupies 20% of the territory of Azerbaijan, forced the country to rely on its other neighbours when delivering its oil and gas products to the world market. These issues placed a heavy burden on the Azerbaijani economy.

In the interest of boosting its economy further, Azerbaijan has also established trading partnerships with more than 147 countries around the world. Its chief imports are reported to be food, machinery, electric equipment and parts, vehicles and parts, chemical products, medical and surgery equipment, while, perhaps unsurprisingly, its principal exports are crude oil, other products related to oil, natural gas, electricity and chemicals.[91]

During the two decades of its existence as a republic, the country has adopted various codes relating to foreign investment in an attempt to grant space to its market economy for growth. The chief elements of these codes are the law concerning the protection of foreign investment, the law on investment activity, the law on privatisation of the state property, and related presidential decrees.[92] These laws provide numerous crucial state guarantees to the investors, concerning non-discrimination, freedom of capital movement, stability of legislation, compensation for expropriation and right of entry to international arbitration.[93] The Azerbaijani government also implemented crucial legislation in the energy sector, notably the law on energy, the law on the use of energy resources, the law on subsoil and the law on natural monopolies.[94]

Despite more recent sluggishness, Turkey remains a dynamic, growing economy. According to the International Monetary Fund, the country is an emerging market economy and is mainly developed and industrialised.[95] Turkey is an upper-middle income state with relatively few natural resources. Its main natural resources are mineral (coal, chromate, copper, boron), steel and petroleum. The country does not have rich oil reserves; however, its economy is presently in transition from a high degree of dependence on agriculture and heavy industry. Although

91 For further details, see the State Statistical Committee of Azerbaijan, available at <www.stat.gov.az>

92 Energy Charter Secretariat, 'In-depth Review of the Investment Climate and Market Structure in the Energy Sector of Azerbaijan' (2005) available at <www.encharter.org/index.php?id=141>

93 Ibid.

94 Ibid.

95 IMF, 'World Economic Outlook 2011: Tensions from the Two-Speed Recovery Unemployment, Commodities, and Capital Flows' (Washington, 2011) 173–4, available at <www.imf.org/external/pubs/ft/weo/2011/01/pdf/text.pdf>

Turkey is not an oil-producing country, it plays a major role as a transit country in international energy projects.

There are number of significant oil and gas pipeline projects in which Turkey has a role, such as the BTC crude oil pipeline, the Trans-Anatolian Natural Gas Pipeline (TANAP) project and the Kirkuk–Ceyhan oil pipeline project. The TANAP project aims to transfer Azerbaijani natural gas via Turkey to Europe. The project was announced on 17 November 2011 at the Third Black Sea Energy and Economic Forum in Istanbul. This major natural gas pipeline project is expected to commence in 2018. The Kirkuk crude oil pipeline project links Turkey and Iraq. However, the pipeline has been sabotaged by the PKK terrorist group (Kurdish Worker's Party) on occasion in the past and is still not in full working order. The relative success of the BTC project renders it one of the most important oil pipeline projects in realising Turkey's national goals in the oil sector. This major oil pipeline project has been in full operation since 2006 and provides a million barrels of oil from Azerbaijan through Georgia to Turkey per day.[96]

According to the United Nations' world investment survey, between 2008 and 2010 Turkey ranked as the 15th most attractive country for FDI in the world.[97] This assessment leads one to question how Turkey gained this status in such a short period. There is no doubt that Turkey's foreign investment policy and new legislative reforms have played an effective role in the attraction of FDI and economic development of the country. In 2003, Turkey enacted significant legislative reforms[98] to develop its investment environment. The new reforms contain three significant legislative acts that intend to remove bureaucratic red tape, ensure equal treatment to both domestic and foreign investors, and protect foreign investors' rights to meet international standards. FDI law provides a definition of foreign investors and foreign direct investment; moreover, it also identifies integral principles of FDI, such as freedom to invest, national treatment, expropriation and nationalisation, dispute settlement and other areas related to foreign investment. Turkey is also a prolific exporter of products such as foodstuffs, clothes and automobiles. In addition, the country exports mineral fuels and oils, tobacco and steel, and trade partnerships with countries from a number of regions across the world play a crucial role in the Turkish economy. The European Union is Turkey's largest trade partner. The Ankara agreement signed between EU and Turkey to establish a customs union in 1995 was the catalyst for this. This agreement enables goods to travel between two entities without any barriers (zero tariffs).

While it is apparent that trade has been a strong driver of the economic growth recently witnessed in Azerbaijan and Turkey, neither country can yet be defined as numbering among the most economically free nation states.

96 Baku–Tbilisi–Ceyhan (BTC) Caspian Pipeline, available at <www.hydrocarbons-technology.com/projects/bp>

97 United Nations Conference on Trade and Development, 'World Investment Prospect Survey 2008–2010', available at <www.unctad.org/en/docs/wips2008_en.pdf>

98 Foreign Investment Law No. 4875, 17 June 2003.

Baku–Tbilisi–Ceyhan crude oil pipeline project: timeline, importance and issues

The BTC is a crude oil pipeline project which spans three countries and runs from the Caspian Sea to the Mediterranean coast. The aim of this project is to transport Caspian crude oil from the Azeri–Chirag–Gunashli (ACG) fields in the Caspian basin via Tbilisi in Georgia to a Turkish port on the Mediterranean Sea for delivery to the Western market. The project's pipeline which runs underground along its whole length, measures 1,768 km (1,099 miles) in total: 443 km of which span Azerbaijan, 249 km in Georgia, and 1,076 km in Turkey.[99] This mega project was organised by an international consortium (Main Export Pipeline participants) and led by British Petroleum (now known as BP plc). This project was seen by Western governments as a vehicle via which the Russian monopoly of the delivery of oil supplies from the Caspian region might be terminated.

The first negotiations regarding the BTC project commenced in 1992, just after Azerbaijan declared itself a republic independent of the former Soviet Union. In spring 1992, the Turkish prime minister, Suleyman Demirel, visited the new independent Turkic countries, including Azerbaijan, and proposed that a pipeline route should be planned for the economic development and promotion of the strategic importance of the region. Initially, it was thought that a pipeline from Azerbaijan would run through Georgia or Armenia. This was found to present too great a political risk due to the unresolved war between Armenia and Azerbaijan over the status of Nagorno-Karabakh and the close military and economic ties between Armenia and Russia. This left, as the only option, the circuitous Azerbaijan–Georgia–Turkey route, longer and financially more expensive to build than the Armenian route.[100]

On 29 October 1998, the President of Azerbaijan, Heydar Aliyev, the President of Georgia, Eduard Shevardnadze, the President of Kazakhstan, Nursultan Nazarbayev, the President of Turkey, Suleyman Demirel, and the President of Uzbekistan, Islam Karimov, met in Ankara to submit and sign the Ankara Declaration. With this declaration the parties officially acknowledged the importance and necessity of the construction of more than one pipeline, commercially optimising oil and natural gas exports to the rest of the world.[101] These countries also confirmed their support for routing the pipeline from Baku to the Turkish Mediterranean port of Ceyhan. Present to witness the declaration was the US Energy Secretary, Bill Richardson.

On 18 November 1999, at the meeting of the Organisation for Security and Cooperation in Europe in Istanbul, the intergovernmental agreement which

99 British Petroleum available at <www.bp.com>

100 Z. Baran, 'The Baku-Tbilisi-Ceyhan Pipeline: Implications for Turkey', Chapter 6 in S. F. Starr & S. E. Cornell, *Baku–Tbilisi–Ceyhan Pipeline: Oil Window to the West* (Washington, DC: Central Asia-Caucasus Institute & Silk Road Studies Program ,2005) 105.

101 *Hurriyet Daily News*, available at <www.hurriyetdailynews.com/default.aspx?pageid=438&n=timeline-of-the-baku-tbilisi-ceyhan-pipeline-2006-07-13>

formally established the foundations of the BTC project was signed by representatives of Azerbaijan, Georgia and Turkey. The then US president, Bill Clinton countersigned the accord as a witness. In addition to this intergovernmental treaty, the signatory states also signed HGAs between the project consortium and Azerbaijan–Georgia–Turkey. The HGAs were ratified by Azerbaijan on 26 May 2000, in Georgia on 29 May 2000, and by Turkey on 22 June 2000.

Stabilisation clauses inserted in host governmental contracts caused considerable alarm to civil rights groups when it became apparent that such contracts enabled BTC sponsors to contract outside the rule of law. Indeed, the provisions of the agreement extend a wide range of privileges and immunities to investors. Moreover, the main purpose of this agreement is to grant immunity to the investor and third parties (such as insurers) from the domestic law of the host state. Notably, the BTC agreement established a unique legal regime contrary to other similar energy investment contracts. It goes without saying that when the economic, environmental and social importance of industries in which stabilisation clauses have been used is considered, it is of no surprise that they have been the subject of debate and criticism by civil rights groups interested in the promotion of sustainable development.[102] BP came under fire for its stabilisation clauses because they prevented the three aforementioned host countries from passing new human rights legislation through their national parliaments and required the host states to compensate them for contravening the clause. This restricted the states' capacity to actively honour their obligations to promote or protect human rights under international law.[103] Amnesty International made the following criticisms regarding the economic equilibrium clauses inserted in the host governmental agreement signed between BTC investor consortium and the Turkish government:

> While Turkey remains bound by its international human rights obligations, it has undertaken in the Host Government Agreement (HGA) to pay the consortium substantial compensation for any changes in law or other actions that will disturb the economic equilibrium of the project. It is thus caught between two sets of requirements – to live up its undertakings to its citizens and to live up to its undertakings to the consortium. Each step in the former direction will carry the price tag of damages – which can easily amount to many millions of pounds. In this way, the HGA creates disincentives for Turkey to become more integrated into international human rights norms. At the very least, it may have to enter reservations exempting the project from any new international standards it subscribes to. The effect of being faced with punitive costs for protecting the human rights of those affected

102 A. Sheppard & A. Crockett, 'Are Stabilisation Clauses a Threat to Sustainable Development?', Chapter 14 in M. C. Segger, A. Newcombe & M. Gehring (eds), *Sustainable Development in International in International Investment Law* (The Hague: Kluwer, 2010) 338–9.

103 Amnesty International, 'Human Rights on the Line: The Baku-Tbilisi-Ceyhan Project' (London, 2003) 5.

by the pipeline is likely to have a chilling effect on Turkey's ability to improve its general human rights record.[104]

In December 2003, the BTC Co published a legal document called 'Human Rights Undertaking'.[105] With regard to this undertaking, compensation clauses in the HGA would not be valid in the event of new laws being adopted or introduced for environmental and human rights issues. It is reasonable to assume that this publication was prompted by the criticism and intended to go some way in appeasing such objections.

Structure of the book

The book consists of three parts which are divided into the following chapters:

Part I

The work begins with a general introduction and the framework of the research.

Chapter 1 includes the definition of key terminology and concepts that are central to this book, such as host governmental energy investment contracts and stabilisation clauses. It also provides an overview of political risk, as well as a geographical, economic and political background to Azerbaijan and Turkey. Understanding political risks is very important in order to assess why energy investment contracts are exposed to conflict and also to understand why stabilisation clauses are used as a form of risk management in host government energy investment contracts.

Chapter 2 attempts to define what constitutes indirect expropriation and reviews the mechanisms that can be employed by foreign investors to guard against it. The chapter starts by providing an overview of indirect expropriation. It then moves on to address the differences between direct and indirect expropriation. Several case studies are cited in order to illustrate what distinguishes the two phenomena. Next, the types of government measure that may constitute indirect expropriation are addressed. This chapter also seeks to provide criteria for distinguishing between non-compensable government measures and indirect expropriation with reference to the approaches and findings of international investment tribunals. This is exemplified by comparing and contrasting the bilateral investment treaties of Azerbaijan and Turkey and their treaty provisions concerning indirect expropriation. Following this, the tools for mitigating the threat of indirect expropriation are assessed and the question of what mechanism (s) can be used by foreign investors against the risk of indirect expropriation is addressed.

104 Ibid.
105 The BTC Human Rights Undertaking, available at <http://subsites.bp.com/caspian/Human%20Rights%20Undertaking.pdf>

Part II

Part II forms the core of this book and is composed of Chapters 3 to 5.

In Part II, stabilisation clauses and internal and external factors are examined and exemplified through a comparative study of Azerbaijan and Turkey.

Chapter 3 examines the stabilisation clauses inserted in HGAs by foreign investors as a political risk management device. The chapter addresses several issues including the typology, validity and efficacy of stabilisation clauses. Chapter 3 seeks to examine how stabilisation clauses manage political risk, in particular regulatory change, which is applicable to energy projects, changes of contractual terms and indirect expropriation. This chapter also makes reference to the ongoing debate between legal scholars in the field on the validity and efficacy of stabilisation clauses. Through the analysis of this chapter the following questions will be answered:

- To what extent are stabilisation clauses effective in protecting investments, or, conversely, in contradiction of their intended guardianship purpose, do they instead disenfranchise the sovereign rights of the host states?
- Do stabilisation provisions constitute a threat for environmental and human rights issues?

Chapter 4 seeks to nominate the external factors which may force host states to include stabilisation clauses in energy investment contracts. This chapter analyses the range of external factors, other than the will of investors, which may force a host state to agree to have a stabilisation clause included in its energy investment agreements as well as their effect on the regulatory powers of states. Chapter 4 examines the role of rating agencies, project finance lenders and political risk insurers in relation to the investor and the host state and their influence regarding the inclusion of stabilisation clauses in agreements. This chapter also provides a legal analysis of the BTC agreements from the perspective of Turkey and Azerbaijan and compares their relative bargaining positions in negotiating the contract. The following question is posed:

- Do rating agencies, project finance lenders and political risk insurers play an active role in lobbying for the inclusion stabilisation clauses in host governmental contracts?

Chapter 5 focuses on internal factors in Azerbaijan and Turkey and whether the legislation, constitutional guarantees and political structure of these countries facilitate stability in energy investment projects. The analysis takes into account each country's FDI laws and constitutional promises, and the legal status of their international agreements under domestic law as well as their respective political regimes. In the case of Turkey, the guarantees available to foreign investors under the country's defunct FDI law (Law for Encouragement of Foreign Capital No.

6224) and the new FDI (FDI Law No. 4875) laws are compared. Finally, this chapter attempts to answer the following questions:

- How effective are different political regimes in promoting FDI and giving consent to stabilisation clauses in Azerbaijani and Turkish HGCs?
- What has caused Azerbaijan and Turkey to agree to contractual stability in the BTC host governmental agreements?

The purpose of the comparison here is to explore the similarities and differences between state guarantees under the countries respective laws, investment policies and political regimes.

Part III

Chapter 6 pulls together the strands of the research in order to present the internal and external factors that motivate states to agree to stabilisation clauses. This chapter also proposes recommendations to the Azerbaijani and Turkish governments for the improvement of legislation, political structure and policies in order to be in a stronger position to negotiate energy investment contracts in their own interests.

Bibliography

Legislation and guides

Foreign Investment Law No. 4875 17 June 2003

Cases and arbitral awards

Generation Ukraine, Inc. v Ukraine, ICSID Case No ARB/00/9, Award of 16 September 2003, 44

Internet websites

www.imf.org/external/pubs/ft/weo/2011/01/pdf/text.pdf
www.miga.org/documents/WIPR10ebook.pdf
http://stats.oecd.org/glossary/detail.asp?ID=5990
http://subsites.bp.com/caspian/Human%20Rights%20Undertaking.pdf
http://unctad.org/en/docs/iteiit20054_en.pdf
www.acc.com/vl/public/Article/loader.cfm?csModule=security/getfile&pageid=16024
www.bakerbotts.com/~/media/files/ideas/publications/2007/03/building-a-cross border-pipeline/files/goolsby-rowley-pgt-march-2007/fileattachment/goolsby-r owley-pgt-march-2007.pdf
www.bp.com
www.encharter.org/index.php?id=141

www.hurriyetdailynews.com/default.aspx?pageid=438&n=timeline-of-the-baku-tbilisi-ceyhan-pipeline-2006-07-13
www.irmi.com/expert/articles/2000/wagner10.aspx
www.silkroadstudies.org/component/jifile/download/OGY3YmRkZDdkMWVlNmQ3YmRmMzk5NzI2YzNjOWI1MjU=/btc-6-pdf.html
www.stat.gov.az
www.tilj.org
www.unctad.org/en/docs/wips2008_en.pdf
www.hydrocarbons-technology.com/projects/bp
www.encharter.org
www.ogel.org

Books and monographs

Allan, G. & Skinner, C., *Handbook for Research in the Social Science.* Brighton: Falmer Press, 1991

Bayulgen, O., *Foreign Direct Investment, Oil Curse and Democratization: A Comparison of Azerbaijan and Russia, Business and Politics.* Cambridge: Cambridge University Press, 2010

Bickman, L. & Rog, D. J., *Handbook of Applied Social Research Methods.* London: Sage Publications, 1998

Cameron, P. D., *International Energy Investment Law: The Pursuit of Stability.* Oxford: Oxford University Press, 2010

Erkan, M., *International Energy Investment Law, Stability through Contractual Clauses,* Energy and Environmental Law and Policy Series. Alphen aan den Rijn: Kluwer Law International, 2011

Ebel, R., *Caspian Energy Resources: Implication for the Arab Gulf, Emirates Centre for Strategic Studies and Research.* Lebanon: Ithaca Press, 2000

Garner, B. A., *A Dictionary of Modern Legal Usage*, 3rd edn. New York: Oxford University Press, 2011

Hober, K., *Investment Arbitration in Eastern Europe: In Search of a Definition of Expropriation.* New York: Juris Publishing, 2007

Hoffman, S. L., *The Law and Business of International Project Finance*, 3rd edn. Cambridge: Cambridge University Press, 2008

Johnston, D., *International Exploration Economics, Risk and Contracts Analysis.* Tulsa, OK: PennWell Books, 2003

Johnston, D., *International Petroleum Fiscal Systems and Production Sharing Contracts.* Tulsa, OK: PennWell Books, 1994

LaxH. L., *Political Risk in the International Oil and Gas Industry.* Boston, MA: International Human Resources Development Corporation, 1983

Mazeel, M., *Petroleum Fiscal System and Contracts.* Hamburg: Diplomica Verlag, 2010

Smith, E. E., *International Petroleum Transactions*, 2nd edn. Denver, CO: Rocky Mountain Mineral Law Foundation, 2000

Sornarajah, M., *International Law on Foreign Direct Investment*, 2nd edn. Cambridge: Cambridge University Press. 2004

Yescombe, E. R., *Principles of Project Finance.* San Diego, CA: Academic Press, 2002

Chapters in books

Baran, Z., 'The Baku–Tbilisi–Ceyhan Pipeline: Implications for Georgia', Chapter 6 in S. F. Starr & S. E. Cornell (eds), *Baku–Tbilisi–Ceyhan Pipeline: Oil Window to the West*, Washington, DC: Central Asia-Caucasus Institute & Silk Road Studies Program, 2005

DufeyA. & Kazimova, R., 'Baku–Tbilisi–Ceyhan Project: Implications of Project Finance', Chapter 12 in S. Leader and D. Ong (eds). *Global Project Finance, Human Rights and Sustainable Development.* Cambridge: Cambridge University Press, 2011

Sheppard, A. & Crockett, A., 'Are Stabilisation Clauses a Threat to Sustainable Development?' Chapter 14 in M. C. C. Segger, A. Newcombe& M. W. Gehring (eds), *Sustainable Development in International in International Investment Law.* The Hague: Kluwer, 2010

Articles, seminars/conference and research papers

Al-Faruque, A. 'Validity and Efficacy of Stabilisation Clauses: Legal Protection vs. Functional Value', *Journal of International Arbitration*, Vol. 23, No. 4 (2006) 317–336

Askerov, G., 'Oil and Gas Pipeline Strategy of a Landlocked Countries: Case of Azerbaijan', *Khazar Journal of Humanities and Social Sciences*, Vol. 3, No. 4 (2000) 5

Bindemann, K., 'Product Sharing Agreements: An Economic Analysis', *Oxford Institute for Energy Studies*, WPM25, October (1999) 1

Bossley, L. (HIS Energy Group), 'Political Risk: A Hedge Too Far', *Petroleum Economist* (October 2002) 33

Boulos, A. J., 'Assessing Political Risk', available at www.ipaa.org/wp-content/uploads/2017/01/PoliticalRisk.pdf

Camal, G., 'BP Keeps Unchanged Azerbaijan's Proved Oil Reserve Estimates', available at www.azernews.az/oil_and_gas/114751.html

Comeaux, P. E. & Kinsella, N. S., 'Reducing Political Risk in Developing Countries: Bilateral Investment Treaties, Stabilisation Clauses, and MIGA & OPIC Investment Insurance', *New York Law School Journal of International and Comparative Law*, Vol. 15 (1994) 4

Dulaney, M. &Merrick, R., 'Legal Issues in Cross-Border Oil and Gas Pipelines', *Journal of Energy and Natural Resources Law*, Vol. 23 (2005) 247

Goolsby, G. & Rowley, M., 'Building a Cross-Border Pipeline: For Multi-National Projects, Host Government Agreements Can Reduce Risk and Create a Stable Investment Environment', available at <www.bakerbotts.com/~/media/files/ideas/publications/2007/03/building-a-crossborder-pipeline/files/goolsby-rowley-pgt-march-2007/fileattachment/goolsby-rowley-pgt-march-2007.pdf>

Kolo, A., 'Managing Political Risk in Transnational Investment Contracts', Centre for Petroleum and Mineral Law Policy (CPMLP), Professional Paper No. PP11 (1994) 2

Likosky, M., 'Contracting, Regulatory Issues in the Oil and Gas and the Metallic Mineral Industries', *Transnational Corporations*, Vol. 18, No. 1 (2009) 14

Lovells International Law Firm/Association of Corporate Counsel, 'Sino-Foreign Oil and Gas Industry: Legal Risk Comparative Analysis' (November 2005) 2, available at <www.acc.com/vl/public/Article/loader.cfm?csModule=security/getfile&pageid=16024>

Maniruzzaman, A. F. M., 'The Pursuit of Stability in International Energy Investment Contracts: A Critical Appraisal of Emerging Trends', *Journal of World Energy and Business*, Vol. 1, No. 2 (2008) 154

Moran, T. H., 'Political and Regulation Risk in Infrastructure Investment in Developing Countries: Introduction and an Overview', *CEPMLP*, Vol. 5–6 (1999)

Neto, J. S. C., 'Risk-bearing Service Contracts in Brazil', *Journal of Energy and Natural Resources Law*, Vol. 3 (1985) 114

Norton, S. D., 'The Natural Environment as a Salient Stakeholder: Non-Anthropocentrism, Ecosystem Stability and the Financial Markets', *Business Ethics: A European Review* Vol. 16, No. 4 (2007) 390

OECD, 'International Investment Law: A Changing Landscape', OECD Working Paper (2005) 45

OECD, 'Indirect Expropriation and Right to Regulate in International Investment Law', OECD Working Papers on International Investment Law (2004) 3–4

Quinley, K. M., 'Managing Political Risks', *The Risk Report*, Vol. 24, No. 7 (March 2002)

Sacco, R., 'Legal Formants: A Dynamic Approach to Comparative Law', *American Journal of Comparative Law*, Vol. 39, No. 1 (1991) 5

Talus, K., Looper, S. & Otillar, S., 'Lex Petrolea and Internationalization of Petroleum Agreements: Focus on Host Government Contracts', *Journal of World Energy Law Business*, Vol. 5, No. 3 (2012) 183

United Nations Conference on Trade and Development, 'World Investment Prospect Survey 2008–2010', available at <www.unctad.org/en/docs/wips2008_en.pdf>

Valera, J. L., 'Political Risks for International Oil Companies Investing in Latin America', *OGEL Journal of Oil, Gas and Energy Law Intelligence* 4 (2006) 1, available at <www.ogel.org>

Vinogradov, S. V., 'Cross-border Oil and Gas Pipelines: Legal and Regulatory Regimes', Association of International Petroleum Negotiators (AIPN) (2001) 7.

Waelde, T. W. & Ndi, G., 'Stabilizing International Investment Commitments: International Law versus Contract Interpretation', *Texas International Law Journal*, Vol. 31, No. 2 (1996), 216

Waelde, T. W., 'Managing the Risk of Sanctions in the Global Oil & Gas Industry: Corporate Response under Political, Legal and Commercial Pressures', *Texas International Law Journal*, Vol. 36 (2001) 183–184

Wagner, D., 'Defining Political Risks', October 2000, available at <www.irmi.com/expert/articles/2000/wagner10.aspx>

Wallace, S. C., 'Symposium: Energy and International Law: Development, Litigation and Regulation', *Texas International Law Journal*, Vol. 36 (2001) 54, available at <http://www.tilj.org>

Reports

Amnesty International, 'Human Rights on the Line: The Baku–Tbilisi–Ceyhan Project', (London, 2003)

Cotula, L., 'Investment contracts and sustainable development: How to make contracts for fairer and more sustainable natural resource investments', *Natural Resource Issues*, No. 20 IIED (2010)

Energy Charter Secretariat, 'In-depth Review of the Investment Climate and Market Structure in the Energy Sector of Azerbaijan' (2005), available at <www.encharter.org/index.php?id=141>

Hober, K., 'Ownership of the Oil and Gas Resources in the Caspian Sea: Problems and Solution – International Arbitration and Contractual Clauses', Stockholm Arbitration Report 1 (2004)

IMF, 'World Economic Outlook 2011: Tensions from the Two-Speed Recovery Unemployment, Commodities, and Capital Flows' (Washington, 2011)

Shemberg, A., 'Stabilisation Clause and Human Rights: A Research Project Conducted for IFC and the United Nations Special Representative to the Secretary General on Business and Human Rights', IFC/SRSG Research Paper, 11 May (2009)

The Economist Intelligence Unit, 'Democracy Index 2017: Free Speech under Attack', available at <http://pages.eiu.com/rs/753-RIQ-438/images/Democracy_Index_2017.pdf>

UNCTAD, 'World Investment Report 2002: Benchmarking FDI Performance and Potential' (2002) 26–31, available at <www.unctad.org/en/docs/wir2002p1ch2_en.pdf>

UNCTAD, 'Taking of Property', UNCTAD Series on Issues in International Investment Agreements (2000)

UNCTAD, *Investor State Disputes Arising from Investment Treaties: 'A Review'* (New York and Geneva, 2005)

World Bank Group, *World Investment and Political Risk Report (2010): Investing in a Low Carbon Economy* (New York and Geneva, 2010)

2 Indirect expropriation

Introduction

The protection of a foreign investor's property ownership against direct expropriation or nationalisation has long been a consideration for international corporations, and, up until the 1980s, was one of the most disruptive kinds of government interference in investment projects. From the start of the new millennium, a shift occurred with the emergence of indirect expropriation soon becoming the single most significant threat to investment contracts in the energy sector as well as the most impactful form of intervention a state could set in motion.[1] This type of government intervention may result from measures that a host country enacts in order to gain greater control over commercial activities in its territory by adopting new regulations, even where such a regulation does not specifically target an investment.[2] In contrast with direct expropriation, which has the aim of physically taking the private property:

> indirect expropriation cases are those where, by means of administrative or legislative procedures, the state in question causes a unilateral change in contract conditions such that the investor is unable to recover the expected quasi rents[3] of the business under the original contractual framework.[4]

International tribunals and scholars in conventional literature have focused on the notion of direct and indirect expropriation in their decisions, and in their various publications. Although there are numerous sources regarding this phenomena:

1 R. Dolzer, 'Indirect Expropriation: New Developments?', *11 N.Y.U. Environmental Law Journal* Vol. 11 (2002) 64–5.

2 S. H. Nikiema, 'Indirect Expropriation', Best Practices Working Paper Series (International Institute for Sustainable Development, 2012) 1available at <www.iisd.org/pdf/2012/best_practice_indirect_expropriation.pdf>

3 Quasi rent is defined as the expected cash flow that the stakeholder will not be able to recover if he/she abandons the operation.

4 M. A. Abdala & P. T. Spiller, 'Damage Valuation of Indirect Expropriation in International Arbitration Cases', *American Review of International Arbitration*, Vol. 14 (2003) 449.

the doctrine and case law on expropriation in international law remain somewhat unsettled. Several factors may explain why this is so. These include the diversity of interest at play, divergence in cultural, economic and legal concepts of property, different understandings of the role of the state, and a general heterogeneity in state practice.[5]

An overview of indirect expropriation

'An indirect form of expropriation in which a government measure, although not on its face affecting a transfer of property, results in the foreign investor being deprived of its property or its benefits.'[6] In other words, while indirect expropriation does not technically undermine the investment title of the foreign investors, it nevertheless considerably diminishes that foreign investor's ability to run their business activities freely or reduces the benefit that they expect to obtain from the investment. When does indirect expropriation occur? Broadly, indirect expropriation occurs 'through interference by a state in the use of that property or with the enjoyment of the benefits even where the property is not seized and the legal title to the property is not affected'.[7] What is the approach of bilateral investment treaties (BITs) and multilateral investment treaties (MITs) to indirect expropriation phenomena? In general, all BITs and MITs provide articles that refer to expropriation.

Article 1110 of the North American Free Trade Agreement (NAFTA) provides that 'no party may directly or indirectly nationalise or expropriate an investment of an investor of another party in its territory or take a measure tantamount to nationalisation or expropriation of such an investment'.[8] In a similar way, the Energy Charter Treaty, under Article 13, precludes host states from taking any measures 'having effect equivalent to nationalisation or expropriation'.[9] Modern BITs generally "refer to direct and indirect expropriation and measures "tantamount" or "equivalent" to expropriation."[10]

However, it should be noted that investment treaties steer clear of providing a definition of what exactly indirect expropriation is. Instead of simply defining

5 L. Fortier & S. L. Drymer, 'Indirect Expropriation in the Law of International Investment: I Know it When I See It', *ICSID Review – Foreign Investment Law Journal*, Vol. 19, No. 2 (2004) 293–4.

6 A. Newcombe & L. Paradell, *Law and Practice of Investment Treaties: Standards of Treatment* (Alphen aan den Rijn: Kluwer Law International, 2009), 323.

7 C. Yannaca-Small, 'Indirect Expropriation and the Right to Regulate in International Investment Law', Organisation for Economic Co-operation and Development, (2004) 3–4, available at <www.oecd.org/daf/inv/investment-policy/WP-2004_4.pdf>

8 NAFTA agreements entered into force on 1 January 1994, reprinted in 32 ILM 289 and 605 (1993).

9 ECT is a significant instrument for the promotion of international cooperation in the energy industry. ECT was signed in December 1994 and entered into force on 16 April 1998. Article 13 of the Agreement can be found on the official website of the organisation < www.encharter.org>

10 See, e.g., Art. 5 of the Netherlands/India BIT (1995), cited in M. Erkan, *International Energy Investment Law: Stability through Contractual Clauses* (Alphen aan den Rijn: Kluwer Law International, 2011) 62.

indirect expropriation, they prefer to employ the aforementioned terms in order to understand indirect expropriation.[11] This begs the question as to how exactly the identification of indirect expropriation is to be made. The classification of host government measures ought to be determined via a case-by-case examination of the precise facts.[12] It is true that in the *Feldman* case the NAFTA tribunal provided 'that each determination under Article 1110 is necessarily fact specific'. This case-by-case approach is also supported by the modern BITs. For instance, the 2004 Canada BIT model stated that 'The determination of whether a measure or series of measures of a Party constitute an indirect expropriation requires a case-by-case, fact-based approach…'.[13]

Distinguishing between direct and indirect expropriation

In the context of direct expropriation, the government measure aims to transfer the legal rights of a foreign investor's ownership to the host country or to the benefit of a third person by applying a sovereign law system.[14] Thus, 'the taking can be readily discerned by examining the *lex situs* [15] of that property'.[16] However, in the case of indirect expropriation, the property rights of the investor are violated in a more subtle way than occurs in a case of direct expropriation. The significant divergence in indirect expropriation is that a host government measure may, in essence, have the same impact on the property interests of the international investor as direct taking.[17] More importantly, even though the government measure does not dispute, alter or affect the legal title of the property, the property's revenue-producing potential is dramatically reduced by the acts attributable to the host state.[18]

11 J. W. Salacuse, *The Law of Investment Treaties*, (New York: Oxford University Press, 2009) 150.
12 A. Reinnisch, 'The Legality of Expropriation', Chapter 11 in P. Muchlinski, F. Ortino & C. Schreuer (eds), *The Oxford Handbook of International Investment Law* (New York: Oxford University Press,: 2008) 438.
13 See, e.g., Canadian 2004 Model BIT, Annex B 13(1).
14 A. W. Rovine, *Contemporary Issues in International Arbitration and Mediation* (Leiden: Martinus Nijhoff Publishers, 2007) 35; see also M. Sornarajah, *The International Law on Foreign Investment*, (Cambridge: Grotius Publications, 1994) 282.
15 *Lex situs* means law of the place where the property is located. See B. A. Garner, *A Dictionary of Modern Legal Usage*, 2nd edn (New York: Oxford University Press, 1995) 526.
16 J. Paulsson & Z. Douglas, 'Indirect Expropriation in Investment Treaty Arbitration', in N. Horn & S. Kroll, *Arbitrating Foreign Investment Disputes* (The Hague: Kluwer International Law, 2004) 151.
17 Rovine (n. 14 above) 39.
18 Paulsson & Douglas (n. 16 above) 152; see also the tribunal's standing in the case of *Compañía Del Desarrollo De Santa Elena, S.A. VS. Costa Rica*, Final Award (ICSID Case No. ARB/96/1, 17 February 2000), 15 ICSID Rev. FILJ (2000) 457, section 77, available at <www.worldbank.org/icsid/cases/santaelena_award.pdf>. The tribunal asserted in this case that 'there is ample authority for the proposition that a property has been expropriated when the effect of the measures taken by the state has been to deprive the owner of title, possession or access to the benefit and economic use of his property'.

Moreover, what is the basic foundation of the investor's property interest? A commercial interpretation of the property interests of an foreign investor to compensation for expropriation (indirect) is upheld in some cases, such as *Pope & Talbot* and *S. D. Myers*,[19] and is also supported by scholars in legal literature. According to Wealde and Kolo, 'The key function of property is less the tangibility of "things", but rather the capability of the combination of rights in a commercial and corporative setting and under a regulatory regime to earn a commercial rate of return'.[20] After providing a definition of the modern understanding of property, can it be asserted that any measures taken by a host state are subject to compensation claims?

According to a widely recognised international principle, 'A state is not liable for economic injury which is a consequence of *bona fide* "regulation" within the accepted police power of state'.[21] The identification of host government acts of direct expropriation is reasonably straightforward, as compared indirect taking. In addition, expropriation or nationalisation is normally performed on a given date and on the basis of an explicit national policy.[22] However, the determination of indirect expropriation is more complex, and thus a host state act cannot easily be held to account. Furthermore, indirect expropriations are frequently upheld 'under the guise of a policy in which the deprivation of the owner's property is not an explicit purpose, and they do not necessarily have a clear date when it can be said that the owners have been deprived of their title to the expropriated property'.[23]

The direct expropriation of an alien investor's property can take various forms, ranging from the outright nationalisation of all economic sectors of an industry as part of a host state's economic policy to the specific taking of a private property under the terms of a legislative or administrative act.[24] Indirect expropriation includes creeping and regulatory expropriation. It should be noted that distinguishing these two forms is fraught with complication.[25] Unlike straightforward expropriation, indirect expropriation manifests itself

19 A. Kawharu, *Property Rights and Sustainability: The Evolution of Property Rights to Meet Ecological Challenges*, ed. D. Grinlinton & P. Taylor (Leiden: Martinus Nijhoff Publishers, 2011) 350.

20 T. W. Waelde & A. Kolo, 'Environmental Regulation, Investment Protection and "Regulatory Taking" in International Law', *International and Comparative Law Quarterly*, Vol. 50 (2001) 835.

21 *Sedco Inc. v National Iranian Oil Co.,* Interlocutory Award 9 Iran-U.S Cl. Trib. Rep. 248, 275(1985); see also J. M. Wagner, 'International Investment, Expropriation and Environmental Protection', *Golden Gate University Law Review*, Vol. 29(1999) 517.

22 See World Investment Report, FDI Policies for Development: National and International Perspectives, (New York and Geneva: United Nations Publication, 2003) 111, available at <www.unctad.org/en/docs//wir2003_en.pdf>

23 Ibid.

24 OECD, *Private Sector Development and in the Middle East and North Africa: Supporting Investment Policy and Governance in Iraq* (OECD Publication, 2010) 67.

25 M. Sornarajah, *The Pursuit of Nationalised Property* (Dordrecht: Kluwer Academic Publishers, 1986) 278–94, cited in World Investment Report (n. 22 above) 111.

through the impact of laws and regulations that subject the foreign investor to discriminatory taxes and legislation, impinge on the control of business management and enforce the cancellation of licences and permits among other side effects.[26]

The measures taken by a host government should be considered with a fact-based determination as to 'whether the sovereign state has engaged in a taking or merely exercised its right to regulate industry'.[27] The creeping and regulatory expropriations which constitute indirect expropriation are subject to compensation as far as comprehensive literature and arbitral awards report. However, one must take into account that the right to compensation for indirect expropriation is riddled with paradox.[28] In general, most sovereign states avoid paying compensation to alien investors for the impact of regulatory alterations 'resulting from legislative, executive and judicial decisions, although such changes may cause losses as or more severe than outright expropriation'.[29] In light of this overview of the subject, it is opportune to discuss exactly what constitutes indirect expropriation.

The types of host state measures that may constitute indirect expropriation

The question of which measures taken by a host state constitute indirect expropriation under international law is a complex one. The subject matter has not yet been given a definitive delineation either by international tribunals or legal scholars. A number of examples can be listed of the measures which may be taken by a host state over the course of an investment project; however, the determination of which regulatory measures are and are not non-compensable remains vague. It is true that not all state measures interfering with property are regarded as constituting expropriation under international law.

With regard to state measures, Brownlie has asserted that

> state measures, prima facie[30] a lawful exercise of powers of governments, may affect foreign interest considerably without amounting to expropriation. Thus, foreign assets and their use may be subjected to taxation, trade restrictions involving licences and quotas or measures of devaluation. While special facts

26 R. Schaffer, F. Agusti and B. Earler, *International Business Law and its Environment*, 7th edn (Boston, MA: Cengage Learning, 2009) 611.

27 Ibid.

28 A. Newcombe, 'Regulatory Expropriation, Investment Protection and International Law: When Is Government Regulation Expropriatory and When Compensation Should Be Paid?' LLM Thesis, University of Toronto (1999) 8.

29 Ibid.

30 The definition of *prima facie* is at first sight; as it seems at first.

> may alter the interpretation of cases, in principle, such measures are not unlawful and do not constitute expropriation.[31]

By highlighting such examples, the author touches on the police power notion. Although this notion will be examined separately, it is also worth mentioning briefly how it is addressed in legal discourse.

The police power notion has been identified in several conventions and case law and has recognised the criteria of non-compensable takings in the context of police power. For instance, the first protocol of the European Convention of Human Rights deemed the regulatory measures taken by governments to be non-compensable. In fact, Article 1 of the Convention states that:

> Every natural or legal person is entitled to the peaceful enjoyment of its possessions. No one should be deprived of his possessions except in the public interest and subject to the conditions provided for by the law and by the general principles of international law.

It also goes on to state that the preceding provisions shall not, however, in any case impair '*the right of a state to enforce such laws as it deems necessary to control the use of property in accordance with the general interest or to secure the payment of taxes or other contributions or penalties*' (emphasis added).[32] In the light of the above quotation, it is fair to conclude that Article 1 of the protocol, specifically references the police power notion.

Similarly, the Harvard Draft Convention on the International Responsibility of States for Injuries to Aliens provides that:

> An uncompensated taking of an alien property or deprivation of the use or enjoyment of the property of an alien which results from the execution of laws; from a general change in the value of currency; from the action of the competent authorities of the State in the maintenance of public order, health, morality; or from the valid exercise of belligerent rights or otherwise incidental to the normal operation of the laws of the State shall not be considered wrongful.[33]

The given provision has also found a place in the *Saluka Investment* case.
The arbitral panel said that the above-quoted passage in the Harvard Draft Convention is subject to four important exceptions:

31 I. Brownlie, *Principles of Public International Law*, 6th edn (Oxford: Oxford University Press, 2003) 509.

32 See the First Protocol to the Convention for the Protection of Human Rights and Fundamental Freedoms, Paris (20 March 1952), cited in Human Rights Review 2012, available at <www.equalityhumanrights.com/uploaded_files/humanrights/hrr_firstprotocol.pdf>

33 *Saluka Investment BV (Netherlands). v The Czech Republic* (Partial Award) of 2 March 2006, para 256, available at <https://arbitrationlaw.com/sites/default/files/free_pdfs/Saluka%20Investments.pdf>

(a) It is not a clear and discriminatory violation of the law of the State concerned;
(b) It is not the result of a violation of any provision of Articles 6 to 8 [of the Draft Convention];
(c) It is not an unreasonable departure from the principles of justice recognised by the principal legal systems of the world;
(d) It is not an abuse of the powers specified in this paragraph for the purpose of depriving an alien of his property.[34]

The tribunal proceeded to conclude that 'these exceptions do not, in any way, weaken the principle that certain takings or deprivations are non-compensable. They merely remind the legislator or, indeed, the adjudicator, that the so-called "police power exception" is not absolute'.[35] Moreover, the 1967 OECD Draft Convention on the Protection of Foreign Property also recognises the police power notion in the following statement: 'measures taken in the pursuit of a State's "political, social or economic ends" do not constitute compensable expropriation.'[36] As previously mentioned, a similar contribution was also provided in the United States Third Restatement of the Law of Foreign Relations.[37]

State measures are not exhaustive; a number of state measures can be exemplified, however, in practice. The following measures are the most frequently applied by host governments: excessive or discriminatory taxation,[38] interference of contract rights,[39] interference with management rights,[40] revocations of licence or denial of government permits.[41]

34 Ibid., para 257.
35 Ibid., para 258.
36 OECD Draft Convention on the Protection of Foreign Property (12 October 1967), 71 *ILM* 117.
37 Restatement of Third of Foreign Relations Law of United States vol. 1 (1987), section 712, comment (g). According to Restatement of Third of Foreign Relations Law's section 712, 'A state is not responsible for loss of property or for other economic disadvantage resulting from bona fide general taxation, regulation, forfeiture for crime, or other action of the kind that is common accepted as within the police power of states, if it is not discriminatory…'.
38 See the case *of Revere Copper and Brass Inc. v Overseas Private Investment Corporation*, 24 August 1978, 56 ILR 268.
39 See *CME Czech Republic BV v Czech Republic* (Partial Award) 13 September 2001.
40 See *Starrett Housing Corp. v Iran*, 19 December 1983, 4 Iran–US CTR 122: *Tippetts, Abbett, MacCarty, Stratton v TAMS-AFFA Consulting Engineers of Iran*, 22 June 1984, 6 Iran–US CTR 219; *PSEG Global, Inc. et al v Republic of Turkey* (ICSID Case No. ARB/02/5) (2007), Award 19 January 2007.
41 See *Goetz and Others v Republic of Burundi*, 2 September 1998, 6 ICSID Reports 5; *Middle East Cement Shipping and Handling Co. S.A. v Arab Republic of Egyp*t, 12 April 2002, 7 ICSID Reports 178; *Metalclad Corporation v United Mexican States*, 30 August 2000, ICSID Reports 209.

Excessive or discriminatory taxation

Host states may use their power to impose taxes as a means to limit and curtail the business activities of alien investors within their territory. To this end, it can be said that the freedom to regulate tax is a sovereign right and cannot be subject to any limitation or restriction. Indeed, there is no rule or restriction imposed or recommended on this measure by international law.[42] However, 'while taxation, even if onerous, may be a legitimate means of raising public revenue, it is possible for taxes to be so high that they are confiscatory and constitute expropriation'.[43] Disproportionate tax increases and discriminative or abusive taxation in the petroleum industry are not new phenomena.[44] Furthermore, excessive or repetitive tax measures are instruments frequently applied by a variety of state authorities, with government collusion[45] 'under cover of what appears on the surface, and at first sight, to formally be the proper application of tax audit, tax assessment, and tax collection procedures'.[46]

The *Yukos* [47]case is a good example of this practice; it is also the most dramatic case to have occurred in recent years. In the Yukos case, the Russian Federal Government required the tax authorities to carry out a reassessment of the tax returns from the Yukos Company, which is privately owned. After the reassessment, penalties and interest charges amounting to 100% of total sales were imposed on the company by the Russian tax authorities and were collected over a three-year period. As a result of these penalties and charges, the company was economically and legally crippled and fell victim to bankruptcy. Numerous claims were brought by the shareholders of the company, through the Energy Charter Treaty (ECT) dispute settlement process.[48]

The arbitration process of the *Yukos* case took ten years under the ECT and the dispute between Russia Federation and the shareholders of the Yukos Company resolved finally on July 2014 by the decision of the Arbitral Tribunal sitting in The Hague. The Permanent Court of Arbitration (PCA) ruled that Russia explicitly violated its commitments and obligations under the ECT by expropriating the Yukos Oil Company. For this reason, the Russian Federation was ordered to pay $50 billion to the former Yukos shareholders. This may conceivably have been the

42 M. Sornarajah, *The International Law on Foreign Investment*, 3rd edn (Cambridge: Cambridge University Press, 2010), 405.
43 Salacuse (n. 10 above) 301.
44 T. Waelde, 'International Law of Foreign Investment: Towards Regulation by Multilateral Treaties' CEPMLP Research Paper CP1/2000, 19.
45 M. Sornarajah, *The International Law on Foreign Investment*, 2nd edn (Cambridge: Cambridge University Press: 2004) 393.
46 Ibid. at 342.
47 *Yukos Universal Limited (Isle of Man) v The Russian Federation*, PCA Case No AA 227, UNCITRAL.
48 For further information about the *Yukos* case, see also P. D. Cameron, *International Energy Investment Law: The Pursuit of Stability*, (Oxford, Oxford University Press, 2010) 189.

highest sum awarded as compensation in investment arbitration history. It is clear that Russia learned an expensive lesson from the *Yukos* case. However, the question of whether Russia is able to pay such a high amount of compensation to the former shareholders remains outstanding.

The *Yukos* case was not the first example of an excessive tax regime to be recorded. When the agenda of the International Centre for Settlement of Investment Disputes (ICSID) is examined, it is evident that there are several cases relevant to this subject.[49] In the first decade of this century, oil and gas prices soared dramatically. The increase in price in the petroleum industry spurred petroleum-producing states on to introduce new taxes for the petroleum sector or increase pre-existing tax rates. In the interests of obtaining a larger share of the cake, or as a result of resource nationalism, some host states in Latin America have frequently indulged in tax-hiking measures. The Venezuelan Hydrocarbons Law[50] best illustrates this tactic. The late president of Venezuela, Hugo Chavez, announced radical new government measures with regard to hydrocarbon law and imposed a new tax regime specifically directed at the petroleum industry.[51] The government measures were served as an ultimatum to Western petroleum companies – that is, 'pay up or get out'. In accordance with the new tax regime, all alien oil and gas companies had to pay 'income tax at the rate of 50% instead of the previous "preferential rate" of 34%'.[52] There is no doubt that the sudden enforcement of such tax reforms had a major impact on international alien petroleum companies in Venezuela.

Interference in contract rights

Governments can take action for reasons of public policy; however, such reasons should not alter or adversely affect the contractual rights of investors. In other words, a state measure should not prevent an alien investor from benefitting from the contractual arrangements they originally entered into.[53] International customary law protects an alien investor's contractual rights against expropriation. Similarly, investment treaties include expropriation provisions which protect alien investors' contractual rights against any type of expropriation. Nevertheless, it

49 See the following cases regarding taxation: *Revere Copper and Brass Inc. v Overseas Private Investment Corporation*, 24 August 1978, 56 ILR 268; *Sedco Inc. v National Iranian Oil Co.*, Interlocutory Award 9 Iran-US Cl. Trib. Rep. (1985); *Philips Petroleum Co., Iran v Islamic Republic of Iran*, 21 Iran-US Cl. Trib. Rep. 79.

50 Decreto con Fuerza de Ley Organica de Hidracarburos (Decree with Force of Organic Law of Hydrocarbons), Decree No. 1,510, 2 November 2001, Official Gazette No. 37, 323.

51 Freshfields Bruckhaus Deringer, 'Venezuela: Proposed Measures Against Oil and Gas Investors' (May 2005) 1, also available at <www.freshfields.com/uploadedFiles/SiteWide/Knowledge/Venezuela%20-%20proposed%20measures%20against%20oil%20and%20gas%20investors.pdf>

52 Ibid.

53 S. Ripinskyi & K. Williams, *Damages in International Investment Law* (London: British Institute of International and Comparative Law, 2008) 9.

should be noted that investment treaties must be examined on a case-by-case basis to determine whether the investment treaty embodies contract rights under the treaty's definition of investment.[54] As mentioned above, the violation of a contract may lead to the loss of the contractual rights of an investor and deprive him/her of any benefit issuing from the investment. To this end, a significant question ought to be asked: does every violation of contract amount to indirect expropriation? This is not the case, even if contractual rights are breached.[55] There are various tribunal decisions that prove that not every instance of state interference in contractual rights is deemed to amount to indirect expropriation. For instance, in the NAFTA case of *Waste Management Inc. v United Mexican States*, the tribunal distinguished between the cautious expropriation of a right under a contract and non-compliance by the state with its contractual commitments:

> The mere non-performance of contractual obligations is not to be equated with a taking of property, nor (unless accompanied by the other elements) is it tantamount to expropriation. Any private party can fail to perform its contracts, whereas nationalization and expropriation are inherently a governmental act.[56]

A comparable decision was upheld by the tribunal in the ICSID case of *Parkerings-Compagniet As v Lithuania*. On consideration of this case, a cumulative condition is required by the tribunal in order to deem that the contractual rights are expropriated by the state interference. These cumulative conditions are as follows:

> First, a breach of an agreement will amount to an expropriation only if the State acted not only in its capacity of party to the agreement, but also in its capacity of sovereign authority, that is to say using its sovereign power. Second, a breach of contract, if there should be one is, itself, not always sufficient to amount to an indirect expropriation within the meaning of the BIT. An investor faced with a breach of an agreement by the State counter-party should, as a general rule, sue that party in the appropriate forum to remedy the breach. Third, the breach of the Agreement, *in casu* the termination of the agreement, must give rise to a substantial decrease of the value of the investment.[57]

As Parkerings-Compagniet had not met the conditions required by the tribunal, the company's claim regarding the expropriation of contractual rights was rejected.

54 Ibid.
55 Salacuse (n. 10 above) 304.
56 *Waste Management Inc. v United Mexican States (Waste Management II)* ICSID Case No. ARB (AF)/00/3 NAFTA Award, 30 April 2004.
57 *Parkerings-Compagniet As v Lithuania*, ICSID Case No. ARB/05/08, Award September (2007) paras 443–56.

Interference with management rights

The exercise of management control over an investment is a significant right of an alien investor. If an alien investor's actual control over its own management is removed, thereby causing disruption to its commercial activities due to governmental intervention, then this unlawful state interference can be deemed indirect expropriation. When can such a situation emerge and in what way does such a government action affect the investor? As mentioned above, this governmental action eliminates the actual management control of the investor 'by either physically and/or legally impeding the investor to continue his or her management tasks or by replacing the investor-controlled management by government appointed-management'.[58] The direct effects this can have include temporary losses in business revenues, potential delays to scheduled projects and a number of other knock-on effects to business planning, staff morale and so on, not to mention the taking of an international company. How can this occur? For instance, a host government may arrest or deport the alien investor or other persons who are in charge of the business activities of the company.

The *Biloune v Ghana* case illustrates this point. Mr Biloune, a Syrian national, established a company of which he was a 60% shareholder. The company held an agreement with their Ghanaian partners to build a hotel resort complex. After a substantial part of its construction had been completed, business activities were halted and the construction demolished on the decision of the government authorities. Afterwards, Mr Biloune was arrested and expelled from the country. This was a clear-cut case of expropriation. The Tribunal stated that:

> The conjunction of the stop work order, the demolition, the summons, *the arrest, the detention*, the requirement of filing assets declaration forms, and *the deportation* of Mr Biloune without possibility of re-entry had the effect of causing the irreparable cessation of work on the project. Given the central role of Mr Biloune in promoting, financing and managing MDCL, his expulsion from the country effectively prevented MDCL from pursuing the project. In the view of the Tribunal, such prevention of MDCL from pursuing its approved project would *constitute constructive expropriation* of MDCL's contractual rights in the project and, accordingly, the expropriation of the value of Mr Biloune's interest in MDCL, unless the respondents can establish by persuasive evidence sufficient justifications for these events.[59]

As there was no strong evidence found to support the Government of Ghana's actions, the tribunal concluded its statement with the following words: '[T]he Government of

58 Reinnisch (n. 12 above) 453; see also Sornarajah (n. 42 above) 400; Salacuse (n. 10 above) 304.

59 *Biloune and Marine Drive Complex Ltd* v *Ghana Investments Centre and the Government of Ghana*, UNCITRAL ad hoc Tribunal, Award on Jurisdiction and Liability, 27 October 1989, 95 ILR 183, 209 (emphasis added).

Ghana, by its act and omission, culminating with Mr Biloune's deportation, constructively expropriated MDCL's assets, and Mr Biloune's interest therein.'

Revocations of licence or denial of government permits

The cancellation of permits and licences of foreign investors is regarded as regulatory taking. If such a regulatory taking is made without due process of law, which is one of the main criteria of lawful taking, then this taking becomes discriminatory and could amount to a compensable taking. If an alien investor's licence or permits are cancelled, one can categorically affirm that the said alien investor's business activities will be unfavourably affected. It is worth mentioning here that, generally, modern investment treaties provide protection against the cancellation of licences and permits.[60] The *Goetz* case best illustrates the issue of the cancellation of licences or permits. In this case, Goetz's free zone status was cancelled by Burundi, without any formal taking of property. The ICSID tribunal held that 'the government's action fell within the concept of measures having the effect of being similar to expropriation, i.e., they constituted a direct expropriation'.[61] The awards, decisions and the confines of international arbitral tribunals will be analysed in detail and their contribution to answering the question of what constitutes indirect expropriation will be discussed in the following sections; however, it would be appropriate to mention briefly the environmentally motivated cancellation of licences and permits.

The revocation of licences on environmental grounds is a growing occurrence. In order to protect the environment, sovereign states prefer to cancel investors' licences or permits. Such revocation of licences or cancellation of permits are not usually held to be a compensable taking.[62] In the case of *Murphyores Ltd v The Commonwealth*, [63] a concession right was provided by the Australian government to two American companies for sand-mining on Fraser Island, close to the Great Barrier Reef. Shortly after the start of the operation, an environmental study was conducted in the area, which found that sand-mining jeopardised the ecological balance of the Great Barrier Reef and recommended that all operations should urgently be halted. The Australian government revoked all the licences it had previously granted and terminated all sand-mining activities. In the ensuing case, the Australian High Court ruled that the actions of the Australian government did not constitute a compensable taking; consequently, any related compensation claims were rejected.

An issue that causes great concern among alien investors is the possibility of facing unexpected regulatory or administrative actions with the aim of environmental protection after the contract is signed.[64] At this point, two significant factors should be evaluated: first, whether the new environmental regulations in the

60 For instance, US 2004 BIT model.
61 *Goetz v Burundi*, ICSID Case No. ARB/95/3 at 26.
62 Sornarajah (n. 42 above), 403.
63 See *Murphyores Inc., Pty Ltd v Commonwealth* (1976) 136 CLR 1; [1976] HCA 20.
64 G. Verhoosel, 'Foreign Direct Investment and Legal Constraints on Domestic Environmental Policies: Striking a Reasonable Balance between Stability and Change', *Law and Policy in International Business*, Vol. 29 (1998) 451,478.

administrative law system have discriminatory intent, or are designed to attain ends other than those they purport to.[65] It is also necessary to pose the question: can the host state cancel the licences and permits of alien investors on environmental grounds? According to Sornarajah, 'the cancellation is usually a punitive measure for not abiding by the purpose behind the regulation or conditions to which the licence is subject'.[66]

What, then, is the real purpose of host governments in such cases? Perhaps, the actual purpose is to force the investor out and give them no other option but to sell the investment to the host state. If this is the case, the actions of the host state are unlawful; this deliberate regulatory action 'constitutes indirect expropriation and requires compensation'.[67] The second possibility is that the administrative system of the host state imposes new environmental regulations in order to protect the environment and/or the health of its citizens and, in order to do so, resorts to revoking the licence and permits of the investor. Can a regulatory action of this kind be deemed indirect expropriation? The simple answer is no: a measure thus motivated would be classed as legitimate police power regulation. In the *Sedco* case the international tribunal asserted that it is 'an accepted principle of international law that a State is not liable for economic injury which is a consequence of *bona fide* "regulation" within the accepted police power of states'.[68]

Criteria for the distinction between legitimate regulation (non-compensable regulation) and indirect expropriation

In the previous section, it was stated that while some state measures may amount to indirect expropriation and therefore warrant the payment of compensation, other types of state interference may not constitute indirect expropriation, as they are simply examples of the host state exercising its sovereign right to regulate. This prompts the question: in what respects can legitimate regulation be distinguished from indirect expropriation? Unfortunately, this question is at the heart of an unresolved issue on the agenda of international investment law. More importantly, although international investment tribunals and legal scholars are not necessarily at loggerheads, they have nonetheless failed to provide 'a definitive test establishing when measures attributable to the host state breach the dividing line between legitimate regulation and compensable indirect expropriation'.[69] As mentioned above, making an exact distinction is not always straightforward, as there is no formula available to determine the boundaries between legitimate regulation and

65 For instance, governments may impose some restrictions on investors or cancel licence and permits of investors to make them to sell the investment.

66 Sornarajah (n. 42 above), 402.

67 Wagner (n. 21 above) 418.

68 *Sedco Inc. v National Iranian Oil Co.*, Interlocutory Award 9 Iran-U.S Cl. Trib. Rep. 248, 275 (1985).

69 Z. A. Al Qurashi, ' Investment Protection under International Petroleum Agreements: an Analysis of Pertinent Arbitral Jurisprudence', PhD Thesis, University of Dundee (2004) 145–6.

indirect expropriation.[70] This is due to the fact that host government measures are broad in scope and do not neatly fit into contractual formulae.[71] The case of *Generation Ukraine, Inc. v Ukraine* exemplifies the difficulty in distinguishing between non-compensable regulation and indirect expropriation:

> Predictability is one of the most important objectives of any legal system. It would be useful if it were absolutely clear in advance whether particular events fall within the definition of an 'indirect' expropriation. It would enhance the sentiment of respect for legitimate expectations if it were perfectly obvious why, in the context of a particular decision, an arbitral tribunal found that a governmental action or inaction crossed the line that defines acts amounting to an indirect expropriation. But there is no checklist, no mechanical test to achieve that purpose. The decisive considerations vary from case to case, depending not only on the specific facts of a grievance but also on the way the evidence is presented, and the legal bases pleaded. The outcome is a judgment, i.e. the product of discernment, and not the printout of a computer programme.[72]

Over the years, many scholars and arbitral tribunals have attempted to provide a watertight definition for the sort of interference that may be said to constitute indirect expropriation. Professor Christie furnished perhaps the most articulate description. According to the author:

> It is evident that the question of what kind of interference short of outright expropriation constitutes a 'taking' under international law presents a situation where the common law method of case by case development is pre-eminently the best method, in fact probably the only method, of legal development.[73]

In order to draw an accurate division between legitimate non-compensable regulations and indirect expropriation requiring compensation, arbitral tribunals have thus far distinguished the two phenomena with reference to the following criteria: (i) the degree of interference with the alien investor's property right, (ii) the purpose and context of the state measure, (iii) the legitimate expectation of the investor and (iv) proportionality.

The degree of interference with investor's property rights

This approach, which entails an assessment of the degree of interference with an investor's property rights, is commonly consulted by arbitral tribunals and

70 Paulsson & Douglas (n. 16 above) 145.
71 Ibid. at 146.
72 *Generation Ukraine, Inc. v Ukraine*, ICSID Case No ARB/00/9, Award of 16 September 2003, ILM 44 (2005) 404, para 20.29.
73 G. C. Christie, 'What Constitutes a Taking of Property Under International Law?', *British Year Book of International Law*, Vol. 38 (1962) 307, 338.

legal academic literature. This has become known as 'sole effect' doctrine. The determining element of whether an indirect expropriation has taken place, according to this assessment, is solely as a result of the effect of the governmental regulatory measure on the investment.[74] More fundamentally, *sole effect* doctrine disregards the purpose of the government's regulatory measure – the main consideration of this doctrine is the severity of the economic impact of the measures on the investment and the duration of host government control.[75]

Severe economic impact and loss of effective control

When the outcomes of international tribunals are compared, it can be surmised that they generally treat the severity of the economic impact incurred by a host governmental regulatory action as an imperative principle in determining whether the measure taken by the government constitutes an indirect expropriation and is subject to compensation or not. International tribunals have frequently rejected the compensation demands of investors, as the measure taken by the host state was not substantial and/or did not deprive investors of all or most of the economic benefits that they expect from the investment.[76] The *CMS v Argentina* tribunal is a good case in point. CMS, a US-based transmission company, claimed that the Argentinian government's decision to suspend a tariff adjustment formula for gas transportation for the duration of an economic crisis in the country constituted an indirect expropriation.

After consideration of the investor's claim, the tribunal affirmed that 'the essential question is to establish whether the enjoyment of the property has been effectively neutralised' as 'the standard...where indirect expropriation has been contended is that of substantial deprivation'.[77] In this case, even though the tribunal recognised that the measure taken by the government provoked a dispute which impacted on the company's business operations, the tribunal decreed that there was no substantial deprivation and hence the expropriation provision of the Argentina–US BIT was not violated by the Argentinian government. The tribunal also underlined that 'the investor is in control of the investment; the government does not manage the day-to-day

74 M. Solanes & A. Jouravlev, *Revisiting Privatization, Foreign investment, International Arbitration, and Water* (Santiago, Chile: United Nations, 2007) 60, available at <www.palermo.edu/Archivos_content/derecho/pdf/Revisiting-privatization-foreign-investment.pdf>

75 Cameron (n. 48 above) 223; see also M. Erkan, *International Energy Investment Law: Stability through Contractual Clauses* (Alphen aan den Rijn: Kluwer Law International, 2011), 87; Salacuse (n. 10 above) 308.

76 Yannaca-Small (n. 7 above) 55; see also UNCTAD, *Taking Property*, Series on Issues on International Investment Agreements (New York and Geneva: United Nations, 2000) 36; see also *Metalclad Corp. v United Mexican States*, ICSID; additionally Facility Case No. ARB (AF)/9701, 30 August 2000, para 13.

77 *CMS Gas Transmission Company v The Argentine Republic*, ICSID Case No. ARB/01/8 Award (12 May 2005) 262.

operations of the company; and the investor has full ownership and control of the investment'.[78]

Conversely, in the *Starrett Housing Corp. v Iran* case, the expropriation claim was based on the appointment of Iranian managers to an American housing project. The tribunal found that an indirect expropriation occurred through the appointment of an Iranian manager to the company operation. The tribunal held that:

> [I]t is recognised by international law that measures taken by a state can interfere with property rights to such an extent that these rights are rendered so useless that they must be deemed to have been expropriated, even though the state does not purport to have expropriated them and the legal title to the property formally remains with the original owner.[79]

Furthermore, in the *Tippetts v TAMS-AFFA* case, Tippetts had established a partnership with an Iranian company before the advent of revolution in the country. In the wake of the revolution, the Iranian government appointed a new Iranian manager to the partnership. In this case, the tribunal did not regard the appointment of an Iranian manager *per se* as an expropriation. However, the tribunal regarded the actions of the manager to constitute an expropriation. The tribunal held that:

> While assumption of control over property by a government does not automatically and immediately justify a conclusion that the property has been taken by the government, thus requiring compensation under international law, such a conclusion is warranted whenever events demonstrate that the owner was deprived of fundamental rights of ownership and it appears that this deprivation is not merely ephemeral...[80]

A similar approach was taken by the tribunal in the case of *Metalclad Corp. v United Mexican States. Metalclad* is an American waste disposal company which had acquired land for the development and operation of hazardous waste landfill in Mexico. In the said case, the Metalclad Company fulfilled all of the legal requirements defined by environmental and planning regulations and the project construction permit was granted by the federal government of Mexico. Nevertheless, although the Mexican federal government initially agreed to grant the permit, the municipality of Guadalcazar successively overturned this decision. Under NAFTA, the severe economic impact and loss of effective control placed

78 Ibid. at 263.

79 *Starrett Housing Corp v Iran*, Interlocutory Award No ITL 32-24-1 (10 December 1983), reprinted in 4 Iran-US CTR 122 at 154.

80 *Tippetts, Abbett, McCarthy, Stratton v TAMS-AFFA*, Award No 141-7-2, 29 June 1984, reprinted in 6 Iran-US CTR 219.

the state's actions in the category of expropriation defined by Article 1110. The tribunal referenced this article in its award and stated that there was:

> incidental interference with the use of the property which has the effect of depriving the owner in whole or significant part, of the use or reasonably to be expected economic benefit of property even if not necessary to the obvious benefit of the state...[81]

In delivering its final decision, the tribunal stated that the host government action deprived the company of its ability to use its property for its own purpose and the evidence of this deprivation sufficed to determine that expropriation had taken place.[82]

Also handled by NAFTA tribunals was the *Pope & Talbot v Canada* case. Pope & Talbot is an American investor with a Canadian subsidiary that manufactured and exported softwood lumber from mills in British Columbia to the United States. The investor claimed that Canada's export control regime breached NAFTA Article 1110. The company went on to assert that the export control regime was a measure tantamount to expropriation because its effect deprived the investor of its ability to sell products in its traditional and natural market in the US. Canada refuted these assertions and in its defence claimed that the implemented regulation was non-discriminatory and was an expression of the state's police power and therefore non-compensable. The tribunal found that although the implementation of an export control regime did impact on the profits of Pope & Talbot, the investor was still technically able to sell its products abroad at a profit because sales abroad were not completely prohibited as a result of the regulatory measure of the state. In relation to the Canadian contention, the tribunal stated that 'mere interference is not expropriation; rather, a significant degree of deprivation of fundamental rights of ownership is required'.[83] The panel concluded that 'the degree of interference with the investment's operations due to the Export Control Regime did not rise to the level of expropriation (creeping or otherwise)'.[84]

Similar elements, or the lack thereof, came into play in *Marvin Roy Feldman Karpa (Feldman) v United Mexican States,* [85] in which the tribunal rejected a claim of indirect expropriation. Marvin Roy Feldman Karpa is a US national who lodged a claim on behalf of the CEMSA, a registered alien trading company and exporter of cigarettes from Mexico. When Mexico subsequently withdrew its attractive tax rebate, Feldman claimed that he was 'no longer able to engage in his

81 *Metalclad Corp. v United Mexican States* (ICSID Additional Facility Case No. ARB (AF)/97/1), 30 August 2000, para 103.
82 Erkan (n. 75 above) 90.
83 *Pope & Talbot, Inc. v Government of Canada*, Interim Award (26 June 2000) at para 96.
84 Ibid., para 102.
85 *Marvin Roy Feldman Karpa (CEMSA)* v *United Mexican States of Mexico* (2002), ICSID Case No ARB (AF) 99/1, Award, IIC 157 (2002).

business of purchasing Mexican cigarettes and exporting them, and has thus been deprived completely and permanently and potential economic benefits from that particular activity'.[86] As an owner of the trading company, Feldman claimed that this action of the Mexican government constituted indirect expropriation and violated Article 1110 of NAFTA. The tribunal found that expropriation did not occur because 'the regulatory action has not deprived the Claimant of control of his company, interfered directly in the internal operations of the company or displaced the Claimant as the controlling shareholder… Thus, this tribunal believes there has been no taking…'[87]

In *Occidental Exploration and Production Co. (OEPC) v The Republic of Ecuador*,[88] Occidental claimed that the host country's refusal to refund to Occidental the value added tax, to which it was entitled under Ecuadorian law, constituted indirect expropriation of its investment. The tribunal investigated this claim and concluded that there had been no indirect expropriation. The tribunal cited the precedent of the *Metalclad* case to assert that the measure in question did not constitute indirect expropriation since 'the criterion of "substantial deprivation" was not fulfilled, since in fact there has been no deprivation of the use of the investment, let alone measures affecting a significant part of the investment'.[89]

There are a number of such cases in the archives of NAFTA and ICSID tribunals. One that is particularly worthy of note is the first case to be based on an indirect expropriation claim under the Energy Charter Treaty. In *Nykomb Synergetics Technology AB v Latvia*, [90] Nykomb claimed that the non-payment of double tariffs constituted an indirect expropriation. The ECT tribunal found that regulatory takings may amount to expropriation or its equivalent but 'the decisive factor for an action to be deemed as crossing the line drawing the borderline towards expropriation must primarily be the degree of possession taking or control over the enterprise the disputed measures entail'.[91] The tribunal found that in the existing case 'there is no possession taking of Windau or its assets, no interference with the shareholders' rights or with the management's control over and running of the enterprise – apart from ordinary regulatory provisions laid down in the production license, the off-take agreement, etc.'. The tribunal concluded that 'withholding of payments at the double tariff does not qualify as an expropriation or the equal vent of an expropriation under the Treaty'.[92]

86 Ibid., para 109.
87 Ibid., para 152.
88 *Occidental Exploration &Production Co. v The Republic of Ecuador*, Final Award, LCIA Case No. UN3467 of 1 July 2004, 43 ILM 1248 (2004).
89 Ibid., para 89.
90 *Nykomb Synergetics Technology AB v Latvia*, Award, SCC Case No 118/2001, IIC 182 (2003), 16 December 2003.
91 Ibid., para 33.
92 Ibid.

Duration of host government control

The previous section sought to assess the scope of interference with property rights by posing the following questions: how much of the property is affected by the state measure? How much is the value of investment diminished in the light of tribunals' decisions? The duration of the measure taken by the host state is another significant benchmark. This is crucial because the measure simply tests whether the regulations had a severe enough economic impact on the investor's property rights, but this may have been a relatively short-lived problem.[93] Some arbitral tribunals have taken into consideration the length of time for which the host state exerted influence over the investor's property. In *S. D. Myers v Canada*, the NAFTA tribunal stated:

> [A]n expropriation usually amounts to a lasting removal of the ability of an owner to make use of its economic rights, although it may be that, in some contexts and circumstances, it would be appropriate to view a deprivation as amounting to an expropriation, even if it were partial or temporary.[94]

In the present case, the NAFTA tribunal disregarded the expropriation claim made regarding a temporary export ban on hazardous waste for disposal, as the duration of the state measure was 18 months. The tribunal decreed that this was insufficient to constitute indirect expropriation. A parallel can be found in the case of *BG Group v Argentina*.[95] The tribunal adjudicating in this case also came to the conclusion that no expropriation had occurred as the measure taken by the Republic of Argentina would not have had a permanent impact upon BG, and also because no substantial deprivation was endured by BG's shareholdings.[96]

The purpose test

The second test utilised by tribunals to determine whether indirect expropriation has occurred or not is the 'character of the governmental measure', also known as the 'purpose approach'. 'Proponents of this theory consider the governmental measure as a challenge to the investor in a contextual framework that allows, indeed requires, a weighing and balancing of factors including the purpose as well as the effect of the measure.'[97] In a broad sense, if the intention of a governmental measure is legitimate in that it is made for a public purpose such as public health, safety, morals or environmental protection, the measure is normally deemed a

93 In doctrine, Professor Christie touched upon the importance of the time factor in his article. See Christie (n. 73 above) 331.

94 *S. D. Myers Inc. v Government of Canada*, Partial Award, 13 November 2000, 40 ILM (2001) 1408, para 283.

95 *BG Group Plc. v the Republic of Argentina*, UNCITRAL Arbitration, Final Award, IIC 321 (2007), 24 December 2007.

96 Ibid., paras 270–1.

97 Fortier & Drymer (n. 5 above) 313; Cameron (n. 48 above) 227; Yannaca-Small (n. 7 above) 64.

police power exercise which merits no compensation.[98] It should be borne in mind that if governmental measures are imposed for public benefit, this cannot amount to indirect expropriation, unless the government demonstrates clear intent to deprive the alien investor.

While states may limit their sovereign rights by signing up to international agreements and contracts, these limitations should not be regarded as all-encompassing as sovereign states do retain their policing power to adopt measures to regulate their economic, financial, environment, human rights and other relevant interests for the public benefit. With regard to the police power notion, it is fair to say that host governments are free to exercise their powers to restrict international investors' property rights without the payment of compensation in pursuance of a legitimate purpose. To this end, could it be claimed that such regulatory measures taken by the host state are to the detriment of foreign investors in realising the profit expected from their investment? The answer is not straightforward, because while international law recognises the police power of a state, due to its sovereignty, 'foreign investment law recognises the concept of regulatory expropriation'.[99] The implications of this grey area continue to present challenges in host government and investor relationships and for those who attempt to legislate and uphold the law.

Much attention has been given to this tension in international tribunals and several attempts have been made in tribunals to settle disputes by claiming regulatory expropriation. It should also be noted that finding evidence and proving a state's discriminatory intention is no mean feat.[100] The *Sea-Land* case[101] best illustrates this difficulty. In this case, the tribunal set out the standards by which the government's actions would be judged as follows:

> [A] finding of an expropriation would require, at very least, that the Tribunal be satisfied that there was deliberate governmental interference with the conduct of Sea Lands' operations, the effect of which was to deprive Sea-Land of the use and benefit of its investment.[102]

The tribunal ruled that no expropriation had occurred in this case.[103]

The purpose test was also applied in the context of NAFTA jurisprudence in *S. D. Myers v Canada* [104] 'but in conjunction with an effects test'.[105] S. D. Myers is a US hazardous waste disposal company which operated a PCB

98 Christie (n. 73 above) 338; see also Cameron (n. 48 above) 227.
99 S. P. Subedi, *International Investment Law: Reconciling Policy and Principle*, 2nd edn (Portland, OR: Hart Publishing, 2012) 157.
100 Cameron (n. 48 above) 227.
101 *Sea-Land Services Inc. v Iran*, 6 Iran-US CI. Trib. Rep. 149 (1984), 166.
102 Ibid.
103 Ibid.
104 *S. D. Myers. Inc. v Government of Canada*, Partial Award of 13 November 2000, 40 ILM 1408 (2001) para 285.
105 Cameron (n. 48 above) 227.

waste treatment service in Ohio. The Canadian Ministry of the Environment had banned the commercial export of waste from a synthetic chemical compound of PCB under its Environmental Protection Act. The company claimed that the Canadian ban amounted to expropriation because the ban deprived the company of business opportunities and violated NAFTA Article 1110. The Canadian government contended that the ban was a measure taken in the interests of the environment. The NAFTA UNCITRAL tribunal accepted that 'international law makes it appropriate for tribunals to examine the purpose and effects of governmental measures'; however, 'it must look at the real interests involved and *the purpose and effects of the government measure*'.[106]

A similar verdict was reached by the ICSID tribunal in *Olguin v Paraguay*. The tribunal stated that 'expropriation therefore requires a teleological driven action for occur it to occur; omissions, however egregious they may be, are not sufficient for it to occur; omissions, however egregious they may be are not sufficient for it to take place'.[107] Taking into consideration the latter two cases, it is apparent that the tribunals accepted the purpose approach by referring to the purpose and effect of the government measure. Notably, although these last two cases can be good examples of the purpose approach, there are also some counter-examples of tribunals with regard to this test. For instance, in *Philips Petroleum Co. Iran v Islamic Republic of Iran*, the tribunal stated that 'a government's liability to compensate for expropriation of alien property does not depend on proof that the expropriation was intentional'.[108] A comparable decision was reached in *Metalclad v Mexico*, where the tribunal asserted that there is no need to decide or regard the motivation or intention of the adaptation of the Ecological Decree.[109]

Legitimate expectations of investors

The investor's reasonable and legitimate expectations test is the other significant criterion which tribunals evaluate. The aim of this test is to ascertain whether or not an investor's legitimate expectation has been adversely affected. It should be borne in mind that the indirect expropriation claim 'must be objectively reasonable and not based entirely upon the investor's subjective expectations'.[110] More importantly, it is the responsibility of the investor to provide evidence that 'his/her investment was based on a state of affairs that did not include the challenged regulatory regime'.[111] It has been asserted that this doctrine is commonly linked with fair and equitable treatment standards; nevertheless, it plays a significant role

106 *S. D. Myers. Inc. v Government of Canada* (n. 105 above) paras 281, 285 (emphasis added).
107 *Olguin v Republic of Paraguay*, ICSID Case No. Arb/98/5 26 July 2001, para 84.
108 *Philips Petroleum Co. v Islamic Republic of Iran* (n. 50 above).
109 *Metalclad Corp. v United Mexican States*, (ICSID Additional Facility Case No. ARB (AF)/97/1), 30 August 2000, para 111.
110 Yannaca-Small (n. 7 above) 68.
111 Ibid.

in determining the law applicable to indirect expropriation.[112] It goes without saying that each alien investor expects to attain specific economic benefits from the investment they made. Generally speaking, most governments in today's business world actively invite investors and create expectations by introducing new laws or announcing new welcoming programmes. Such announcements and favourable laws may be the major driving factors in an investor's decision to pursue a venture in a host country. The following cases under NAFTA and ICSID best illustrate how tribunals regard the legitimate expectation criterion when assessing alleged indirect expropriation.

As mentioned above, in the *Metalclad* case the company had met all the necessary requirements and the project construction permit had been granted by the Mexican federal government. Naturally, the company had counted on the guarantee given to it before the project commenced. As a result, the tribunal held that

> these measures, taken together with the representations of the Mexican federal government, on which *Metalclad* relied, and the absence of a timely, orderly or substantive basis for the denial by the municipality of the local construction permit, amount to an indirect expropriation.[113]

The tribunal delivered a similar verdict in the *TECMED* case.[114] In this case, the Spanish company Tecnicas was required to renew its licence in order to continue operating in the landfill; however, the Mexican State agency refused the licence renewal request of the investor. The ICSID tribunal found that the measures taken by the Mexican state agency amounted to expropriation and held that

> even before the claimant had made its investment, it was widely known that the investor expected its investments in the landfill to be long term and that it took this into account to estimate the time and business required to recover such investment and obtain expected return...such expectations should be considered legitimate...[115]

In *Methanex Corp v United States of America*,[116] the tribunal's approach exhibited key differences to the *TECMED* case. In that case, the claimant alleged that the ban levied by the Californian government on the sale and use of the gasoline additive methyl tert-butyl ether (MTBE) had been tantamount to an expropriation. Therefore the loss of the company needed to be compensated. In its defence, the US asserted that the prohibition of the MTBE was necessary and justifiable

112 Cameron (n. 48 above) 226; see also Reinnisch (n. 12 above) 448.
113 *Metalclad* (n. 109 above) para 107.
114 *Tecnicas Medioambentales TECMED S.A. v the United Mexican States*, ICSID Case No. ARB (AF)/00/3 (2004) (*TECMED* hereinafter).
115 Ibid., para 150.
116 *Methanex Corporation v United States of America*, Final Award on Jurisdictions and Merits, 2 August 2005.

because the substance in question can contaminate drinking water, thereby categorising their claim as motivated by public purpose. The tribunal rejected the investor's claim and provided instructive statements in the context of the legitimate expectation of investors. In this regard, the tribunal held that with reference to international law, non-discriminatory measures were taken by the host state for the public purpose that did not constitute expropriation as long as specific commitments were provided by the state 'to the then putative foreign investor contemplating investment that the government would refrain from such regulation'.[117] It is apparent that the tribunal did not concentrate on, in the first instance, whether an expropriation had taken place; it instead focused its attention on determining whether the measure taken by the Californian government was for public purpose and could therefore be deemed legitimate.

The proportionality test

Another significant test is the proportionality of the measures taken by the host government. In determining whether a host government's measure constitutes an indirect expropriation, tribunals have also examined whether the measure taken by the government is reasonably proportional to the purpose the government seeks to attain.[118]The focus of this analysis is the impact of the measure taken against alien investors versus the impact on host state nationals.[119] As was stated by the tribunal in the *TECMED* case, there had to be 'a reasonable relationship of the proportionality between the charge or levy imposed on the foreign investor and the aim sought to be realised by any expropriatory measure'.[120]

Moreover, the proportionality test is frequently referred to in the jurisprudence of the European Court of Human Rights (ECHR). In *James and Others v The United Kingdom*, the court stated:

> Not only must a measure depriving a person of his property pursue, on the facts as well as in principle, a legitimate aim 'in the public interest', but there must also be a reasonable relationship of the proportionality between the means employed and the aim sought to be realised. This latter requirement is also expressed by the notion of the 'fair balance' that must be struck between the demands of the general interest of the community and the requirements of the protections of the individual's fundamental rights… The requisite balance will not be found if the person concerned has had to bear 'an individual and excessive burden'.[121]

Even though the proportionality test is applied most frequently in the context of ECHR, the investment arbitral tribunals have also applied the test in

117 *Methanex* (n. 116 above) Part IV, chapter D, para 7.
118 Salacuse (n. 10 above) 313.
119 Ibid.
120 *TECMED* (n. 114 above) para 122.
121 *James and Others v the United Kingdom* (21 February 1986) Series A No. 98, para 50, European Court of Human Rights.

determination of indirect expropriation, such as the *TECMED case* and, more recently, the *Azurix case.* [122]

Sole effect versus police power

Throughout the previous section, selected case studies have served to illustrate how a number of arbitral tribunals have adopted differing approaches to distinguish between non-compensable regulatory measures and indirect expropriation. Taking into account this overview, it is fair to state that not one of the principles applied clearly prevailed over the others, and it can be concluded that is difficult to predict what an investment tribunal's approach will be from one case to the next. It can be claimed that having no precise criteria at hand creates an uncertain atmosphere in international investment law. This uncertainty is

> not only a problem for the investment or state involved arbitration, but that also undermines the legitimacy of investment law as a whole, as it remains unclear what rights investment law grants to foreign investors and to what degree it interferes with the sovereignty of states to regulate their economic order.[123]

What can be asserted with conviction is that, generally speaking, the sole effect test and the purpose approach are more frequently applied than any of the other available methods in tribunals, and for this reason an important question needs to be addressed regarding these two approaches: should investment tribunals concentrate on merely the sole effects of the measure taken by the host state or ought they to focus on police power doctrine?

According to Dolzer, the effect of the host state measure ought to be the sole criterion[124] and little weight should be given to the purpose of the state in establishing the measure.[125] Conversely, Al-Qurashi argues that sole effect doctrine should not be the only approach and exclusive criterion applied by tribunals.[126] In other words, investment tribunals should not pay less attention to or single out the police power approach, because focusing on one specific principle may lead tribunals more frequently to reach verdicts that disadvantage the host state. Naturally, in the long term, any measures taken by the host state could be seen as a threat for investors and interpreted as having an impact on an alien investor's property rights. For this reason, before investing in a foreign country, investors

122 *Azurix Corp. v Argentine Republic* (ICSID Case No. Arb/01/12), Annulment Proceeding, Decision of the Ad Hoc Committee, 1 September 2009.

123 M. Perkams, 'The Concept of Indirect Expropriation in Comparative Public Law: Searching for Light in the Dark', Chapter 4 in S. W. Schill, *International Investment Law and Comparative Public Law* (Oxford: Oxford University Press, 2010) 111.

124 Dolzer (n.1 above) 64; Reinnisch (n. 12 above) 405.

125 Salacuse (n. 10 above) 316.

126 Z. A. Al-Qurashi, 'Indirect Expropriation in the Field of Petroleum', *Journal of World Investment and Trade*, Vol. 5, No. 6 (2004) 897, 907, cited in Erkan,(n. 76 above) 93.

should be aware of the risks that arise from regulatory change which may affect their business operations or property rights.[127]

Generally speaking, it is clear that tribunals aim to reach conclusions regarding the discussion of whether the state measure constitutes indirect expropriation and the host government is liable to pay compensation as a consequence of bona fide domestic regulation. What has been found in this section is that there is inconsistency between these two approaches. Perhaps the fairest approach from the point of view of both parties is to give due consideration of both doctrines in determining whether the actions amount to indirect expropriation.

Bilateral investment treaties of Azerbaijan and Turkey and their treaty provisions concerning indirect expropriation

The bilateral investment treaty (BIT) is one of the most significant tools to attract foreign direct investment in a developed or developing country. Each developed state regards the BIT as a catalyst for economic growth and development of their countries. In addition to their attempts to attract investors into their territories, they commit to providing a favourable investment environment to investors from their own country. In that respect, it can be stated that through BITs, industrialized countries obtain legal promises or indeed protections for domestic investors based on international law. Unlike national domestic laws on foreign direct investment (FDI), which can also suggest safeguards and encouragements to alien investors but are liable to change with a change of government, no state can unilaterally modify international law or the provisions that exist under BITs.[128] The first BIT to be signed was between Pakistan and Germany on 25 November 1959. Since 1959, 2,963 BITs have been concluded around the world.[129]

The lifespan of such treaties can be 10–20 years, with continuing coverage normally for 20 years after the termination of investment agreements made while they are in force.[130] Despite the fact that 2,963 BITs to date have been entered into between many diverse states, the safeguards and guarantees they include are more or less similar. They are designed to cover the following five elements: (i) protection from expropriation without compensation; (ii) most favoured nation provisions; (iii) national treatment provisions; (iv) fair and equitable treatment; (v) methods of dispute settlement. However, save for a few exceptions, the vast majority of BITs do not define indirect expropriation, even though it is possible that state actions may constitute indirect expropriation. It could be concluded that rather than depending on tribunals to determine whether or not a state action constitutes indirect expropriation, it might be more appropriate and help avoid future deliberation if states determined in their BITs what possible state action

127 Ibid.
128 Subedi (n. 99 above) 81–2.
129 International Investment Agreements Navigator, available at <http://investmentpolicyhub.unctad.org/IIA>
130 Subedi (n. 99 above) 82.

may be classed as indirect expropriation as well as providing a clear definition of indirect expropriation.

The following sub-sections examine the BIT models of Azerbaijan and Turkey to investigate whether their BIT provisions define indirect expropriation or illustrate what possible state actions may cause indirect expropriation

Azerbaijan

Since 1991, Azerbaijan has enacted a significant number of laws and initiatives designed to facilitate foreign investment in its territory. To become part of a global economy, to participate in the activities of international organisations and to sign international agreements have been the goals Azerbaijani governments aspired to. Azerbaijan signed its first raft of BITs with a number of developed and developing countries during 1990s. By 1999, the country had signed 17 BITs with its neighbours and major trading partners outside the Caucasus region that included some OECD countries, such as Turkey, Germany, France and the United Kingdom. Between 1999 and 2013, the country concluded 28 more BITs, with some EU member states as well as other non-EU states such as Egypt, Qatar and Israel. In total, Azerbaijan has concluded 45 BITS. The main objective of these agreements was to supply fair, foreseeable, transparent and non-discriminatory principles for foreign investors in its territory. Notably, all Azerbaijani BITs include an expropriation clause and specifically address 'direct and indirect' expropriation phenomena. For instance, the Azerbaijan–Finland BIT (2003) addresses this in Article 6 of the treaty:

> Investments by investors of a Contracting Party in the territory of the other Contracting Party shall not be expropriated, nationalised or subjected to any other measures having the effect, either directly or indirectly, equivalent to expropriation or nationalisation (hereinafter referred to as 'expropriation') except for a public interest, on a non-discriminatory basis, under due process of law and against prompt, adequate and effective compensation.[131]

It is clear that this expropriation clause explicitly recognises the existence of both direct and indirect expropriation. However, the article does not define exactly what single action or combination of actions may be deemed indirect expropriation or exactly which outcomes may constitute indirect expropriation. As stated above, traditional BITs do not proffer a definition for possible state actions that may constitute indirect expropriation. Moreover, it should also be noted that between 1994 (when the first BIT was entered into with Turkey) and the present, no indirect expropriation case has emerged against Azerbaijan. In addition to BITs, Azerbaijan has also signed a number of agreements in parallel to prevent

131 See Article 6 of the Agreement between Republic of Azerbaijan and Republic of Finland on Promotion and Protection of Investment (2003), available at <http://investmentpolicyhub.unctad.org/Download/TreatyFile/231>

double taxation.[132] Azerbaijan's concluded BITs include provisions consistent with Azerbaijani foreign investment law (1992). During the examination, it was realised that the law on foreign investment provides investment security through national treatment provisions and free transfer of funds (after payment of taxes), in harmony with the BITs signed by Azerbaijan. It is to be recommended that Azerbaijan continues to enter into more BITs to further accelerate the flow of investment into its territory.

Turkey

In order to attain the most liberal FDI regime possible, Turkey has entered into BITs with 82 countries since 1962. The first BIT was signed with Germany and was followed by a BIT with the US in 1986. While 74 BITs have so far been approved by the Turkish parliament, the remainder are yet to enter into force. The defining feature of the Turkish BIT model is the compatibility of their key provisions with international investment protection standards, such as: (i) application of national treatment; (ii) most favoured national treatment to alien investor; (iii) guarantee of free transfer of profits; (iv) the terms and conditions of expropriations; (v) compensation for losses; (vi) provisions for international arbitration. It should be noted that, like Azerbaijan, the Turkish BIT model also specifically addresses direct and indirect expropriation. For instance, according to Article 3(1) of the Yemen–Turkey BIT (2011):

> Investments shall not be expropriated, nationalized or subject, directly or indirectly, to measures of similar effects except for a public purpose, in a non-discriminatory manner, upon payment of prompt, adequate and effective compensation, and in accordance with due process of law and the general principles of treatment provided for in Article II of this Agreement.[133]

Similar to the Azerbaijani BIT model, the Turkish BIT's provision specifically references the phenomenon of indirect expropriation. However, neither country's BITs identify what indirect expropriation is or name the possible state actions that may constitute indirect expropriation. The China–India BIT model[134] could serves as useful future reference for Turkey and Azerbaijan in this respect as it successfully defines indirect expropriation phenomena and references the state actions that can be deemed to constitute indirect expropriation.

132 Azerbaijan has signed double taxation agreements with 53 countries. Available at <www.azernews.az/business/111044.html>

133 Article 3(1), Agreement between the Republic of Turkey and the Republic of Yemen Concerning the Reciprocal Promotion and Protection of Investments (2011), available at <http://unctad.org/Sections/dite_tobedeleted/iia/docs/bits/turkey_yemen.pdf>

134 See Section III (Article 5) of Protocol to the Agreement between the Republic of India and the People's Republic of China on Promotion and Protection of Investments. The agreement is available at <http://unctad.org/sections/dite/iia/docs/bits/India_China.pdf>

It is worth noting that before the current Turkish FDI Law No. 4875 was enacted in 2003, the country used the Law for the Encouragement of Foreign Capital No. 6224. Despite the fact that the old FDI law provided some guarantees to foreign investors, no provisions were made for expropriation. For this reason, BITs signed before the new law was passed were not in compliance with the provisions of the old FDI law. However, on the adoption of new FDI, this problem was dealt with because the new law regulates against expropriation. It can be affirmed with confidence that the provisions of the new law and the clauses in BITs are in harmony and comply with each other.

During the last decade, Turkey has accelerated the number of BITs it has entered into, not only with developed countries but also with developing states from different regions, such as Afghanistan, Jordan, Yemen, Thailand and the Philippines. Entering into bilateral relationships with developed and developing countries demonstrates the Republic of Turkey's efforts to develop its economy as well as improve its political relationships. In order to boost its BITs, the country has also entered into a number of supplementary agreements with several countries in parallel to its BITs. For example, in order to prevent double taxation, Turkey has signed double taxation prevention treaties with 76 countries. The benefit of these agreements is that tax paid in one of the two countries can be offset against tax payable in the other, thus preventing double taxation. Also, in order to foster greater freedom of movement for its expatriates, Turkey has also signed social security agreements with 22 countries.

Unlike Azerbaijan, Turkey has had an indirect expropriation claim lodged against it. As a result of the growing demand for electricity, the country decided to liberalise its energy sector during the 1980s. According to this policy, Turkey allowed private companies to establish facilities for the generation of electricity that they could then sell to the government, and also offered incentives to the companies including Treasury Guarantees. In 1994, PSEG,[135] a US-based company, signed a Concession and Implementation Contract with the government of Turkey for the establishment of a coal-fired power plant and an adjacent coal mine. Subsequently, a dispute arose between the parties as to whether the Concession Contract included a final agreement of key terms and what those terms were. Meanwhile, the legal framework of the agreement also underwent a change with the enactment of Law No. 4828 in 2001, which eliminated the possibility of the claimants obtaining a Treasury Guarantee for the project (the corresponding legal provisions were annulled by the Turkish Supreme Court in 2002). According to the claimant, all these events, viewed in conjunction, reflected Turkey's intent to damage the claimant's investment. The Tribunal found that Turkey was in violation of the fair and equitable treatment obligation but dismissed all other claims. In determining the compensation payable, the Tribunal rejected the 'fair market value' standard because no expropriation had been found and because there was no damage to productive assets.

135 *PSEG Global, Inc. et al v Republic of Turkey* (ICSID Case No. ARB/02/5) (2007), Award 19 January 2007.

Tools for mitigating indirect expropriation risk

Although Chapter 3 specifically focuses on stabilisation clauses *per se*, it is also worth briefly mentioning here stabilisation clauses along with other legal instruments used in the management of indirect expropriation risk. There are ranges of devices available to the host state for it to utilise against alien investors: states may introduce new laws and regulations, which terminate or change the condition of a previously agreed contract. More dramatically, the state may use its sovereign powers to unlawfully expropriate the alien investor's property directly or indirectly as well as the property rights of the foreign investor. In order to defend themselves from such violations by the state, there are also some mechanisms available to alien investors to protect them against those measures taken by the host state that affect their business operations.[136] Energy investment-related projects are based on profit, efficiency and sustainability, just like any other type of investment. Therefore, in order to be in a favourable position in the contract and protect the investment against indirect expropriation, foreign investors may require stabilisation clauses from host states. According to Cameron, the stabilisation clauses inserted in a host government contract are one way of managing risk.[137] From the perspective of the investor, inserting such clauses in an investment contract has the benefit of safeguarding their rights; however, accepting such clauses and agreeing to them in long-term investment contracts may serve as a disincentive for host governments inasmuch as it attempts to limit the use of its police power.[138]

Conclusions

A significant proportion of this chapter was devoted to examining documented examples of indirect expropriation phenomena. It has been acknowledged that the definition of indirect expropriation is a conundrum in the sphere of international investment law. Modern investment treaties go some way to resolving that conundrum. As previously mentioned, while traditional treaties do not provide a definition of indirect expropriation, some modern investment treaties make mention of indirect expropriation under the definition of investment. This kind of definition of investment not only covers tangible assets but also takes into account the intangible rights of the investors. The interpretation that can be made of this fact is that the expropriation clauses in the BITs 'may not only protect physical property, such as land and buildings, but also intangible forms of

136 W. Waelde & G. Ndi, Stabilizing International Investment Commitments: International Law versus Contract Interpretation', *Texas International Law Journal*, Vol. 31 (1996) 234. The inclusion of a '[s]tabilisation...clause [is] meant to restrain a government from subsequently abrogating or otherwise intervening by exercise of state powers in investment agreements concluded with foreign companies'.

137 P. D. Cameron, 'Stabilisation in Investment Contracts and Changes of Rules in Host Countries: Tools for Oil & Gas Investors', *AIPN, FINAL REPORT*, 5 July (2006) 9.

138 L. Cotula, 'Reconciling Regulatory Stability and Evolution of Environmental Standards in Investment Contracts: Towards a Rethink of Stabilisation Clauses', *Journal of World Energy Law and Business*, Vol. 1, No. 2 (2008).

property, such as contractual rights, intellectual property rights, and government business concession'.[139]

Furthermore, there are various state measures, as described above, that may constitute indirect expropriation, such as an excessive or discriminatory tax regime, interference with the management rights of the investor, interference with contractual rights, revocation of licence and denial of permits. These are all typical examples of indirect expropriation. It should, however, also be noted that, more recently, measures related to environmental or human rights issues have also been used by states as justification for interference in the energy sector. Regardless of the differences between any given type of state intervention and the reasons behind the indirect taking, the fact is that the alien investor's return on investment may be significantly reduced by these forms of state intervention. In an effort to find a resolution to these issues, investment arbitral tribunals have turned their focus to the problem and, as a result of this, have created invaluable guidance on the issues arising from indirect expropriation. Nonetheless, the impact of the state measure on the profit that investors expect is not always considered by the investment tribunals, in particular in the case of regulatory taking.

In other words, the question of distinguishing non-compensable regulatory state measures and indirect expropriation is, as yet, an unresolved one and continues to act as a major obstacle in international law. As outlined previously, there are several tests that are applied by arbitral tribunals. From an examination of case law, it is evident that the classification of government measures depends on the specific facts and circumstances of each case. The tests applied by the tribunals concentrate on the severe economic impact on the investment, the legitimate expectation of the investor and the character of the government measure – that is, the purpose and context of the measure and proportionality criteria. It should also be noted that these tests are not exact formulas that are consistently applied by tribunals. From examples of case law, the only common conclusion that can be drawn regarding regulatory taking is that the state's regulatory activity should not be unlawful and must be fair and proportional. There are two main doctrines perhaps most frequently employed in the determination of whether a government measure constitutes an indirect expropriation or not. These are the sole effect doctrine and police power doctrine.

There is no definite evidence that investment tribunals more frequently apply a particular approach. In other words, no one doctrine has been favoured over others in case law. What can be said is that perhaps sole effect doctrine tends to come down on the side of the investor. It could be suggested that during the determination process tribunals ought to consider not only sole effect doctrine as it suggests a bias in favour of investors, but also police power doctrine, as this understanding is based on the state's right to regulate.

139 J. W. Salacuse, *The Three Laws of International Investment: National, Contractual and Interventional Frameworks for Foreign Capital*, 1st edn (Oxford: Oxford University Press, 2013) 394.

Perhaps this combination of doctrines constitutes the fairest approach, removing the uncertainty around the question of distinguishing non-compensable regulatory measures and indirect expropriation. It must be taken into account that, as is always the case in law, law systems can be subject to revision, and indeed can be altered by a state at any time if it adopts various regulatory measures. It is fair to assume that the adoption or revision of an existing legal system is more frequent in developing states than would be the norm in developed countries. In order not to leave themselves exposed to the effects of such changes, alien investors should be conscious that those changes may occur at any time and that it is advisable for them to seek specific guarantees to protect their investments.

The bilateral investment treaties of Azerbaijan and Turkey were also examined in this chapter. It was found that both countries have entered into a number of BITs with different countries. It is to be recommended that Azerbaijan extend its bilateral treaty investment relations with a large number of states in order to attract more investors into its territory. In this respect, Turkey is comparatively much more established. Moreover, the provisions regarding expropriation in the BITs of both countries are not descriptive in defining indirect expropriation and what measures may or may not constitute indirect expropriation. It is true that most BITs do not adequately address this; however, if Azerbaijan and Turkey follow certain existing modern BIT models, such as that of China–India, or other similar treaties which explicitly define indirect phenomena, they would thereby improve the prospects of attracting capital into their economies. Generally speaking, if countries around the world inserted an explicit and comprehensive definition of indirect expropriation, rather than simply alluding to it in their BITs, this would be of great assistance to tribunals in determining what state action may/may not constitute indirect expropriation As a political risk manager, stabilisation clauses represent one of the best guarantees of all those contractually available in the petroleum industry. The following chapter will lend its focus to the stabilisation clause in detail.

Bibliography

Legislation (national and international) and guides

Agreement between Republic of Azerbaijan and Republic of Finland on Promotion and Protection of Investment (2003), available at <http://investmentpolicyhub.unctad.org/Download/TreatyFile/231>

Agreement between the Republic of Turkey and the Republic of Yemen Concerning the Reciprocal Promotion and Protection of Investments (2011), available at <http://unctad.org/Sections/dite_tobedeleted/iia/docs/bits/turkey_yemen.pdf>

Decreto con Fuerza de Ley Organica de Hidracarburos (Decree with Force of Organic Law of Hydrocarbons), Decree No. 1,510, 2 November 2001, Official Gazette No. 37, 323, available at <www.freshfields.com/uploadedFiles/SiteWide/Knowledge/Venezuela%20-%20proposed%20measures%20against%20oil%20and%20gas%20investors.pdf>

Energy Charter Treaty (ECT) Reader Guide, available at <www.encharter.org>
North American Free Trade Agreement (NAFTA) Between the Government of Canada, the Government of Mexico and the Government of the United States, 17 December 1992, reprinted in 32 ILM 289 and 605 (1993), came into force 1 January 1994
OECD Draft Convention on the Protection of Foreign Property, (12 October 1967), 71 *ILM*
Restatement (Third) of the Foreign Relations Law of the United States (1987) 117
The European Convention for the Protection of Human Rights and Fundamental Freedoms, Protocol No. 1 (18 May 1954), Paris. Available at <www.equalityhumanrights.com/uploaded_files/humanrights/hrr_firstprotocol.pdf>

Cases and arbitral awards

Azurix Corp. v Argentine Republic (ICSID Case No., Arb/01/12), (1 September 2009)
BG Group Plc. v The Republic of Argentina, UNCITRAL Arbitration, Final Award, IIC 321(2007), 24 December 2007
Biloune and Marine Drive Complex Ltd *v* Ghana Investments Centre and the Government of Ghana, UNCITRAL ad hoc Tribunal, Award on Jurisdiction and Liability, 27 October 1989, 95 ILR 183, 209
CME Czech Republic BV v Czech Republic (Partial Award) 13 September 2001
CMS Gas Transmission Company v The Argentine Republic, ICSID Case No. ARB/01/8 Award (12 May 2005) 262
Compañía Del Desarrollo De Santa Elena, S. A. v Costa Rica, Final Award, ICSID Case No. ARB/96/1 (17 February 2000), 15 ICSID Rev. FILJ (2000) 457, available at <www.worldbank.org/icsid/cases/santaelena_award.pdf>
Generation Ukraine, Inc. v Ukraine, ICSID Case No ARB/00/9, Award of 16 September 2003, 44
Goetz and Others v Republic of Burundi, 2 September 1998, ICSID Case No. ARB/95/3
James and Others v The United Kingdom (21 February 1986) Series A, No. 98, European Court of Human Rights
Marvin Roy Feldman Karpa (CEMSA) v United Mexican States of Mexico (2002) ICSID Case No. ARB (AF) 99/1, Award, IIC 157(2002)
Metalclad Corporation v United Mexican States, 30 August 2000, ICSID Reports 209
Methanex Corporation v United States of America, Final Award on Jurisdictions and Merits, 2 August 2005
Middle East Cement Shipping and Handling Co. S.A. v Arab Republic of Egypt, 12 April 2002, 7 ICSID Reports 178
Murphyores Inc., Pty Ltd v Commonwealth (1976) 136 CLR 1; [1976] HCA 20
Nykomb Synergetics Technology AB v Latvia, Award, SCC Case No. 118/2001, IIC 182 (2003), 16 December 2003
Occidental Exploration and Production Company v the Republic of Ecuador, Final Award, and LCIA Case No. UN3467 of 1 July 2004, 43 ILM 1248(2004)
Parkerings-Compagniet As v Lithuania, ICSID Case No. ARB/05/08 Award Sept. (2007)
Philips Petroleum Co., Iran v Islamic Republic of Iran, 21 Iran-U.S. Cl. Trib. Rep.79
Pope & Talbot, Inc. v Government of Canada, Interim Award (26 June 2000), available at <www.biicl.org/files/3922_2002_pope_&_talbot_v_canada.pdf>
PSEG Global, Inc. et al v Republic of Turkey (ICSID Case No. ARB/02/5) (2007), Award 19 January 2007

Revere Copper and Brass Inc. v Overseas Private Investment Corporation, 24 August 1978, 56 ILR 268

S. D. Myers Inc. v *Government of* Canada, Partial Award, 13 November 2000, 40 ILM (2001) 1408

Saluka Investment BV (Netherlands) v The Czech Republic (Partial Award) of 2 March 2006

Sea-Land *Services* Inc. v Iran, 6 Iran-U.S. CI. Trib. Rep. 149 (1984), 166

Sedco Inc. v National Iranian Oil Co., Interlocutory Award 9 Iran-U.S Cl. Trib. Rep. 248 , 275 (1985)

Starrett Housing Corp v Iran, Interlocutory Award No ITL 32-24-1, Award 19 December 1983, reprinted in 4 Iran-US CTR 122

Tecnicas Medioambentales TECMED S.A v the United Mexican States, ICSID Case No. ARB (AF)/00/3, (2004)

Tippetts, Abbett, McCarthy, Stratton v TAMS-AFFA, No 141–147, 6 Iran-US CTR Rep. 219 (29 June 1984)

Waste Management Inc. v United Mexican States (Waste Management II) ICSID Case No. ARB (AF)/00/3 NAFTA Award 30 April 2004

Yukos Universal Limited (Isle of Man) v the Russian Federation, PCA Case No. AA 227, UNCITRAL

Internet websites

http://investmentpolicyhub.unctad.org/IIA

http://investmentpolicyhub.unctad.org/Download/TreatyFile/231

http://unctad.org/en/Docs/psiteiitd15.en.pdf

www.equalityhumanrights.com/uploaded_files/humanrights/hrr_firstprotocol.pdf

www.freshfields.com/uploadedFiles/SiteWide/Knowledge/Venezuela%20-%20proposed%20measures%20against%20oil%20and%20gas%20investors.pdf

www.palermo.edu/Archivos_content/derecho/pdf/Revisiting-privatization-foreign-investment.pdf

www.pca-cpa.org/showpage.asp?pag_id=1149

www.unctad.org/en/docs//wir2003_en.pdf

www.unctad-docs.org/files/UNCTAD-WIR2011-Full-en.pdf

Books and monographs

Al-Qurashi, Z.A., 'Investment Protection under International Petroleum Agreements: an Analysis of Pertinent Arbitral Jurisprudence', PhD Thesis, University of Dundee, 2004

Brownlie, I., *Principles of Public International Law*, 6th edn. Oxford: Oxford University Press, 2003

Cameron, P. D., *International Energy Investment Law: The Pursuit of Stability*. Oxford: Oxford University Press, 2010

Erkan, M., *International Energy Investment Law: Stability through Contractual Clauses*, Energy and Environmental Law and Policy Series. Alphen aan den Rijn: Kluwer Law International, 2011

Garner, B. A., *A Dictionary of Modern Legal Usage*, 2nd edn. New York: Oxford University Press, 1995

Newcombe, A., 'Regulatory Expropriation, Investment Protection and International Law: When Is Government Regulation Expropriatory and When Compensation Should Be Paid?' LLM Thesis, University of Toronto, Toronto, 1999

Newcombe, A. & Paradell, L., *Law and Practice of Investment Treaties: Standards of Treatment* (Alphen aan de Rijn: Kluwer Law International, 2009), 323

OECD, *Private Sector Development and in the Middle East and North Africa: Supporting Investment Policy and Governance in Iraq*, OECD Publication, 2010

Ripinskyi, S. & Williams, K., *Damages in International Investment Law*. London: British Institute of International and Comparative Law, 2008

Rovine, A.W., *Contemporary Issues in International Arbitration and Mediation*. Leiden: Martinus Nijhoff Publishers, 2007

Salacuse, J. W., *The Law of Investment Treaties*. Oxford: Oxford University Press, 2009

Salacuse, J. W., *The Three Laws of International Investment: National, Contractual and Interventional Frameworks for Foreign Capital*, 1st edn. Oxford: Oxford University Press, 2013

Schaffer, R., Agusti, F. & Earler, B., *International Business Law and its Environment*, 7th edn. Boston, MA: Cengage Learning, 2009

Solanes, M. & Jouravlev, A., *Revisiting Privatization, Foreign investment, International Arbitration, and Water*. Santiago, Chile: United Nations, 2007, available at <www.palermo.edu/Archivos_content/derecho/pdf/Revisiting-privatization-foreign-investment.pdf>

Sornarajah, M., *The Pursuit of Nationalized Property*. Dordrecht: Kluwer Academic Publishers, 1986

Sornarajah, M., *The International Law on Foreign Investment*, Cambridge: Grotius Publications, 1994

Sornarajah, M., *The International Law on Foreign Investment*, 2nd edn. (Cambridge: Cambridge University Press: 2004)

Sornarajah, M., *The International Law on Foreign Investment*, 3rd edn. Cambridge: Cambridge University Press, 2010

Subedi, S.P., *International Investment Law: Reconciling Policy and Principle*, 2nd edn. Portland, OR: Hart Publishing, 2012

Chapters in books

Kawharu, A., 'International Law's Protection of Foreign Owned Property against Uncompensated Expropriation: Preserving Host State Regulatory Freedom', Chapter 15 in P. Grinlinton & P. Taylor (eds) *Property Rights and Sustainability: The Evolution of Property Rights to Meet Ecological Challenges*. Leiden: Martinus Nijhoff Publishers, 2011

PaulssonJ. & Douglas, Z., 'Indirect Expropriation in Investment Treaty Arbitration' in N. Horn & S. Kroll (eds) *Arbitrating Foreign Investment Disputes*. The Hague: Kluwer International Law, 2004

Perkams, M., 'The Concept of Indirect Expropriation in Comparative Public Law: Searching for Light in the Dark', Chapter 4 in S. W. Schill (ed.) *International Investment Law and Comparative Public Law*. Oxford: Oxford University Press, 2010

Reinnisch, A., 'The Legality of Expropriation', Chapter 11 in P. Muchlinski, F. Ortino & C. Schreuer (eds), *The Oxford Handbook of International Investment Law*. New York: Oxford University Press, 2008

Articles, seminars/conference and research papers

Abdala, M. A. & Spiller, P. T., 'Damage Valuation of Indirect Expropriation in International Arbitration Cases', *American Review of International Arbitration*, Vol. 14 (2003) 449

Al-QurashiZ.A., 'Indirect Expropriation in the Field of Petroleum', *Journal of World Investment and Trade*, Vol. 5, No. 6 (2004) 897–907

Christie, G.C., 'What Constitutes a Taking of Property Under International Law?' *British Year Book of International Law*, Vol. 38 (1962) 307–338

Cotula, L. 'Reconciling Regulatory Stability and Evolution of Environmental Standards in Investment Contracts: Towards a Rethink of Stabilisation Clauses', *Journal of World Energy Law and Business*, Vol. 1, No. 2 (2008) 158–179

Dolzer, R., 'Indirect Expropriation: New Developments?', *N.Y.U. Environmental Law Journal*, Vol. 11 (2002) 64–65

Fortier, L. & Drymer, S. L., 'Indirect Expropriation in the Law of International Investment: I Know it When I See It', *ICSID Review – Foreign Investment Law Journal*, Vol. 19, No. 2 (2004) 293–294

Nikiema, S. H., 'Indirect Expropriation', Best Practices Working Paper Series, (International Institute for Sustainable Development) (2012) 1, available at <www.iisd.org/pdf/2012/best_practice_indirect_expropriation.pdf>

Verhoosel, G., 'Foreign Direct Investment and Legal Constraints on Domestic Environmental Policies: Striking a "Reasonable" Balance between Stability and Change', *Law and Policy in International Business*, Vol. 29 (1998) 451–478

Waelde, T., 'International Law of Foreign Investment: Towards Regulation by Multilateral Treaties', CEPMLP Research Paper CP1/2000, 19.

Waelde, T. W. & Kolo, A., 'Environmental Regulation, Investment Protection and "Regulatory Taking" in International Law', *International and Comparative Law Quarterly*, Vol. 50 (2001) 835

Waelde, T. W. & Ndi, G. 'Stabilizing International Investment Commitments: International Law versus Contract Interpretation', *Texas International Law Journal*, Vol. 31 (1996), 234–260

Wagner, J. M., 'International Investment, Expropriation and Environmental Protection', *Golden Gate University Law Review*, Vol. 29 (1999) 517

Yannaca-Small, C., 'Indirect Expropriation and the Right to Regulate in International Investment Law', Organisation for Economic Co-operation and Development (2004) 3–4, available at <www.oecd.org/daf/inv/investment-policy/WP-2004_4.pdf>

Reports

Cameron, P. D., 'Stabilisation in Investment Contracts and Changes of Rules in Host Countries: Tools for Oil & Gas Investors', *AIPN Final Report*, 5 July 2006

UNCTAD, *Taking Property*, Series on Issues on International Investment Agreements. New York and Geneva: United Nations (2000)

UNCTAD, *World Investment Report, FDI Policies for Development: National and International Perspectives*. New York and Geneva: United Nations (2003)

Part II

Mitigating political risks through stability provisions

3 Stabilisation clauses

Introduction

The insertion of stabilisation clauses in international investment agreements is the contractual feature most frequently required by foreign investors in their quest to obtain a stable investment environment. The motivation behind this lies in the scale and scope of the investment and the complex nature of economic development agreements. Over the course of an energy investment relationship an investor may sink billions of pounds or dollars into the venture; meanwhile, as evidenced in the previous chapter of this book, the host country has a high degree of control over the fate of the investment made within its territory. The inclusion of stabilisation clauses is intended to guard the investment against the damage incurred by unilateral changes to, or termination of, energy investment contracts at any point in the course of the project. In other words, by agreeing to such clauses the host state reassures the foreign private investor that certain aspects of its laws will be 'frozen' and the contractual arrangement will not be altered or terminated by the legislative or administrative activities of the host government during the lifespan of the project.

Although stabilisation clauses would appear to grant some guarantees to foreign investors, it is important to test this assumption by posing the following questions. To what extent are stabilisation clauses effective in protecting investments or, conversely, in contradiction of their intended guardianship, do they instead disenfranchise the sovereign rights of the host state? And do stabilisation provisions constitute a threat for environmental and human rights issues?

General implications of stabilisation clauses

In the literature several commentators have sought to offer definitions for this contractual article. According to Brownlie, 'the term "stabilisation clause" relates to any clause contained in an agreement between a government and a foreign legal entity by which a government party undertakes neither to annul the agreement nor to modify its terms, either by legislation or by administrative measures'.[1]

A similar description has been provided by Bernardini. According to this author, stabilisation clauses are an attempt to defend an alien investor by 'restricting the legislative or administrative power of the State, as sovereign in its country and legislator in its own legal system, to amend the contractual regulation or even to annul the agreement'.[2] In the case of *Amoco Int'l Fin. Corporation v Government of the Islamic Republic of Iran*, a definition was provided by the tribunal. The tribunal defined stabilisation clauses as 'contract language which freezes the provision of a national system of law chosen as the law of the contract as of the date of the contract, in order to prevent the application to the contract of any future alterations of this system.'[3]

In light of the above definitions, the purpose of stabilisation clauses should be explored. According to Sornarajah, 'the aim of the stabilisation clause was to ensure that future changes in the legislation of the host state did not vary the terms of the contract on the basis of which entry was made'.[4] The author goes on to state that inclusion of such clauses in an investment contract provide immunity to an alien investor from a wide range of potential threats to their interests, for instance, 'taxation, environmental controls and other regulations as well as to prevent the destruction of the contract itself before the contract expires'.[5] Furthermore, in Cotula's words, the purpose of the stabilisation clause is to 'stabilise the terms and conditions of an investment project, thereby contributing to manage non-commercial (that is fiscal, regulatory) risk'.[6]

In a similar vein, according to Professor Cameron, in international energy contracts, the term 'stabilisation' applies to all of the mechanisms, contractual or otherwise, designed to protect, during the lifespan of the contract, the benefit of certain economic and legal conditions which host states and foreign investors considered to be suitable at the time they were agreed.[7] The question of why alien private investors seek to freeze the contractual terms and conditions and the law of

1 I. Brownlie, *Principles of Public International Law*, 6th edn (Oxford: Oxford University Press, 2003), 526.
2 P. Bernardini, 'Stabilization and Adaptation in Oil and Gas Investments', *Journal of World Energy Law and Business*, Vol. 1, No. 1 (2008) 100.
3 *Amoco Int'l Fin. Corporation v Government of the Islamic Republic of Iran*, 16 Iran-U.S. Cl. Trib. Rep. 189, 239 (1987).
4 M. Sornarajah, *The International Law on Foreign Investment*, 3rd edn (Cambridge: Cambridge University Press, 2010) 281.
5 Ibid. at 282.
6 L. Cotula, 'Regulatory Takings, Stabilization Clauses and Sustainable Development', Session 2.2: The Policy Framework for Investment: The Social and Environmental Dimensions', OECD Global Forum on International Investment 27–28 March (2008) 5, available at <www.oecd.org/investment/globalforum/40311122.pdf>
7 P. D. Cameron, *International Energy Investment Law: The Pursuit of Stability*, (Oxford: Oxford University Press, 2010) 70 (hereinafter Cameron, *The Pursuit of Stability*).

host states by inserting such clauses during the lifespan of the contract is also explained by Sornarajah:

> The foreign corporation stood at a disadvantage in any agreement it made with the host state, as the host state had the legislative power to alter the impact on the contract of any event that took place within its territory or to affect any contractual right or right to property that was located within its territory. Such a power flowed from its sovereignty. It was in the interest of the foreign corporation to neutralise this power.[8]

What can be understood from the above definitions is that stabilisation clauses satisfy alien investors' expectations and provide a wide range of protections from discriminatory changes which may adversely affect the terms and conditions of energy investment contracts. However, it should also not be disregarded that although the main purpose of a stabilisation clause is to deter the application of subsequent alterations of host state legislation to the contract, stabilisation clauses may go as far as to discourage the host state from adopting new laws or reforming its legal system at all. How and where this affects environmental or human rights are the issues yet to be tackled in this chapter.

The following section examines the types of stabilisation clauses with regard to the different types of contracts that may exist between a host state and an investor.

Typologies of stabilisation clauses

The stabilisation clauses that may be inserted into investment contracts may be categorised into four significant types. The first type of stabilisation clause is the freezing clause. This clause is designed to insulate alien investors from subsequent unilateral host governmental actions during the lifespan of the agreement.[9] Such clauses are intended to 'fix' or 'freeze' the governing law of the contract between parties, the fiscal regime and other available indispensable investment conditions.[10] This 'fixing' or 'freezing' of the law is applicable to the contract once the contract is made and is applied throughout the lifespan of the project.[11] Notably, this clause creates one of the following two scenarios: either the state accepts that any changes to legislation enacted after the date of the contract will not apply to the contract, or where there is a

8 Sornarajah (n. 4 above) 281.

9 A. Sheppard & A. Crockett, 'Are Stabilisation Clauses a Threat to Sustainable Development?', Chapter 14 in M. C. C. Segger, A. Newcombe & M. W. Gehring (eds), *Sustainable Development in International Investment Law* (The Hague: Kluwer, 2010) 336.

10 T. W. Waelde & G. Ndi, 'Stabilizing International Investment Commitments: International Law versus Contract Interpretation', *Texas International Law Journal*, Vol. 31, No. 2 (1996) 260 (hereinafter Waelde & Ndi, 'Stabilizing International Investment Commitments').

11 A. Al-Faruque, 'Validity and Efficacy of Stabilisation Clauses: Legal Protection vs. Functional Value', *Journal of International Arbitration*, Vol. 23, No. 4 (2006) 319.

discrepancy between the provisions of the contract and any new legislation, any new legislation inconsistent with the clause will not apply to the contract.[12]

This type of stabilisation clauses has also been called a 'stabilisation clause in *stricto sensu*'. This is a more immoderate version which attempts to impose a definitive check on the legislative power of the host countries. A more thorough comprehension of the workings of the stabilisation clause in *stricto sensu* can be gained through the provision of an example. The concession agreement between the State of Iran and the Anglo Iranian Oil Company in 1933 provided that:

> The concession shall not be annulled by the Government of and the terms therein contained shall not be altered either by the general or special legislation in the future or by the administrative measures or any other acts whatever of the executive authorities.[13]

Another type of stabilisation clause is often referred to as the *intangibility* clause. In the context of this type of clause, the government may not modify or abrogate the contract unless both parties achieve mutual consent. In other words, the host state is not allowed to alter the contract without first obtaining the consent of the investor. This type of clause freezes the contract between the parties, but not the law of the host state in a dispute. It is noteworthy that this type of clause does not include any explicit waiver of legislative sovereignty; rather, it aims to preclude unilateral modification of the contract by the host country.[14] In this regard it is worth supplying some illustrative examples of the intangibility clause. Article 33 of the concession agreement between the Ruler of Abu Dhabi and three Japanese companies provided as follows: 'The mutual consent of the Ruler and the companies shall be required to annul or modify the provisions of this agreement.'[15] Another notable example of an intangibility clause can be found in an oil contract between the Government of Qatar and Holcar Oil Company. Article 33 is a textbook example of this type of stabilisation clause. It provides that: '[W]ithout prejudice to the Government's prerogative of sovereign powers the mutual consent of the Parties hereto shall be required to annul, amend or modify the provisions of this Agreement.'[16]

12 D. Clinch & J. Watson, 'Stabilisation Clauses – Issues and Trends', Herbert Smith Freehills LLP 2010, available at <www.lexology.com/library/detail.aspx?g=c5976193-1acd-4082-b9e7-87c0414b5328>

13 Z. A. Al-Qurashi, 'International Oil and Gas Arbitration', *OGEL, Journal of Oil, Gas and Energy Law Intelligence* Vol. 3, (2005), 181–2.

14 A. Al-Faruque, 'Stability in Petroleum Contracts: Rhetoric and Reality', PhD Thesis, University of Dundee (2005) 108.

15 Article 33 of the Concession Agreement between the Ruler of Abu Dhabi and Maruzen Oil Co. Ltd.; Daikyo Oil Co. Ltd. And Nippon Mining Co. Ltd., 6 December 1967, Selected Documents of the International Petroleum Industry, 1967, p. 137 cited in Al-Qurashi (n. 13 above) 181.

16 Exploration and Product Sharing Agreement between the Government of Qatar and Holcar Oil Co., 1 January 1976, Art. 33, Selected Documents of the International Petroleum Industry, 1967, 249, cited in M. Erkan, *International Energy Investment Law: Stability through Contractual Clauses* (Alphen aan den Rijn: Kluwer Law International, 2011) 105.

In light of the latter two examples, it is apparent that the intangible clause requires mutual consent of the parties in order to modify the terms and conditions of the agreement. When the nature of the intangibility clause is considered, requirement for consent from the parties seems fair and consensual; otherwise the contract could be altered at any time by the host state. More importantly, the main differences between the two types of clauses described thus far is that while the stabilisation clause in *stricto sensu* aims to protect the investor from any host government legislative activities which may affect the contract, the latter clause protects investors and prevents host states from acting as a unique authority to modify the contract, by requiring mutual consent.

The third type of stabilisation clauses are hybrid clauses. This type of stabilisation clause belongs in the category of stabilisation clauses which can be regarded as 'traditional'. Stabilisation clauses in *stricto sensu* and intangibility clauses are the main components of hybrids. An exemplary case study of how such clauses can be found in combination in a concession agreement between Libyan Am. Oil Co. and the Libyan Arab Republic. The contract provided that:

1 The Government of Libya, the Commission and the appropriate provincial authorities will take all steps necessary to ensure that the Company enjoys all the rights conferred by this Concession shall not be altered except by mutual consent of the parties.
2 This Concession shall throughout the period of its validity be constructed in accordance with the Petroleum Law and the Regulations in force on the date of execution of the Agreement of Amendment by which this [paragraph] (2) was incorporated into this Concession Agreement. Any amendments to or repeal of such regulations shall not affect the contractual rights of the Company without consent.[17]

Stabilisation clauses in *stricto sensu*, intangibility and hybrid clauses are all forms of freezing clause which are, in turn, categorised as traditional types of stabilisation clause. Generally speaking, the purpose of traditional stabilisation clauses is to negate the applicability of a law or fiscal regime. In other words, these traditional stabilisation clauses are intended to neutralise the power of a host country by safeguarding an agreement from alteration or threat by any subsequent legislative activities undertaken by the host state without first achieving mutual consent. Reference to the UN resolution on the principle of permanent sovereignty over natural resources helps demonstrate the inconsistency with internationally sanctioned principles that these types of clauses can represent. The resolution regards sovereignty as a unique and inalienable right of the state and asserts the free will of states to exercise their power over their natural resources and stipulates that such power cannot be restricted by a contract. When juxtaposed with the freezing effect that traditional stabilisation clauses exert over the applicable law and fiscal regime of the contracting state, there is an obvious conflict. This contradiction presents

17 *Liamco v Libya*, 62 I.L.R. 170.

questions about the validity and efficacy of stabilisation clauses which will be explored in more detail in the following section, following an assessment of the second category of stabilisation clauses.

Another type of stabilisation clause provides that the agreement between the parties shall be performed consistently with 'good will' or in 'good faith', hence precluding unilateral alteration or termination.[18] What this means is that the host state should avoid unilaterally altering or terminating the contract by using its legislative and executive power.[19]

Another type of stabilisation clause is the economic equilibrium clause which can be categorised in modern stabilisation clauses. The purpose of this type of clause is to restore economic balance between the host state and investor through the application of the renegotiation mechanism.[20] Such clauses are also called economic equilibrium clauses, economic stabilisation clauses or balancing clauses.[21] An accurate definition of these clauses was provided in the Baku–Tbilisi–Ceyhan (BTC) Agreement:

> Economic Equilibrium means the economic value to the Project Participants of the relative balance established under the Project Agreements at the applicable date between the rights, interests, exemptions, privileges, protections and other similar benefits provided or granted to such Person and concomitant burdens, costs, obligations, restrictions, conditions and limitations agreed to be borne by such Person.[22]

It is fair to say that the main difference between freezing clauses and economic equilibrium clauses is the latter's aim to stabilise the economic return of the investor rather than stabilise the legal or fiscal structure. In this type of clause, the state is allowed to make changes and introduce new laws that may have an impact the project.[23] However, in this scenario, the host government and foreign investor

18 C. T. Curtis, 'The Legal Security of Economic Development Agreements', *Harvard International Law Journal*, Vol. 29 (1998) 347; M. T. B. Coale, 'Stabilization Clauses in International Petroleum Transactions', *Denver Journal of International Law and Policy*, Vol. 30 (2002) 223.

19 Erkan (n. 16 above) 106.

20 Waelde & Ndi, 'Stabilizing International Investment Commitments' (n. 10 above) 266.

21 See, P. D. Cameron, 'Stabilisation in Investment Contracts and Changes of Rules in Host Countries: Tools for Oil & Gas Investors', AIPN, Final Report, 5 July 2006, 74 (hereinafter Cameron, 'Tools for Oil & Gas Investors'); see also Al-Faruque (n. 14 above) 100. It should be noted that in order to avoid any terminological ambiguity, the term 'stabilisation clauses' in this work covers all forms of stabilisation clauses.

22 Generally, see the BTC agreements, Appendix 1 of the Georgian HGA; Appendix 1 of the Turkish HGA and Appendix 1 of the Azerbaijani HGA.

23 According to Shemberg, these exemptions are not specifically emphasised in the contract: A. Shemberg, 'Stabilisation Clause and Human Rights: A Research Project Conducted for IFC and the United Nations Special Representative to the Secretary General on Business and Human Rights', IFC/SRSG Research Paper, 11 May (2009) vii.

agree on the economic benefit the investor may expect from the project and pledge their willingness to renegotiate the contract to safeguard the investor's economic position; otherwise the host government will be bound to pay compensation to the foreign investor. In other words, the economic equilibrium clauses provides that 'if any government action adversely affects the economics of the project for the companies, then the terms of the agreement will be readjusted to keep the companies in the same financial position as provided by the contract on the date it was signed'.[24]

In contractual practice, traditional freezing and economic equilibrium clauses are frequently applied simultaneously[25] within the same contract as well as separately.[26] There is no doubt that when the freezing type is used on its own, it can be very effective. Nevertheless, when these two clauses are employed in unison, the economic equilibrium provision 'lays down the outcome of the host state's breach of promise contained freezing clause that it makes to the contracting partner'.[27]

According to some legal scholars, economic equilibrium clauses can be divided into the following three categories:[28] (i) stipulated economic balancing; (ii) non-specified economic balancing and (iii) negotiated economic balancing.

Stipulated economic balancing decrees that the adjustment made can be automatic or achieved in the manner provided for in the agreement.[29] The Model Offshore Production Sharing Agreement of Pakistan best illustrates this category:

(a) The Government undertakes to uphold the fiscal stability of this Agreement and specifically guarantees that the payments to Government stipulated in Articles 6.6, 6.9, 9.1, 9.6, XIII, XXIV shall not be amended or changed with respect to the application of this Agreement.
(b) Where any agency or authority of the Government imposes any tax, cess, fee, duty, levy, or other ancillary payment in addition to the guaranteed payments in Article 31.1(a) as required by the laws of Pakistan other than those

24 R. D. Bishop, 'International Arbitration of Petroleum Disputes: The Development of *Lex Petrolea*', *Yearbook of Commercial Arbitration* , Vol. 23 (1998) 1161.
25 Shemberg (n. 23 above) 19–20.
26 A. F. M. Manirruzzaman, 'International Energy Contracts and Cross-Border Pipeline Projects: Stabilisation, Renegotiation and Economic Balancing in Changed Circumstances', *OGEL, Journal of Oil, Gas and Energy Law Intelligence*, Vol. 4, No. 4 (2006) 1 (hereinafter Manirruzzaman, 'International Energy Contracts and Cross-Border Pipeline Projects').
27 Ibid.
28 F. C. Alexander, 'The Three Pillars of Security of Investment Under PSCs and Other Host Government Contract', Chapter 7 of *Institute for Energy Law of the Centre for American and International Law's 54th Annual Institute on Oil and Gas Law* (Publication 640, Release 54), Lexis Nexis Mathew Bender, February 2003, 7.1, 7.19; see also Cameron, 'Tools for Oil & Gas Investors' (n. 22 above) 31; Manirruzzaman, 'International Energy Contracts and Cross-Border Pipeline Projects' (n. 26 above) 1; Erkan (n. 16 above) 204.
29 Alexander (n. 28 above) 7.19; Cameron, 'Tools for Oil & Gas Investors' (n. 21 above) 31; Erkan (n. 16 above) 204.

> concerning health, safety and environmental and related matters of public interest, Government Holdings shall consult with Contractor on appropriate measures in order to compensate Contractor for such unfavourable impacts caused by such amendments. After having quantified the unfavourable impacts, the Government Holdings share of Profit Oil and Profit Gas shall be adjusted in such a manner that the overall fiscal balance is maintained.[30]

According to Manirruzzaman, 'in stipulated Economic Balancing provisions various prescriptions for affecting the balance are stipulated'.[31] To this end, it can be said that in the above given agreement 'the Pakistani Model Contract stipulates for the adjustment of the government holdings share of the profit oil and profit gas'.[32]

In the case of non-specified economic balancing, there is no need to supply in the agreement for the manner of such adjustments or to stipulate that it ought to be the result of mutual agreement of the contracting parties.[33] The Azerbaijan PSA of 1998 offers a practical example:

> [In] the event that any Governmental Authority invokes any present or future law, treaty, intergovernmental agreement, decree or administrative order which contravenes the provision of this agreement or adversely or positively affects the rights or interests of Contractor hereunder, including, but not limited to, any changes in tax legislation, regulations, or administrative practice, or jurisdictional changes pertaining to the Contract Area, the terms of this Agreement shall be adjusted to re-establish the economic equilibrium of the Parties, and if the rights or interests of Contractor have been adversely affected, then SOCAR [The National Company] shall indemnify Contractor (and its assignees) for any disbenefit, deterioration in economic circumstances, loss or damages that ensure therefrom.[34]

With regard to the above-cited contract, Cameron asserts that

> the role of SOCAR in the contract underlines an important point. In a number of cases the host country's NOC will play a central role in the operation of fiscal stabilisation. It may provide for adjustment by paying any additional taxes out of its share of profit petroleum or royalty under a PSA or it may reimburse the IOC directly out of general revenues. Under a rate of

30 [Undated] Art. XXXI cited in Manirruzzaman, 'International Energy Contracts and Cross-Border Pipeline Projects' (n. 26 above) 4, for further details, see n. 8 of the author's article.

31 Ibid. at 6.

32 Ibid.

33 Alexander (n. 28 above) 7.19; P. D. Cameron, 'Tools for Oil & Gas Investors' (n. 21 above) 31; Erkan (n. 17 above) 204.

34 The Azerbaijan Union Texas/Commonwealth Production Sharing Agreement, 1998, Art 22(2), cited in Erkan (n. 16 above) 205.

> return system, the NOC could pay from its share of royalty and/or excess profits tax.[35]

As a third category, negotiated economic balancing offers the opportunity to contracting parties to meet and discuss how amendments ought to be made to the contract in the event of host state intervention which has the potential to adversely affect the original equilibrium of the contract.[36] The following serve as examples of the practical application of the negotiated economic balancing type of economic equilibrium clauses.

Article 17.1 of the Vietnam Model Product Sharing Contracts of 2004 states:

> If after the effective date, existing laws and regulations are amended or annulled new laws and regulation are introduced in Vietnam…in any case adversely affecting the economic rights or benefits expected by the contractor from this…*the parties shall meet and consult promptly with each other and make such changes to this contract* as are necessary both to maintain the Contractor's rights, benefits and interests hereunder and to ensure that any revenues or incomes or profits…derived or to be derived under this contract…shall not in any way be diminished as a result of such changes…[37] (emphasis added)

The Egyptian concession agreement 2002 includes the following provisions:

> In case of changes in existing legislation or regulations applicable to the conduct of Exploration, Development and production of Petroleum, which take place after the Effective Date, and which significantly affect the economic interest of this Agreement to the detriment of or which imposes on CONTRACTOR an obligation to remit to the A.R.E. (Arab Republic of Egypt) the proceeds from sales of CONTRACTOR's Petroleum, CONTRACTOR shall notify EGPC (the NOC) of the subject legislative or regulatory measure. *In such case, the Parties shall negotiate possible modifications to this Agreement designed to restore the economic balance thereof which existed on the Effective Date.* The Parties shall use their best efforts to agree on amendments to this Agreement within ninety (90) days from aforesaid notice. These amendments to this Agreement shall not in any event diminish or increase the rights or obligations of CONTRACTOR as these were agreed on the Effective Date. Failing agreement between the Parties during the period referred to above in this Article XIX, the dispute may be

35 Cameron, 'Tools for Oil & Gas Investors' (n. 21 above) 36; Erkan (n. 16 above) 204.
36 Alexander (n. 28 above) 7.19; Cameron, 'Tools for Oil & Gas Investors' (n. 21 above) 31; Manirruzzaman, 'International Energy Contracts and Cross-Border Pipeline Projects' (n. 26 above) 2; Erkan (n. 16 above) 205.
37 Article 17.1 of the Vietnam Model Product Sharing Contracts of 2004, cited in Al-Faruque (n. 14 above) 100.

> submitted to arbitration, as provided in Article XXIV of this Agreement.[38] (emphasis added)

An additional example of the negotiated economic balancing category can be found in the Qatar Model of Exploration and Production Sharing Agreement (1994):

> Whereas the financial position of the Contractor has been based, under the agreement, on the laws and regulations in force at the Effective Date, it is agreed that, if any future law, decree or regulation affects Contractor's financial position, and in particular if the customs duties exceed...percent during the term of the Agreement, both Parties shall enter into negotiations, in good faith, in order to reach an equitable solution that maintains the economic equilibrium of this Agreement. Failing to reach agreement on such equitable solution, the matter may be referred by either Party to arbitration pursuant to Article 31.[39]

The use of a stabilisation clause by contracting parties as a method of economic balancing is in frequent use not only in petroleum production sharing contracts but also in cross-border pipeline projects. The BTC Agreement also contained an economic equilibrium provision no less typical than the previously cited examples:

> The State Authorities are to take all actions available to them to restore the Economic Equilibrium established under the Project Agreements if and to the extent the Economic Equilibrium is disrupted or negatively affected, directly or indirectly, as a result of any change (whether the change is specific to the Project or of general application) in host government's law (including taxes, health, safety and the environment), including changes resulting from:
>
> - The amendment, repeal, withdrawal, termination or expiration of the host government's law;
> - The enactment, promulgation or issues of the host government's law;
> - The interpretation or application of the host government's law (whether by courts, the executive or legislative authorities, or administrative or regulatory bodies);
> - The decision, policies or other similar actions of judicial bodies, Tribunals and courts, the State Authorities;

38 Concession Agreement of 2002 for Petroleum Exploration and Exploitation between Egypt & Egypt General Petroleum Corporations & Dover Investments Limited (East Wadi Araba Area Gulf of Suez) Barrows Company Inc., cited in Cameron, 'Tools for Oil & Gas Investors' (n. 21 above) 31–32; see also Manirruzzaman, 'International Energy Contracts and Cross-Border Pipeline Projects' (n. 26 above) 4; Erkan (n. 16 above) 206.

39 Article 34.12 Equilibrium of the Agreement, Borrows Company Basic Oil Laws and Concession Contracts, Middle East, Supplement 124 (1994) 1, cited in Bernardini (n. 2 above), 110; see also Erkan (n. 16 above) 206.

- Jurisdictional alterations; and
- The failure or refusal of judicial bodies, Tribunals and courts, and/or the State Authorities to take action, exercise authority or enforce the host government's law (a 'change in law').

> The foregoing obligation[s] of the State Authorities to take all actions available to restore the Economic Equilibrium are to include the obligation to take all appropriate measures to resolve promptly by whatever means may be necessary, including by way of exemption, legislation, decree and/or other authoritative acts, any conflict or anomaly between any Project Agreement and the host government's law.[40]

Undoubtedly, economic equilibrium clauses are more convenient than the freezing clause type of stabilisation clauses in terms of their ease of application and functionality. In order to better understand their special character, a comparison should be made in this respect.

Traditional stabilisation clauses are designed to protect alien investors by freezing the legal situation in the host state on the point of signing the contract. Due to their function of freezing the legal regime in the host state, such clauses constitute a challenge to the principle of state sovereignty. Conversely, economic balancing clauses do not pose such a threat to the principle of state sovereignty and instead provide a flexible and dynamic contractual framework for the parties over the course of the investment project in case the host country changes the economic conditions by sovereign act.[41]

In recent years, the use of economic equilibrium clauses in energy investment contracts has surged in popularity worldwide[42] 'mainly because of their flexibility and versatility'.[43] Key to this popularity is the fact that while this type of clause does not strip the host state of its legislative freedoms, it still allows the investor room for manoeuvre. From the perspective of the host government, the state can maintain its sovereign power over natural resources and can adopt new laws to improve its sustainable development goals. For international investors, the application of such a clause can provide better protection and prospects than freezing clauses. Professor Manurizzaman explains why the use of economic equilibrium clause has taken root. According to the author:

40 Article 7.2(x) of the Georgian HGA; Article 21.2 of the Turkish HGA; Article 20.2 of the Azerbaijani HGA. All HGAs are available at <www.bp.com/en_az/caspian/aboutus/legalagreements.html>

41 K. B. Berger, 'Renegotiation and Adaptation of International Investment Contracts: The Role of the Contract Drafters and Arbitrators', *Vanderbilt Journal of Transnational Law*, Vol. 36 (2003) 1361. See also Erkan (n. 16 above) 208.

42 Cameron, 'Tools for Oil & Gas Investors' (n. 21 above) 31.

43 L. Cotula, 'Investment Contracts through a Development Lens', in E. Blanco & J. Razzaque (eds), *Natural Resources and the Green Economy: Re-defining the Challenges for People, States and Corporations*, (Leiden: Martinus Nijhoff Publisher, 2012) 31 (hereinafter Cotula, 'Investment Contracts through a Development Lens').

> The reason for the increasing tendency of International Oil Companies (IOCs) to favour economic balancing provision lies in the fact that if the State's unilateral acts adversely affect the contract the available remedies could be more favourable under the freezing clauses. Thus the breach of a freezing clause itself may result in only lump sum damages which could be far below what the IOC would consider would be necessary to 'keep it whole', whereas in economic balancing clauses the provision for 'Government Pays', 'Government indemnifies' is design to ' keep whole' the IOC on an on-going basis.[44]

It should not be disregarded that in the event of unilateral action by the host government, the parties of the investment contract are under obligation to renegotiate in good faith for the sake of re-establishing the original economic balance.[45]

This discussion would be incomplete without mention of the functionality of such clauses. According to Nwente, economic equilibrium clauses play a significant role in the contract because they 'reconcile the needs of the government and the investor by ensuring stability and flexibility through the adaptation of the petroleum contract to a change in circumstance, while at the same time maintaining the economic equilibrium of the project'.[46] Setting aside the flexible and dynamic nature of economic equilibrium clauses, it is important to ascertain whether those clauses are effective enough in every possible circumstance. According to Nwente, economic equilibrium clauses are not efficient enough at dealing with changes in circumstances brought about by unexpected events outside a change in law or regulations – for instance, marginal discovery or fluctuations in price.[47] For this reason, equilibrium clauses ought to distinguish external events from the events that arise from state action.[48]

The next section examines the legal value and function of stabilisation clauses in energy investment agreements.

Legal importance and functional value of stabilisation clauses

Throughout the previous section the main concepts and arguments concerning the validity and effectiveness of stabilisation clauses were discussed with the benefit of scholarly opinions and case law. Furthermore, 'questions concerning state responsibility for measures affecting contractual rights of an alien (individual or corporation) depend primarily on the law governing the particular contractual

44 A. F. M Manirruzzaman, 'The Pursuit of Stability in Energy Investment Contract: A Critical Appraisal of Emerging Trends', *Journal of World Energy & Business*, Vol. 1, No. 2 (2008) 126 (hereinafter Manirruzzaman, 'A Critical Appraisal of the Emerging Trends').

45 Ibid.

46 B.O.N. Nwete, 'To What Extent Can Stabilisation Clauses Mitigate the Investor's Risks in a Production Sharing Contract?' *Oil and Gas Energy Intelligence (OGEL)*, Vol. 3 (2005) 56.

47 Ibid. at 59.

48 Erkan (n. 16 above) 208.

relationship between state and alien'.[49] It is true that stabilisation clauses in an investment contract freeze the content of the applicable law. For that reason, this section will also point out the validity and effectiveness of stabilisation clauses under the applicable law.

Validity of stabilisation clauses

There is no obstacle to a host state entering into a contractual relationship which contains stabilisation provision as long as the clause complies with its constitutional and legislative requirements.[50] Stabilisation clauses may be regarded as a valid provision in a contract if the contract is legitimately signed by a host state or a state-owned company. However, in some cases a problem may occur if the contract is not signed properly by the contracting state itself.[51] According to Waelde, contractual guarantees granted by the state in the absence of legal authority may result in *ultravires*:

> Contractual drafting techniques cannot modify and expand the powers existing under constitutional and other law for government and legislature to make commitments not to exercise their sovereignty and legislative rights. No argument can be advanced by a foreign investor that he had a legitimate expectation in the validity of such clauses negotiated in the face of questionable legal validity to the extent that he can easily (applying due legal diligence) ascertain their invalidity under their national law. Clauses negotiated under the shadow of *ultravires* and constitutional invalidity cannot generate valid rights simply by appearance or legitimate reliance on the state agency's contracting powers.[52]

For this reason, the validity, or the extent of validity, of stabilisation clauses should be determined in the context of the specific circumstances of each case.[53] Taking into account the considerations outlined above, it is opportune to examine an important court decision. In *SPP Ltd v Egypt*, [54] a joint venture project was signed between the state authorities and the foreign investor. Technically, the state authorities entered into the contract on behalf of the host state. The tribunal held that the host state was not the signatory party of this contract, because the officials

49 F. V. Garcia-Amador, 'State Responsibility in Case of Stabilization Clauses', *Journal of Transnational Law and Policy*, Vol. 2, No. 23 (1993) 23.

50 W. Peter, *Arbitration and Renegotiation of International Investment Agreements*, 2nd revised and enlarged edition (The Hague: Kluwer Law International, 1995) 221.

51 Ibid.

52 Waelde & Ndi, 'Stabilizing International Investment Commitments' (n. 10 above) 242.

53 A. F. Manirruzzaman, 'National Laws Providing Stability of International Investment Contracts: A Comparative Perspective', *Journal of World Investment and Trade*, Vol. 1, No. 2 (2007) 7.

54 *SSP Ltd v Egypt* (1983) 22 ILM 752.

and agents signed the contract on behalf of the minister and host state. Thus, the state was not responsible for the unauthorised or *ultravires* acts of its officials and agents. Somewhat controversially, the reason the court gave for deeming the act of the host government officials to be *ultravires* was that the government agents and officials in question lacked the authority to commit to such contractual obligations on behalf of the state.[55] El-Kosheri and Riad support this argument: 'the legality of the stabilization clauses can only be established on the basis of a public law rule which authorizes the contracting governmental party to include such clauses in the development agreement and to be bound thereby'.[56] In summary, it can be said that stabilisation clauses inserted in a contract would not be regarded as valid unless agreed to and signed by an authority explicitly invested with the authority to do so.

Before examining the validity of stabilisation clauses under national and international law, it is significant to mention the relationship between applicable law and stabilisation clauses. An interaction exists between applicable law clauses and stabilisation clauses since they both modify the law governing the contract, albeit in different ways.[57] There is no doubt that international law principles are, by definition, those that will be applied by an arbitrator in the context of investor–state disputes or agreements, unless the parties of the contract or agreement have specifically determined the applicable law in the agreement in the case that such a disagreement should arise.[58] Thus, it has been suggested that stabilisation clauses in addenda to an investment agreement governed by domestic law will lack the validity of stabilisation clauses.[59] It should be noted that this issue is not a paradox, because parties are able to agree on a specific law to govern the contract, by a choice of law clause which indicates that international law is applicable to the agreement.

To this end, it can be said that determination of the applicable law of an energy investment contract is of significant importance to both the alien investor and the host state. While host states would often prefer their national law to apply to the energy investment contract, it is in the interests of the alien investor that the legal order imposed is the one that is best able to provide a stable and predictable legal environment.[60]

55 Erkan (n.16 above) 109.

56 A. El-Kosheri & T. Riad, 'The Law Governing a New Generation of Petroleum Contracts', *ICSID Review*, Vol. 1(1986) 259, 266; see also Peter (n. 50 above) 222; Erkan (n. 16 above) 109.

57 A. Al-*Faruque*, 'Typologies, Efficacy and Political Economy of Stabilisation Clauses: A Critical Appraisal', *OGEL, Journal of Oil and Gas Energy Law Intelligence*, Vol. 4, No. 5 (2007) 33, available at <www.gasandoil.com/ogel>

58 E. Witten, 'Arbitration of Venezuelan Oil Contracts: A Losing Strategy?' *Texas Journal of Oil, Gas and Energy Law*, Vol. 4 (2009) 67–8, available at <http://tjogel.org/archive/Vol4No1/witten.pdf>

59 Amador-Garcia (n. 49 above) 48–9.

60 R. Dolzer & C. Schreur, *Principles of International Investment Law*, 2nd edn (Oxford: Oxford University Press, 2012) 81.

Naturally, each party in such a situation would seek to convince the other to adopt the law which offers them the most security and confidence. Therefore, reaching a consensus on the applicable law between parties is often no mean feat and relies on the bargaining power and negotiating skills of each party. This competing interest in the choice of law can be a cause of disputes between contracting parties; however, it should be taken into consideration that when conflict arises with regard to choosing the applicable law, both parties may choose 'a combined solution of domestic law and international rules'.[61] In fact, the legal validity and effectiveness of stabilisation clauses included in investment contracts or agreements is a complex issue.[62] The difficulty has been explained by Waelde and Ndi as

> one of the most complex issues in international economic law in view of the fact that standards of arguments from international law (state responsibility, law of treaties) of national law, of conflict of law, both international and national conflict of laws and possibly of an 'international *lex mercatori*' come together and can be arguably applied.[63]

Thus, the following sub-sections examine the issue of the validity of stabilisation clauses under national and international laws.

The validity of stabilisation clauses under domestic law

Historically, most disputes have arisen from concession contracts governed by the national law of the contracting state.[64] Nevertheless, more recently, a new approach known as 'internationalised' contract has taken root. Since it includes stabilisation clauses, it cannot be subject to the domestic law of the contracting state.[65] Nevertheless, it should not be forgotten that even if the contract between the parties is governed by international law, this will not provide full guarantees of stability for the contract because the sovereign right to intervene in a contract when significant interests are at stake is recognised in international law.[66] To this end, it can be said that if the contract between the parties is governed exclusively by the domestic law of the contracting state, 'constitutional and legal constraints on the contractual capacity of that state may have significant legal implications for

61 F. N. Botchway, *Natural Resource Investment and Africa's Development* (Cheltenham: Edward Elgar Publishing Company, 2011) 124.

62 Waelde & Ndi, 'Stabilizing International Investment Commitments' (n. 10 above) 238.

63 Ibid.

64 Coale (n. 18 above) 223. It is worth nothing that according to recent survey there are a number of petroleum contracts governed by the host state's law. See Erkan (n. 16 above) 110.

65 M. E. Dickstein, 'Revitalizing the International Law Governing Concession Agreements', *International Tax and Business Lawyer*, Vol. 6 (1988) 54.

66 C. Greenwood, 'State Contracts in International Law: The Libyan Oil Arbitrations', *British Year Book of International Law*, No. 63 (1982) 53.

the validity and enforcement stabilisation clause'.[67] In addition, it is worth noting that many countries have established significant legal principles that 'have the effect of invalidating a stabilisation clause and making it of no legal effect'.[68]

The established principle which invalidates stabilisation clauses in national law is that the executive organ or parliament of the state may not be constrained or prevented by a contract from performing functions vital to its existence.[69] This legal principle is adopted in English common law and is applicable in many states which have adopted the common law system as part of their internal law. The establishment of this principle was in *Raderiakiebolaget Amphitrite v The King*:

> It is not competent for the government to fetter the execution of an action, which must necessarily be determined by the needs of the community when the question arises. It cannot by contract, hamper its freedom of action in maters which concern the welfare of the State.[70]

The principle is also applicable in many common law states. It is fair to assume that if the contract is subject to the national law of the contracting state which is, in turn, governed by common law, the courts of such countries will deem a stabilisation clause to be invalid.[71]

It should be noted that the insertion of a stabilisation clause in an agreement is not necessarily the best way to provide stability for host states because such stability can also be bestowed upon investors through legislative enactments.[72] At first glance, it could be assumed that if the domestic law of the host state recognises international agreements with stabilisation clauses, the clause is valid under the law of that state. Nevertheless, even if the state authorises stabilisation clauses inserted in international agreements, such statutory guarantees can be revoked or altered on the basis of public need and in the exercise of the host state's power of sovereignty.[73] According to Waelde, 'the legislator can take what he has given; in other words, nothing would prevent the national legislature to retroactively cancel and

67 Al-Faruque (n. 11 above) 333.

68 A. D. Nwokolo, ' Is There a Legal and Functional Value for the Stabilisation Clause in International Petroleum Agreements?', available at <https://uod.app.box.com/s/pwunkrworh8aidrlhu17f56knlt3h6p1 >

69 Waelde & Ndi, 'Stabilizing International Investment Commitments' (n. 10 above) 238; see also A. F. M. Maniruzzaman, 'State Contracts with Aliens: The Question of Unilateral Change by the State in Contemporary International Law', *Journal of International Arbitration*, Vol. 9, No. 4 (1992) 141 (hereinafter Maniruzzaman, 'State Contracts with Aliens').

70 *Raderiakiebolaget Amphitrite v The King* [1921] 3 K.B. 500, 503–4.

71 T. W. Waelde & G. Ndi, *Fiscal Regime Stability and Issues of State Sovereignty in Taxation of Mineral Enterprises* (London: Graham and Trotman, 1995) 76.

72 Timor-Leste, Papua New Guinea, Peru, Panama, Ivory Coast, Bolivia, Venezuela, Columbia and Kazakhstan are good examples of countries which provide stability and enable stabilisation provisions under their legal system.

73 Waelde & Ndi, 'Stabilizing International Investment Commitments' (n. 10 above) 239.

revoke rights awarded, subject possibly, to constitutional and other legal consequences, e.g. the duty to pay compensation under national law'.[74]

As discussed above, a stabilisation clause protects the contract from legislative or regulatory changes. However, the question of how such changes made by the legislative power in the interpretation of the same provision would be evaluated is unclear.[75] In some cases, such changes made by the legislating power may indeed have effects similar to the enactment of a new provision.[76] The recent case of *Duke Energy v Peru* [77] neatly illustrates the relationship between a stabilisation clause and a change in the interpretation of domestic tax law. In this case, the claimant asserted that the Peruvian government had imposed a tax assessment which breached the guarantee of stability that was provided in a Legal Stability Agreement. According to the tribunal's view, the continuity of the existing provisions not only covered a change of specific laws or regulations, but also encompassed changes in interpretation. The tribunal finally held that the Peruvian government was liable for its breach of the tax stabilisation to which it had previously agreed.

Consequently, the legal status of stabilisation clauses is commonly rendered invalid by most domestic law systems. If a guarantee of stability is regarded as valid under national law, the continuity of stabilisation clauses is determined by the legislature of the host state.[78] As previously mentioned, the security that stabilisation clauses offer may be granted by the host state to the investor under their internal law. However, it should be borne in mind that although the stabilisation clause is granted by the host government, as some authors have pointed out, the rules of the game may always change after the contract started.[79] For instance, host states may subsequently invalidate the stabilisation clause with retroactive effect.[80] When such a situation occurs under domestic or international law, the protection of property rights against direct and indirect expropriation would become an imminent priority.[81]

In light of this discussion, it is reasonable to conclude that most developing states which grant concession agreements seek to govern the contract in accordance with their national law system. Even if the host state's governmental action does not breach the contract and complies with domestic law, the government may wield the greater authority of its sovereignty against contract terms that are no longer in its interests to honour and may change the contract with or perhaps

74 Ibid.

75 J. E. Vinuales, *Foreign Investment and the Environment in International Law* (New York: Cambridge University Press, 2012) 342.

76 Ibid.

77 *Duke Energy International Peru Investments No. 1 Ltd v Peru*, ICSID Case No. ARB/03/28, Final Award, 25 July 2008.

78 Waelde & Ndi, 'Stabilizing International Investment Commitments' (n. 10 above) 239.

79 A. Shapira & M. Tabory, *New Political Entities in Public and Private International Law with Special Reference to the Palestinian Entity* (The Hague: Kluwer Law International, 1999) 315.

80 Waelde & Ndi, 'Stabilizing International Investment Commitments' (n. 10 above) 239.

81 Ibid.

without compensation to alien investors. It goes without saying that knowledge of this fact boosts the host state's confidence when a dispute arises between the parties. Contrary to the wishes of the host state, international energy investors may seek to internationalise the agreement and convince the host government that international law should be the governing law of the contract. In these circumstances, the typical behaviour of petroleum investors is to err on the side of caution by doing whatever necessary to ensure that, should a dispute arise, potential misinterpretation of stabilisation clauses in national courts by local judges that may render the clause invalid are avoided. Another reason why investors wish to internationalise the contract is that if a dispute arises between the contracting parties, a private investor may want to defend its case under the dispute resolution mechanisms of international law with a selected independent arbitrator in an unbiased environment.

The validity of stabilisation clauses under international law

Undoubtedly, international law is able to offer a high degree of protection to both the host state and a private investor when conflict arises between the parties. Nevertheless, such protection may not be benefitted from by either of the parties unless it is selected as the governing law of the agreement.[82] Thus, private investors may attempt to control the effects of host state legislation to some degree by insisting that the state accepts that not only the host state's domestic law should be applicable but also the general principles of international law.[83] In this respect, by providing proper recognition of a state's interest in applying its own domestic law, such a choice fetters the state's ability to modify or enforce the law arbitrarily to the detriment of the private investor.[84] In their quest to achieve a better level of protection, private investors frequently seek to internationalise the agreement. In that respect, there is a need to argue whether the insertion of a stabilisation clause in a host government contract is valid under international law when international law is selected as the governing law of the contract and where international investment tribunals stand regarding this question.

As far as the validity of stabilisation clauses under international law is concerned, two significant concepts exist: the doctrine of sanctity of contracts (*pacta sunt servanda*) and the principle of the state's permanent sovereignty over natural wealth and resources.[85] Three divergent views have surfaced in discussions regarding the validity of stabilisation clauses under international law; however, no

82 J. Crawford & W. Johnson, 'Arbitrating with Foreign States and Their Instrumentalities', *International Finance Law Review*, Vol. 5 (1986) 11, 12, cited in Waelde & Ndi, 'Stabilizing International Investment Commitments' (n. 10 above) 241.

83 M. L. Moses, *The Principles and Practice of International Commercial Arbitration* (New York: Cambridge University Press, 2008) 63.

84 A. Redfern & M. Hunter, *Law and Practice of International Commercial Arbitration* (Bath: Sweet & Maxwell, 2004) 92.

85 Waelde & Ndi, 'Stabilizing International Investment Commitments' (n. 10 above) 31.

dominant view has emerged as prevalent to settle the issue. However, a significant number of arbitral cases have taken place and a prescriptive approach to the validity issue of stabilisation clauses under international law has been drafted.

THE THEORY OF INTERNATIONALISED CONTRACTS

The theory of the internationalisation of contracts poses some of the most difficult questions in relation to both public and private international law.[86] The theory suggests that no matter whether the parties decide which law governs the contract, international law may override their choice and is automatically applied in the event of a dispute.[87] In other words, the rights and obligations of the contracting parties are governed in accordance with the rules of international law. One school of legal scholars has articulated the opinion that the principle recommending the choice of international law as the governing law of the contract is to render applicable specific international norms, in particular the doctrine of the sanctity of contract (*pacta sunt servanda*).[88]

The foundation of this view is that any unilateral breach of contract, including stabilisation clauses made by the host state under the contract, directly holds the contracting party responsible under international law.[89] Therefore, the contractual rights of investors cannot be unfavourably affected by the unilateral action of the host state. In order to avoid any unilateral modification, 'investors and his counsel should attempt to internationalise the contract'.[90] To this end, it can be said that the internationalisation of contracts is a method to 'deny effect' to unilateral changes made by states, the legal justification being the 'unrestricted application of the principle of *pacta sunt servanda*'.[91] The *pacta sunt servanda* principle was articulated by Professor Wehberg, who stated 'the principle is valid exactly in the same manner, whether it is in respect of contracts between states or in respect of contracts between states and private companies'.[92]

It is apparent that, according to supporters of this view, international law is the rightful governing law of the contract and that stabilisation clauses have a binding effect and are valid under international law. They imply that any unilateral actions made by host states which violate contractual obligations should be regarded as unlawful, deeming this to be in accordance with the ruling of international law. The view of the second group of scholars differs from the first group of writers, as

86 Manirruzzaman, 'State Contracts with Aliens' (n. 69 above) 309.
87 Ibid.
88 Waelde & Ndi, 'Stabilizing International Investment Commitments' (n. 10 above) 239.
89 Nwokolo (n. 68 above) 11.
90 E. Paasivirta, 'Internationalization and Stabilization of Contracts Versus State Sovereignty', *British Year Book International Law*, Vol. 60 (1989) 315, 317.
91 D. Suratgar, 'Considerations affecting Choice of Law Clauses in Contracts Between Governments and Foreign Nationals', *Indian Journal of International Law*, Vol. 2 (1962) 273.
92 H. Wehberg, 'Pacta Sunt Servanda', *American Journal of International Law*, Vol. 53 (1959) 775, 786.

the second group of commentators believe that internationalising contracts is in conflict with the principle of permanent sovereignty.

PERMANENT SOVEREIGNTY OVER NATURAL RESOURCES NORM

Some legal scholars hold the view that stabilisation clauses with the intended aim of freezing the applicable law are invalid under international law because the state has the right to modify or abrogate the contract entered into with a foreign investor.[93] This view of this second group of writers is rooted in the principle of the state's permanent sovereignty under the United Nations General Assembly and in the following pronouncement: 'The description of this sovereignty as permanent signifies that the territorial State never loses its legal capacity to change the status or the method of exploitation of those resources, regardless of any arrangement that have been made.'[94] The crux of the matter in this view is that being part of an agreement which includes stabilisation provisions creates binding obligations on states; therefore, they cannot waive their sovereign rights under the principle of permanent sovereignty.[95] In other words:

> Indeed a State is able to bind itself towards another State to exercise its sovereign power to legislate insofar as this would lead to a violation of duties which it has established by agreement of an international character. But this does not entail the consequences that a state can by a contract with an individual or with a company limited by shares bind itself to abstain from a full exercise of its right to legislate.[96]

This view holds that stabilisation clauses are invalid under international law because such clauses cannot prevent a state from exercising its sovereign power for the public good. The exercise of such power may be relevant to human rights, environmental protection or any other issues which could be considered vital to the interests of the state and the protection of its citizens and natural environment. The principle of the state's permanent sovereignty over natural wealth and

93 M. Sornarajah, 'The Myth of International Contract Law?', *Journal of World Trade Law*, Vol. 15 (1981) 187, 189, cited in T. J. Pate, 'Evaluating Stabilization Clauses in Venezuela's Strategic Association Agreements for Heavy-Crude Extraction in the Orinoco Belt: The Return of a Forgotten Contractual Risk Reduction Mechanism for the Petroleum Industry', *University of Miami Inter-American Law Review*, Vol. 40, No. 2 (2009) 351; see also Waelde & Ndi, 'Stabilizing International Investment Commitments' (n. 10 above) 244.

94 E. Jiminez de Arechaga, 'State Responsibility of Nationalisation of Foreign Owned Property', *N.Y.U. Journal of International Law and Policy* (1978) 179–80.

95 Waelde & Ndi, 'Stabilizing International Investment Commitments' (n. 10 above) 244.

96 M. Wolff, 'Some Observations on the Autonomy of Contracting Parties in Conflict of Laws', *Transactions of the Grotius Society*, Vol. 35 (1949) 143–50, cited in Paasivirta (n. 91 above) 319.

resources is a *jus cogens* norm; therefore no derogation is allowed.[97] As the Constitution is hierarchically the highest law in a state, it therefore may not be possible to say that a state cannot bind itself by a contract made with an alien investor and restrain its legislative power.[98] In other words, the legislature cannot be bound by its own preceding legislation and always possesses the right to change it.[99] On the topic of permanent sovereignty of states over their natural resources and wealth, divergent views exist which have been the subject of animated debate by scholars. Before setting out these views, the effects of the resolutions of the UN on natural wealth and resources and the Charter of Economic Rights and Duties of States (CERDS) on the binding force of host government contract should be reviewed.

The principle of the permanent sovereignty of states over natural resources in their territory was formally recognised and documented by the UN General Assembly Resolution, 1803.[100] Article (1) of the resolution declares that '[t]he right of peoples and nations to permanent sovereignty over their natural wealth and resources must be exercised in interest of their national development'. What is understood from this article is that states are free to exercise extraction of their natural resources and free to sell them to second or third parties. Furthermore, Article 4 of the resolution bestows upon states the right to nationalise, expropriate or requisition property as long as such activities are done for public purposes, security or national interest, and prompt and adequate compensation is paid. Article (8) of the resolution clearly declares that '[*international*] *investment agreement freely entered into by, or between, sovereign States shall be observed in good faith*; States and international organisations shall strictly and conscientiously respect the sovereignty of peoples and nations over their natural wealth and resources'[101] (emphasis added). To this end it can be said that the principle of permanent sovereignty does not affect the binding power of host government contracts made with private investors.

Moreover, CERDS, which was adopted by the UN General Assembly in 1974, and also embraces the principle of permanent sovereignty. While Article (1) states that '[e]very State has the sovereign and inalienable right to choose its economic system as well as its political...systems in accordance with the will of its people, without outside interference, coercion or threat in any form whatsoever',[102] Article (2)[103] specifically addresses nationalisation and references the principle of permanent sovereignty of states.

Taking into consideration the relevant articles of Resolution 1803 and CERDS, it can be stated that the principle of permanent sovereignty is one of the most significant in international law. With regard to the question posed above, several

97 Brownlie (n. 1 above) 489.
98 Sornarajah (n. 4 above) 282.
99 Ibid.
100 The United Nations Assembly Resolution on Permanent Sovereignty over Natural Resources, G.A, Res. (1803) Article 1.
101 Article 4 of G.A. Res. (1803).
102 Article 8 of G.A. Res. (1803).
103 Article 2 of G.A. Res. (1803).

views have emerged. According to El Sheikh, the contractual agreement between state and private investor cannot be regarded as an alienation of a state's sovereignty, but as a partial and temporary exercise of sovereignty.[104] According to Peter, UN resolutions on the principle of the permanent sovereignty of states over their natural resources do not prevent a contracting state from binding itself by stabilisation provisions.[105] However, according to Sornarajah, when the principle of the permanent sovereignty of states is regarded, stabilisation clauses should be deemed as invalid under international law because the acceptance of such principles puts 'a constitutional limitation on the state in international law to deal with its natural resources'.[106] Erkan criticises Sornarajah's view and argues that perhaps it would be extreme to regard stabilisation clauses as invalid.[107]

MODERATE OPINION

The third group of commentators recognise the validity of stabilisation clauses under international law and their significance in international agreements; however, they express doubt regarding the capacity of such clauses to provide absolute protection to private investors.[108] According to some authors, stabilisation clauses inserted in economic development agreements or investment contracts bind and constrain host governments for a long period of time and are contrary to the principle of permanent sovereignty; 'however, a stabilisation clause limited in time, area and scope, aimed at maintaining unchanged certain material terms and the fiscal regime for a reasonable period, is not incompatible with the principle of permanent sovereignty'.[109] To this end, it can be said that a guarantee given for a specific period of time against nationalisation would be one of the ways of providing guarantees.[110] It is the commentators' belief that the freezing function of stabilisation clauses is only the tip of the iceberg.[111] When interpreting the validity of stabilisation clauses, the whole range of conditions in existence globally need to be taken into consideration. Such conditions can be

104 A. El Sheikh, *The Legal Regime of Foreign Private Investment in Sudan and Saudi Arabia*, 2nd edn (Cambridge: Cambridge University Press, 2003) 334.
105 Peter (n. 50 above) 222.
106 Sornarajah (n. 93 above) 210.
107 Erkan (n. 16 above) 120.
108 Waelde & Ndi, 'Stabilizing International Investment Commitments' (n. 10 above) 244–5.
109 P. De Waart, P. Peters and E. Denters, *International Law and Development* (Dordrecht: Kluwer Academic Publishers, 1988) 81.
110 A. Redfern, 'The Arbitration Between the Government of Kuwait and AMINOIL', *British Year Book of International Law*, Vol. 58 (1985) 100, cited in Al-Qurashi (n. 13 above) 216; see also Paasivirta (n. 90 above) 337.
111 R. Higgins, 'Legal Preconditions for Foreign Investment', IBA-SERL Seminar Proceeding, Mathew Bender, New York (1986) 233–5; see also Paasivirta (n. 90 above) 338; Waelde & Ndi, 'Stabilizing International Investment Commitments' (n. 10 above) 245.

economic and social environments, political factors or the historical relationship between the parties.[112]

The doctrinal writings referenced above demonstrate that there is continuing controversy among legal scholars regarding the validity of stabilisation clauses under international law. No dominant view seems to have prevailed as yet. Although consensus has not been reached among academic writers on the validity issue, a considerable number of arbitral awards have been granted in this respect. Therefore, the following section will merely concentrate on the response of arbitral tribunals to challenges to the validity of stabilisation clauses.

ARBITRAL AWARDS CONCERNING THE VALIDITY OF STABILISATION CLAUSES

The validity of stabilisation clauses and their relationship to the principle of the permanent sovereignty of host states have been the subject of a significant number of arbitration cases in the petroleum industry. The most frequently referred arbitral decision is the case of *Texas Overseas Petroleum Co./California Asiatic Oil Co. v Libyan Arab Republic.* [113] Texaco and Calasiatic are two American petroleum companies which were both granted 14 oil concessions by the Royal Libyan Government between the years of 1955 and 1968.[114] In 1973, following the advent of a revolution in Libya, the new revolutionary government, in a dramatic move, nationalised 51% shares of these two companies' interest in the concession.[115] When Texaco and Calasiatic started the arbitration proceeding as the nature of concession agreements require, 49% of the companies' interests were also nationalised by the same revolutionary Libyan government.[116]

Furthermore, the new revolutionary government did not respond to the companies' request to submit to arbitration; however, when the companies, under clause 28(3), asked the President of the International Court of Justice to appoint a sole arbitrator,[117] the new Libyan government objected on the grounds that the dispute that had arisen between the parties could not be the subject of arbitration as the nationalisation measure taken by the government was an expression of its sovereignty.[118] Professor René-Jean Dupuy, who was the sole arbitrator in the given case, examined the whole issue in detail and cited a number of reasons why compensation should be paid to TOPCO. The arbitrator first rejected the claim of the Libyan government and stated that a concession agreement is not an

112 Ibid.

113 *Texas Overseas Petroleum Co./Californian Asiatic Co. v Libyan Arab Republic,* 17 ILM. 1 (Int'l Arb. Trib. 1977).

114 Greenwood (n. 66 above) 29.

115 Ibid.

116 *Texaco v Libyan Arab Republic* (TOPCO) award, 53 I.L.R. 389 (1978) (hereinafter *TOPCO*).

117 R. B. Von Mehren & P. N. Kourides, 'International Arbitrations between States and Foreign Private Parties: The Libyan Nationalization Cases', *American Journal of International Law*, Vol. 75, No. 3 (1981) 489, cited in Coale (n. 18 above) 233.

118 Ibid.

administrative contract.[119] Professor Dupuy then started to examine the validity and binding effect of stabilisation clauses. Before proceeding to examine the arbitrator's decisions with regard to this subject, it is relevant to cite Article 16 of the concession agreement.

In this case, the concession agreement between the parties contained a stabilisation clause in the Article 16:

1 The Government of Libya will take all the steps necessary to ensure that the Company enjoys all the rights conferred by this Concession. The contractual rights expressly created by this concession shall not be altered except by mutual consent of the parties.
2 This Concession shall throughout the period of its validity be construed in accordance with the Petroleum Law and the Regulations in force on the date of execution of the agreement of amendment by which this paragraph (2) was incorporated into this concession agreement. Any amendment to or repeal of such Regulations shall not affect the contractual rights of the Company without its consent.[120]

Taking into consideration the above provision, the arbitrator found that Clause 16 did not, in principle, impair the sovereignty of the Libyan state, since its entire sovereign legislative and regulatory powers were preserved and such power can only be exercised with respect to citizens or aliens with whom the state has not undertaken contractual obligations.[121] Professor Dupuy went on to assert that the Libyan state, through the exercise of its sovereignty, had undertaken obligations under an agreement governed by international law.[122] In this respect, the arbitrator held:

> The recognition by international law of the right to nationalize is not sufficient grounds to empower a State to disregard its commitments, because the same law also recognizes the power of a State to commit itself internationally, particularly by accepting the inclusion of stabilization clauses in a contract entered into with a private party.[123]

The arbitrator, Dupuy, based on the above reasoning, recognised the validity of stabilisation clauses with the following words:

> Thus, in respect of the international law of contracts, nationalization cannot prevail over an internationalized contract, containing stabilization clauses, entered into between a State and a foreign private company. The situation

119 Ibid.
120 *TOPCO* (n. 116 above).
121 Ibid., at 24.
122 Ibid.
123 Ibid., para 71.

> could be different only if one were to conclude that the exercise by a State of its right to nationalize places that State on a level outside of and superior to the contract and also to the international legal order itself, and constitutes an act of government which is beyond the scope of any judicial redress or any criticism.[124]

In light of the arbitrator's assessments, it can be said that two significant points emerged in the *TOPCO* arbitration. First, the arbitrator internationalised the contract between the parties and he interpreted the stabilisation clauses as a basis to do so. In other words, the arbitrator of the present case held that when the contract is internationalised, the contracting parties act as equals and the host state is responsible for the guarantees that have been provided to the private investor.[125] Second, Professor Dupuy asserted that stabilisation clauses are fully valid and effective as long as the parties concerned have freely entered into them. From the perspective of the arbitrator, it is beyond question that sovereign states may adopt or modify their laws. However, it should be noted that newly adopted laws or changes do not have the power to overturn freely agreed obligations under an international agreement. For this reason, when the host state agrees to stabilisation provisions, it makes a binding legal commitment not to exercise its sovereign power over the course of the investment project. In the case of any changes or the adoption of new laws drafted by the host government, such unilateral actions would be regarded as invalid under international law and the contracting state would be in breach of the stabilisation clauses. Significantly, the decision given by the arbitrator was severely criticised by some authors who believe that the arbitrator's 'interpretation is too rigid and provides unlimited guarantees to private investors'.[126] It is an accepted fact that the petroleum sector is fragile and requires some stability; however, considering the length of a typical energy investment project, they assert that it would be naive not to expect any unilateral actions from host states.

The validity of stabilisation provisions was also examined extensively by the international tribunal in the case of *Government of State of Kuwait v the American Independent Oil Company* (*AMINOIL*).[127] In this case, the ruler of Kuwait granted a 60-year oil concession to American company AMINOIL for the exploration and exploitation of petroleum, starting in 1948.

The agreement between the parties included a stabilisation provision that read as follows:

> The Sheikh shall not by general or special legislation or by administrative measures or by any other act whatever annul this Agreement except as provided in

124 Ibid., para 73.
125 Greenwood (n. 66 above) 29.
126 Al-Qurashi (n. 13 above) 209.
127 *American Independent Oil Company v Kuwait* Award, 24 March, 1982 21 ILM 976 (1982) (hereinafter *AMINOIL).*

> Article 11. No alteration shall be made in the terms of this Agreement by either the Sheikh or the Company except in the event of the Sheikh and the Company jointly agreeing that it is desirable in the interest of both parties to make certain alteration, deletion or addition to this agreement.[128]

In 1961, a supplemental agreement modified the concession agreement between the parties that was signed in 1948 and provided additional financial benefit to the host state and also contained a renegotiation clause. In 1974, the OPEC countries adopted the 'Abu Dhabi formula', which triggered an increase of the tax regime[129] applicable to the agreement. Naturally, the company did not wish to accept the changes to its existing tax regime. Finally, in 1977, the government of Kuwait promulgated Decree Law No. 124 which terminated the concession agreement between the parties.[130] Thereafter, the government of Kuwait acted unilaterally and nationalised the company's assets. AMINOIL instituted ad hoc arbitration and claimed that the government of Kuwait's unilateral action breached the stabilisation provision of the agreement inserted in 1948.[131]

Discussion around the validity of stabilisation clauses becomes the most significant issue in this case. A number of arguments were put forward by the contractually linked parties. On the one hand, AMINOIL argued that the concession agreement between the parties was terminated wrongfully because the contract contained a stabilisation clause.[132] The company asserted that the nationalisation act of Kuwait was a violation of the principle of *pacta sunt servanda* under international law; therefore, this unilateral act of the host state was an unlawful expropriation. On the other hand, the government of Kuwait defended itself against these claims by alleging that the clauses which had been inserted in the agreement had a colonial character and particularly imposed upon Kuwait, despite the fact that the country was still under the protection of the British.[133]

Another argument set forth by the Kuwaiti government was that:

> [S]tabilisation clauses – initially valid and effective – were annulled by the emergence of a subsequent factor in the shape either of the Kuwait Constitution of 1962, or of a public international law rule of *jus cogens* forming part of the law of Kuwait.[134]

128 Article 17 of the 1948 Agreement.
129 T. Begic, *Applicable Law in International Investment Disputes* (Utrecht: Eleven International Publishing, 2005) 87.
130 *AMINOIL* (n. 127 above) at 998.
131 Begic (n. 129 above) 87.
132 G. Delaume, 'Comparative Analysis as a Basis of Law in State Contracts: The Myth of the Lex Mercatoria', *Tulsa Law Review*, Vol. 63 (1989) 575, 606, cited in Coale (n. 19 above) 236.
133 S. K. B. Asante, 'Stability of Contractual Relations in the Transnational Investment Process', *International and Comparative Law Quarterly*, Vol. 28 (1979) 401, 403.
134 *AMINOIL* (n. 127 above) at 1021, para 90.

The tribunal rejected these arguments and held that there is no rule under international law that prevents states from undertaking to proceed to nationalisation during a limited period of time.[135]

Moreover, the tribunal also examined the question of whether stabilisation clauses are able to prohibit nationalisation. In this respect, the tribunal stated that:

> [N]o doubt contractual limitations on the State's right to nationalize are legislatively possible, but what that would involve would be a particularly serious undertaking which would have to be expressly stipulated for, and be within the regulations governing the conclusion of State contracts; and it is to be expected that it should cover only a relatively limited period.[136]

In light of the tribunal's response to this question, it should be noted that the tribunal did not consider that the nationalisation was unlawful because 'the case of nationalisation is certainly not expressly provided against by the stabilisation clauses of the concession'.[137]

The tribunal also added that even if the stabilisation clauses originally sought to prohibit nationalisation, they had ceased to do so due to the fact that the character of the concession agreement had changed and stabilisation clauses had lost their previous possessive absolute character.[138] Consequently, the tribunal reached the conclusion that the takeover of the AMINOIL enterprise was not inconsistent with the concession contract, provided that the nationalisation did not possess any confiscatory character.[139]

What makes this decision significant is that several key questions were answered by the tribunal. The existence of stabilisation clauses under the concession agreement between the contracting parties made tribunals consider the nationalisation right of a host state where a stabilisation clause had been applied. The tribunal recognised the validity of stabilisation clauses in principle; however, the tribunal disregarded the prohibition against changing the agreement in any way except in the event of mutual consent.[140] Furthermore, the tribunal expressed that stabilisation clauses should cover only a 'relatively limited period'. To this end, the approximate length of 'a relatively limited period of time' needs to be ascertained. When the concession agreement between the parties is considered, the contract in question was signed almost 30 years previously. It would have been useful for the tribunal to suggest parameters for the time frames; they instead referred to this in quite general terms.[141]

135 Ibid. at 1021–22, para 90.
136 Ibid. at 1023, paras 94–5.
137 Ibid.
138 Ibid. at 1024, paras 98–101.
139 Ibid. at 1024, para 102.
140 Begic (n. 129 above) 87.
141 Al-Qurashi (n. 13 above) 217.

Another historical but significant oil industry arbitration case is *Aramco v Saudi Arabia*.[142] Aramco is an American petroleum company which had been granted permission by the Saudi government to extract and transport petrol from Saudi Arabia to other countries. Aramco complained that the Saudi government had also entered into an agreement with the Saudi Arabian Maritime Tankers Ltd, which was headed up by the well-known Greek businessman Aristotle Onassis and enjoyed, for over 30 years, the right to transport all the extracted petrol from Saudi Arabia.[143] Aramco claimed that an oil concession agreement was signed between the Kingdom of Saudi Arabia and Aramco in 1933; therefore, the right to extract the oil and its transfer belonged to Aramco.[144] This conflict led the contracting parties to arbitration in 1955. As the concession agreement between the parties included stabilisation clauses, the tribunal examined the clauses and held that '[b]y reason of its very sovereignty within its territorial domain the State possesses the legal powers to grant rights by which it forbids itself to withdraw before the end of the concession'.[145] In 1958, the tribunal reached a verdict, ruling in favour of Aramco, and asserted that the government of Saudi Arabia is bound by the concession agreement with Aramco and that the subsequent agreement with Onassis's company had violated that agreement.[146] The tribunal also recognised the validity of stabilisation clauses under international law.

It should be noted that there are a number of arbitral decisions with regard to the validity issue of stabilisation clauses. In most cases, the tribunals provided appreciable details and good reasoning when they refer to validity of such clauses under international law. However, in *British Petroleum Exploration Company (Libya) Ltd v the Government of the Libyan Arab Republic*,[147] the arbitrator did not refer to stabilisation clauses in his judgment. This case was the first of a series of Libyan nationalisation cases. The stabilisation clauses were contained in Article 16 of the concession agreement. The arbitrator of the present case determined that an agreement was a contractual relationship belonging to the category of administrative contracts and that, by virtue of the stabilisation clause, Libya had limited its 'freedom to change or terminate the concession by unilateral act unless it could be shown that the change was truly in the public interest'.[148] In his decision, the arbitrator did not make reference to the stabilisation clause existing in Article 16. Therefore, this case does not represent a legitimate example of the validity issues surrounding stabilisation clauses.

142 *Saudi Arabia v Arabian American Oil Company (ARAMCO)* 27 I.L.R. 117 (1958).

143 M. R. Samartano, *International Arbitration Law and Practice*, 2nd edn (The Hague: Kluwer International Law, 2001) 160.

144 Cameron, *The Pursuit of Stability* (n. 7 above) 109.

145 *ARAMCO* (n. 142 above) at 168.

146 Cameron, *The Pursuit of Stability* (n. 7 above) 110.

147 *British Petroleum Exploration Company (Libya) Ltd v Government of the Libyan Arab Republic* 53 I.L.R. 297 (1973–1974) 53.

148 R. C. A. White, 'Expropriation of the Libyan Oil Concessions – Two Conflicting International Arbitrations', *International and Comparative Law Quarterly*, Vol. 30, No. 1 (1981) 11, cited in Coale (n. 19 above) 234.

The most recent arbitration involving the Libyan nationalisation case series was *Libyan American Oil Company (LIAMCO) v the Government of the Libyan Arab Republic.*[149] The sole arbitrator in the present case found that the stabilisation clause inserted in Article 16 was 'justified not only by the said Libyan petroleum legislation, but also by the general principle of the sanctity of contracts recognised also in municipal and international law'.[150] The arbitrator went on to compare the consistency of stabilisation clauses 'with the principle of non-retroactivity of laws, which denies retrospective effects to a new legislation and asserts the respect of vested rights (*droits acquis*) acquired under a previous legislation'.[151] Afterwards, he mentioned that 'the rights of a state to nationalise its wealth and national resources is sovereign, subject to the obligation of indemnification for premature termination of concession agreements'.[152] During the examination of LIAMCO's concession agreements, the arbitrator found that these concession agreements were valid and binding; therefore, they could not be validly terminated unless there was 'mutual consent of the contraction parties, in compliance with the said principle of the sanctity of contracts and particularly with the explicit terms of Clause 16 of the Agreements'.[153] The award, however, was not in harmony with the opinions of the arbitrator regarding the validity of the stabilisation clause.[154] Therefore, it is difficult to assess how the stabilisation clause influenced the award in this case.[155]

Efficacy of stabilisation clauses

Doctrinal assessments

The functional value and efficacy of stabilisation clauses in host governmental contracts has been the subject of some debate in conventional literature. Some authors believe that there is no point in expecting a functional protection from stabilisation clauses because international law prohibits arbitrary and unlawful intervention by a state in an international agreement.[156] The reasoning behind this view is that there is no hindrance to the state from taking unilateral action, such as expropriating or nationalising the assets of an investor, as long as such actions are made lawfully, by meeting certain conditions decreed by international law.

Another group of commentators oppose the previous view and argue that stabilisation clauses serve as a secondary protection mechanism, despite the fact that international law bestows protection upon investors against arbitrary and unilateral state intervention. According to the supporters of this view, the function of

149 *Libyan American Oil Company (LIAMCO) v the Government of the Libyan Arab Republic*, Award of 12 April 1977, 62 I.L.R. 140, (1977); 20 I.L.M. 1 (1977).
150 Ibid. at 31.
151 Ibid. at 61.
152 Ibid.
153 Ibid.
154 Coale (n. 18 above) 234.
155 Amador-Garcia (n. 49 above) 44.
156 Waelde & Ndi, 'Stabilizing International Investment Commitments' (n. 10 above) 238.

stabilisation clauses is to provide alien investors extra protection against any '*prima facie* lawful grounds which international law recognises for affecting changes to the concluded agreement'.[157] Similarly, according to Peter, the stabilisation technique has been regarded as 'a strict yardstick for contract performance with its corresponding counterpart of legal consequences for breach of contract'.[158]

The third view to be found in literature is that the inclusion of stabilisation clauses in an investment agreement has a financial function, particularly in the event of their violation. The foundation of this view is that even if a stabilisation clause is deemed not to have any effect on the host state's right to unilaterally change the terms and conditions of the previously agreed agreement, the violation would provide the private investor a special right to compensation as a result of the inclusion of the stabilisation clause.[159] It is important to emphasise that the amount of compensation would be higher than those of other contractual violations should stabilisation provisions be excluded.[160] Such compensation would cover prospective gains or lost profits (*lucrum cessans*).[161]

Do stabilisation provisions constitute a threat to environmental protection and human rights?

In recent years, the petroleum industry has witnessed new concerns in the areas of environmental protection and human rights. It has been vehemently argued that stabilisation provisions in a contract can have a 'chilling effect' on law reform in a host state, particularly in the field of human rights[162] and environmental protection.[163] The foundation of this argument is that stabilisation clauses demotivate or discourage host states from introducing new laws focussing on environmental and social policy. A recent empirical study in this area found that 'contracts from non-OECD countries are more likely than those from OECD countries to insulate the investor from new social and environmental laws or to provide compensation to the investor for compliance with new social and environmental laws'.[164] As previously mentioned, theoretically sovereign states are free to exercise their sovereignty by regulating domestic issues such as the environment, tax, human rights, health and safety and all other areas under the jurisdiction of police power. In this respect, it is vital to discuss whether the inclusion of stabilisation commitments forces the host state to relinquish international treaty obligations in the area of

157 Nwokolo (n. 68 above) 14.
158 Peter (n. 50 above) 226.
159 Ibid.
160 Ibid.
161 Ibid.
162 For further reading, see Shemberg (n. 23 above).
163 L. Cotula, 'Freezing the Balancing Act? Project Finance, Legal Tools to Manage Regulatory Risk, and Sustainable Development', Chapter 6, in S. Leader & D. Ong (eds), *Global Project Finance, Human Rights and Sustainable Development*,(Cambridge: Cambridge University Press, 2011) 162 (hereinafter Cotula, 'Freezing the Balancing Act?').
164 Shemberg (n.23 above) v.

human rights or environmental issues, and whether such regulatory measures taken by host states violate stabilisation commitments.

It is inevitable that such a lucrative industry with the potential to have significant impact on local and regional environmental, social and economic concerns is so exposed to criticism. In other words, considering cases in which stabilisation clauses have been applied, 'it is unsurprising that they have been subjected to scrutiny by persons and organisations concerned with promoting sustainable development'.[165] This criticism is founded on the fact that the adoption of such clauses has the potential to have a grave impact on the contracting state's legislative power and administrative acts, and the judicial decisions of its independent courts. It is, therefore, difficult for a host state to regulate significant issues in the interest of its citizens.[166] In doctrine, some authors argue that traditional stabilisation clauses are inflexible and that they have a restrictive effect on host state policy.[167] Therefore, they assert, the scope of stabilisation clauses should be limited to non-fiscal areas, such as environmental and human rights.[168] According to Leader, 'host-state regulation to promote the full realisation of human rights is outside the scope of the stabilisation clause'.[169] What this means is that state sovereignty is limited by the international obligation to realise fundamental human rights.[170]

In the *Texaco* case, the arbitrator held that host states may forgo their sovereign rights during the lifespan of the investment agreement should a definitive event such as nationalisation occur. However, as far as international treaty obligations are concerned, host states do not have the prerogative to refuse to take the measures that international law obliges.[171] In other words, state sovereignty is limited by international obligations regarding the areas of human rights and environmental concerns. It is true that the general tendency in the petroleum industry is not to insert strict stabilisation provisions in the contract and exclude non-fiscal areas.[172]

For the latter question, it can be said that there is nothing to hinder a sovereign state from exercising its sovereign rights for public good or in the public interest. Nevertheless, 'the functional value of stabilisation clauses cannot be discounted'.[173] Furthermore, since stabilisation clauses do not distinguish between compensable taking or indirect expropriation and non-compensable regulation, legal proceedings would be inevitable to settle this matter in the event that any

165 Sheppard & Crockett (n. 9 above) 338.
166 Manirruzzaman, 'A Critical Appraisal of the Emerging Trends' (n. 44 above) 156.
167 Ibid. at 126.
168 Cotula, 'Freezing the Balancing Act?' (n. 163 above) 163.
169 Ibid.
170 Ibid.
171 Principle 2 of the 1992 Rio Declaration on Environment and Development 13 June 1992, 31 ILM 874 (1992).
172 However, it should also be noted that Shemberg's recent research demonstrates that freezing clauses are still in use to some extent particularly in mining sector. See Shemberg (n. 23 above) 6–7.
173 Manirruzzaman, 'A Critical Appraisal of the Emerging Trends' (n. 44 above) 156.

such measure were taken by a host state. A solution to this problem has been suggested in conventional academic literature by several authors. According to Sheppard and Crocket, 'stabilisation clauses are often narrower in scope than many critics assert, or fear'.[174] The authors believe:

> [T]hose criticism and fears can be assuaged – and the legitimate concerns of investors and lenders that the host government does not denude the project of economic value by changing the rules can be addressed – by appropriate drafting and the incorporation of the international law norms of fair and equitable treatment and legitimate expectation.[175]

Cotula also states:

> [B]est contractual practice clearly defines the scope of stabilisation clauses to ensure that social and environmental matters are not stabilised. This can be done not only by wording the clause around arbitrary, discriminatory or similar treatment, but also explicitly stating that public purpose measures are outside the scope of the clause.[176]

Recent state practice supplies good guidance in this matter. For instance, the 2004 US Model BIT contains the following provision: 'Except in rare circumstances, non-discriminatory regulatory actions by a Party that are designed and applied to protect legitimate public welfare objectives, such as public health, safety and environment, do not constitute indirect expropriation.'[177] In the same vein, Article 12 of the Draft of the Norway Model BIT (2008) contains the following provision:

> Nothing in this Agreement shall be constructed to prevent a Party from adopting, maintaining or enforcing any measure otherwise consistent with the Agreement that it considers to ensure that investment activity is undertaken in a manner sensitive to health, safety or environmental concerns.[178]

BITs offer good guidance by furnishing specific terms for these highly sensitive areas. Similarly, if environmental and human rights and other public interests of a host state were provided for in the contracts and singled out from the scope of stabilisation commitments, then the action of the host state would not amount to indirect expropriation and could not be claimed by an investor to be in violation of the stabilisation clause.

174 Sheppard & Crockett (n. 9 above) 343.
175 Ibid.
176 Cotula, 'Investment Contracts through a Development Lens' (n. 43 above) 33.
177 United States Model Bilateral Investment Treaty, 2004, Annex B Expropriation Section (b) available at <www.state.gov/documents/organization/117601.pdf>
178 It should be noted that due to disagreement on the Norway BIT Model, it did not come into existence.

The BTC pipeline project (I): reactions to the project

The BTC pipeline project has been subject to the criticism of public interest groups who see the legal framework of the HGA as placing the interests of the BTC consortium over human rights, the environment and state sovereignty. One of the claims made by these groups was that Azerbaijan, Georgia and Turkey had agreed to exempt the BTC pipeline project from the rule of local laws, except for obligations arising under the Constitution, and to surrender their right to impose more stringent environmental and social laws over the 40–60-year term of the project.[179] According to non-governmental organisations (NGOs), this undertaking facilitates the transfer of the financial burden of the investor to the government if the host states' governments 'instituted more stringent legislative standards that impacted the project'.[180]

The economic equilibrium form of stabilisation clauses in the HGAs were also subject to NGOs' criticism. The public interest groups claimed that the BTC consortium contract was unlawful on the grounds that it would hinder host governments from delaying project execution should any environmental or social (e.g. health) concerns arise, except in the case of national emergency.[181] This constraint prevents the host state from honouring its international obligations with regard to human rights and the environment; moreover, it actually penalises the host government with heavy compensation for doing so.[182] This effectively inhibits national development during the term of the project that may constitute an improvement in standards of living in that host state.[183]

Another concern voiced by NGOs relates to the privileged status of IGA and HGAs. This establishes the IGA and each HGA as the prevailing legal regime under international law and the laws of each of the three countries, overriding all conflicting domestic law, present and future, thereby rendering the Constitution ineffectual. Under the 'frozen and extremely weakened regulatory environment, the governments are thus less able to respond to new environmental and other threats or to evolving understanding of risk'.[184] For instance, in the case of Georgia, the HGA was invoked to override the Georgian National Water Act in areas where such an override was required in order to grant the pipeline right of

179 Host Government Agreements of the BTC Project (n. 44 above), Article 7.2(x) and 9 (iii) HGA Azerbaijan; Article 7.2(x) and 9.1(iii) of Georgian HGA; and Turkish HGA Article 7.2(x) and 10.1(iii).

180 United States Agency for International Development (USAID), 'Multilateral Development Bank Assistance Proposals: Likely to Have Adverse Impacts on the Environment, Natural Resources, Public Health and Indigenous Peoples, September 2002–October 2004', 29, available at <https://ecd.usaid.gov/repository/mdb/2004O.pdf>

181 Ibid.; see also Azerbaijan HGA, Article 5.2(iii).

182 <www.amnesty.org.uk/press-releases/baku-tbilisi-ceyhan-pipeline-project-puts-human-rights-line>

183 Ibid.

184 N. Hildyards & G. Muttitt, 'Turbo Charging Investor Sovereignty: Investment Agreements and Corporate Colonialism', (2004) 47–48 available at <www.thecornerhouse.org.uk/sites/thecornerhouse.org.uk/files/HGAPSA.pdf >

way.[185] Furthermore, the project agreements also overrode key provisions in Turkish expropriation law which require the price for expropriated property to be negotiated; instead, it was compulsorily purchased, under the emergency law normally invoked only in times of national disaster or war, under the terms of the agreements.[186] BP has countered that the exemptions it obtained were nothing out of the ordinary and are common to the other concession agreements.

Joint Statement, the Security Protocol and the BTC Human Rights Undertaking

As a response to the criticisms about the potential impact of legal framework of the BTC agreements on the autonomy and policy-making discretion of the host states,[187] the project sponsors published several legal documents: *Joint Statement*, the *Security Protocol* and the *BTC Human Rights Undertaking*. A joint statement delivered in May 2003 addressed the standards (environmental, health, safety and social) which would govern project implementation.[188] These standards serve as a baseline for the assessment of changes in law and a ceiling for the limitation of the effects of future legislation.[189] This was executed by interpretation of the IGA which

> commits each state to the application of environmental standards that are no less stringent than those generally applied within member states of the European Union from to time. The HGA and other BTC Agreements give effect to this commitment, and provide a dynamic benchmark that will evolve as EU standards evolve.[190]

In July 2003, the protocol relating to the Provisions of Security for the East–West Energy Corridor (*Security Protocol*) was published to establish the manner in which the host governments of the three signatory states propose to meet their security commitments under the HGAs.[191] Furthermore, in September 2003, the BTC Company produced another legal document, the BTC Human Rights Undertaking, which is a legally binding unilateral deed under English law. The undertaking modified the terms of the stabilisation clauses, excluding previously agreed clauses from being applied to legal changes in the area of human rights, health, safety and the environment. What this means is that the project consortium

185 USAID (n. 180 above) 28.
186 Hildyards & Muttitt (n. 184 above) 47.
187 A. Dufey, and R. Kazimova, 'Baku–Tbilisi–Ceyhan Project: Implications of Project Finance', Chapter 12 in S. Leader and D. Ong (eds), *Global Project Finance, Human Rights and Sustainable Development* (Cambridge: Cambridge University Press, 2011) 382.
188 Cameron, *The Pursuit of Stability* (n. 7 above) 404–5.
189 Ibid.
190 Joint Statement on the Baku–Tbilisi–Ceyhan Pipeline Project 16 May (2003) 1, para 7, available at <http://subsites.bp.com/caspian/Joint%20Statement.pdf>
191 Dufey & Kazimova (n. 187 above) 382.

acquiesces not to assert claims that are inconsistent with host countries' regulations, provided that this is:

> reasonably required by international labour and human rights treaties to which the relevant Host Government is a party from time to time [or]... required in the public interest in accordance with domestic law in the relevant project state from time to time, provided that such domestic law is not more stringent than the highest of European Union standards as referred to in the Project Agreements, including relevant EU directives (EU Standards)...those World Bank Group standards referred to in the Project Agreements, and standards under applicable international labour and human rights treaties.[192]

Through this undertaking, the BTC Company also agrees not to seek compensation under the economic equilibrium clause

> in connection with...any action or inaction by the relevant Host Government that is reasonably required to fulfil the obligations of the Host Government under any international treaty on human rights (including the European Convention on Human Rights), labour, or HSE in force in the relevant Project State from time to time to which such Project States in then a party.[193]

The BTC Company hereby provided guarantees that it would not apply the compensation clauses in the IGA and HGAs if one the host states involved in the project legislated in the interests of human rights, environment, health and safety. From that perspective, it might be said that the Human Rights Undertaking represented a breakthrough and was an innovative work, commissioned by the BTC Company as an overt demonstration of their sensitivity towards human rights issues. As this action resulted in a restriction of the reach of the stabilisation clause in the BTC agreements, host states were thereby rendered freer to legislate. Nevertheless, the scope of the stabilisation clause in HGAs is still considered a murky issue by project investors. Distinguishing between legitimate regulations and compensable regulatory actions of states remains challenging. However, the solution seems to lie in the referencing of bilateral international treaties as a benchmark to define whether a host state measure falls within the exception delineated by this Human Rights Undertaking. Bilateral investment treaties do not address the distinction between legitimate regulations and compensable regulatory actions. Arguably, previous attempts made by international arbitral tribunals in distinguishing compensable from non-compensable regulatory actions of host states may help by providing a frame of reference to define whether a host state's regulatory measure may fall within the exception established by BTC undertaking.

192 BTC Human Rights Undertaking, 22 September (2003) Section 2(a) available at <http://subsites.bp.com/caspian/Human%20Rights%20Undertaking.pdf>

193 Ibid., section 2(d).

Conclusion

Most host government contacts contain stabilisation clauses against discriminatory changes, which may adversely affect the terms and conditions of the contract from the perspective of the host state. When these clauses are inserted in a contract, they reduce political risk for the investor and preserve the fiscal regime;[194] thus, they are the preferred risk management method by investors in the energy industry.[195] In addition, the validity of stabilisation clauses was assessed during this chapter. If domestic law is chosen by the parties to govern the contract, then stabilisation clauses may be exposed to the constitutional and legal restrictions of the host country when the host state makes legislative changes and modifies the governing law. In other words, a right bestowed upon the investor by the state can be taken away at any time by sovereign authority. On the other hand, in order to limit the effects of potentially damaging host government legislation, foreign investors may obligate the host country to agree that the contract should be governed by international law as well as domestic law.[196]

In such a case, a stabilisation clause that is validly entered into may legitimately fetter the host state's ability to modify or unilaterally change the contract or to nationalise assets.[197] It is apparent that this view of stabilisation clauses challenges the principle of the permanent sovereignty of states. In addition, well-established norms of international law and a UN resolution recognise that a host country has full control and power to regulate its natural resources.[198] This means that stabilisation clauses are not the only defence against nationalisation actions of a government. It is true that, in the case of *AMINOIL*, the tribunal held that a stabilisation clause does not forbid a host state from nationalising the property, but it protects against confiscation. To this end, it can be said that there is no power that may hinder a host state from exercising its public interest, as this right is founded in a state's sovereignty. Nevertheless, these clauses should not be regarded as impotent and without legal effect. They are binding and enforceable, because the insertion of such clauses raises the legitimate expectation of a foreign investor. As the legitimate expectation of investors is linked with stabilisation clauses, the violation of stabilisation clauses damages the legitimate expectation of an investor which may in turn seek to be compensated by the host state.[199]

Although stabilisation clauses have been subject to criticism, largely regarding whether they are valid under national and international law, such clauses are still regarded as an essential risk management technique against sovereign risks such as 'nationalisation, expropriation, or the obsolescence bargain in which the host state

194 J. N. N. Emeka, 'Anchoring Stabilization Clauses in International Petroleum Contracts', *International Law*, Vol. 42 (2008) 1317.
195 Waelde & Ndi, 'Stabilizing International Investment Commitments' (n. 10 above) 234.
196 Moses (n. 83 above) 63.
197 Al-Qurashi (n. 13 above) 235.
198 Waelde & Ndi, 'Stabilizing International Investment Commitments' (n. 10 above) 261.
199 Al-Qurashi (n. 13 above) 234.

can use changes in circumstances to improve new requirements on investors'.[200] However, contemporary practice in the area of stabilisation clauses has moved from the traditional freezing genre of the stabilisation clause to a hybrid mechanism combining stabilisation with renegotiation provisions. This combination is called an economic equilibrium clause. The components of economic stabilisation clauses are versatility and stability.[201] As evidenced during the examination of economic equilibrium clauses, these clauses, 'while indeed showing a willingness of the parties to change, can, at the same time represent a very effective means of stabilising the contract'.[202] It is irrefutable that economic equilibrium clauses are highly effective in reducing indirect expropriation risk and the unilateral change of contractual terms.

Stabilisation clauses inserted in investment contracts cannot fetter a host state from engaging in legislative activities in the areas of environmental and human rights. As examined in the *Texaco* case, sovereign states may forgo their sovereign rights and fetter themselves; for instance, they can promise not to nationalise the foreign investor's property. However, it should never be forgotten that a state cannot make promises to foreign investors regarding the non-assignable and inalienable rights which derive from international treaty obligations. When drafting contracts, the best solution is to limit the scope of stabilisation clauses to matters that do not impact on human rights and environmental concerns.[203] Recent BITs prove that state measures related to environmental and human rights cannot amount to indirect expropriation, and so cannot be claimed to be a violation of stabilisation provisions.

Reactions to the BTC project agreements were also explored during this chapter. Following vociferous criticism from several NGOs, the BTC project consortium was forced to backtrack and subsequently issued several legal documents to redefine its position. Through the Human Rights Undertaking, the BTC Company declared that the consortium would not require compensation if Azerbaijan, Georgia or Turkey were to adopt new laws designed to protect human rights or the environment, or in the interests of health and safety. Although it may seem that this undertaking narrowed the scope of the stabilisation clause, to date there has been no attempt made by the signatory states to adopt new laws in the area of human rights and the environment to put this hypothesis to the test. More importantly, the Human Rights Undertaking issued by BP was just a unilaterally executed deed poll. Strictly speaking, it is not a legal contract as it applies to only one party. In the BTC case, the deed poll only binds the consortium. In this regard, it could be said to have the status of a documented promise. Debatably, if human rights and environmental exceptions (defined areas in BTC undertaking) were annexed to each HGA and agreed by each state, this may have constituted

200 Shemberg (n. 23 above) vii.

201 Erkan (n. 16 above) 220; here, the elements of economic equilibrium clauses are called 'flexibility and stability'.

202 Peter (n. 50 above) 241.

203 Cotula, 'Freezing the Balancing Act?' (n. 163 above) 162.

the fairest and perhaps the most favourable solution for both parties. It should, however, be noted that a measure taken by a signatory state can always be subject to a dispute.

After examining the stabilisation clauses, the following two chapters will analyse the driving force(s) influencing host states to agree to insert such clauses in their host governmental contracts. While Chapter 4 merely focusses on external matters, Chapter 5 will examine internal reasons that have forced Azerbaijan and Turkey to accept stability provisions in the HGAs of the BTC project.

Bibliography

Legislation and guides

Rio Declaration on Environment and Development, U.N. Doc., A/CONF.151/5 Rev.1 (1992) 31 ILM 874

The United Nations Assembly Resolution on Permanent Sovereignty over Natural Resources, GA Res.1803 (XVII) 17 U.N. GOAR Supp. (No.17), U.N. Doc. A/5217 (1962)

Contracts

Concession Agreement of for Petroleum Exploration and Exploitation between Egypt & Egypt General Petroleum Corporations & Dover Investments Limited (East Wadi Araba Area Gulf of Suez) 2002

Equilibrium of the Agreement, Borrows Company Basic Oil Laws and Concession Contracts, Middle East, Supplement 124 (1994)

Exploration and Product Sharing Agreement between the Government of Qatar and Holcar Oil Co., 1 January 1976

HGA between and among the Government of the Azerbaijan Republic and the State Oil Company of Azerbaijan Republic, BP Exporation (Caspian Sea) LTD., Statoil BTC Caspian AS, Ramco Hazar Energy Limited, Turkiye Petrolleri A.O, Unocal BTC Pipeline Ltd, Itochu Oil Exploration (Azerbaijan) Inc., Delta Hess (BTC) Limited, 17 October 2000

Host Government Agreement between and among the Government of the Republic of Turkey and the MEP Participants, 18 November 2000

Host Government Agreement between and among the Government of the Republic Georgia and the MEP Participants, 28 April 2000

The Azerbaijan Union Texas/Commonwealth Production Sharing Agreement, 1998

The Concession Agreement between the Ruler of Abu Dhabi and Maruzen Oil Co. Ltd.; Daikyo Oil Co. Ltd And Nippon Mining Co. Ltd., 6 December 1967

Vietnam Model Production Sharing Contracts, 2004, Barrows Basic Oil Laws and Concession Contracts, (Asia and Australasia) Supp. No. 164

Cases and arbitral awards

Amoco Int'l Fin. Corporation v Government of the Islamic Republic of Iran, 16 Iran-U.S. Cl. Trib. Rep. 189, 239 (1987)

British Petroleum Exploration Company (Libya) Ltd v Government of the Libyan Arab Republic, 53 I.L.R. 297 (1973–1974)
Duke Energy International Peru Investments No. 1 Ltd v Peru, ICSID Case No. ARB/03/28, Final Award, 25 July 2008
Libyan American Oil Company (LIAMCO) v the Government of the Libyan Arab Republic, Award of 12 April 1977, 62 I.L.R. 140, (1977) 20 I.L.M.1 (1977)
Libyan American Oil Company (LIAMCO) v the Government of the Libyan Arab Republic, Award of 12 April 1977, 62 I.L.R. 140, (1977) 20 I.L.M.1 (1977)
Raderiakiebolaget Amphitrite v The King [1921] 3 K.B. 500
Saudi Arabia v Arabian American Oil Company, 27 I.L.R. 117 (1958)
SSP Ltd v Egypt (1983) 22 ILM 752
Texaco v Libyan Arab Republic (TOPCO) award, 53 I.L.R. 389 (1978)
Texas Overseas Petroleum Co./Californian Asiatic Co. v Libyan Arab Republic, 17 ILM. 1 (Int'l Arb. Trib. 1977)

Internet websites

http://tjogel.org/archive/Vol4No1/witten.pdf
www.state.gov/documents/organization/117601.pdf
www.thecornerhouse.org.uk/sites/thecornerhouse.org.uk/files/HGAPSA.pdf
www.bp.com/en_az/caspian/aboutus/legalagreements.html
www.gasandoil.com/ogel
www.amnesty.org.uk/press-releases/baku-tbilisi-ceyhan-pipeline-project-puts-human-rights-line

Books and monographs

Al-Faruque, A., 'Stability in Petroleum Contracts: Rhetoric and Reality', PhD Thesis, University of Dundee, 2005
BegicT., *Applicable Law in International Investment Disputes*. Utrecht: Eleven International Publishing, 2005
Botchway, F. N., *Natural Resource Investment and Africa's Development*. Cheltenham: Edward Elgar Publishing Company, 2011
Brownlie, I., *Principles of Public International Law*, 6th edn. Oxford, Oxford University Press, 2003
Cameron, P. D., *International Energy Investment Law: The Pursuit of Stability*. Oxford: Oxford University Press, 2010
Dolzer, R. & Schreur, C., *Principles of International Investment Law*, 2nd edn. Oxford: Oxford University Press, 2012
El Sheikh, A., *The Legal Regime of Foreign Private Investment in Sudan and Saudi Arabia*. 2nd edn. Cambridge: Cambridge University Press, 2003
ErkanM., *International Energy Investment Law: Stability through Contractual Clauses*, Energy and Environmental Law and Policy Series. Alphen aan den Rijn: Kluwer Law International, 2011
Moses, M. L., *The Principles and Practice of International Commercial Arbitration* (New York: Cambridge University Press, 2008) 63.
Peter, W., *Arbitration and Renegotiation of International Investment Agreements*, 2nd revised and enlarged edition. The Hague: Kluwer Law International, 1995

Redfern, A. & Hunter, M., *Law and Practice of International Commercial Arbitration*. Bath: Sweet & Maxwell, 2004

Samartano, M. R., *International Arbitration Law and Practice*, 2nd edn. The Hague: Kluwer International Law, 2001

Shapira, A. & Tabory, M., *New Political Entities in Public and Private International Law with Special Reference to the Palestinian Entity*. The Hague: Kluwer Law International, 1999

Sornarajah, M., *The International Law on Foreign Investment*, 3rd edn. Cambridge: Cambridge University Press, 2010

Vinuales, J. E., *Foreign Investment and the Environment in International Law*. New York: Cambridge University Press, 2012

Waart, P., Peters, P. & Denters, E., *International Law and Development*. Dordrecht: Kluwer Academic Publishers, 1988)

Waelde, T. W. & Ndi, G., *Fiscal Regime Stability and Issues of State Sovereignty in Taxation of Mineral Enterprises*. London: Graham and Trotman, 1995

Chapters in books

Alexander, F. C., 'The Three Pillars of Security of Investment Under PSCs and Other Host Government Contract', Chapter 7 in *Institute for Energy Law of the Centre for American and International Law's 54th Annual Institute on Oil and Gas Law* (Publication 640, Release 54), (Lexis Nexis Mathew Bender, 2003) 7.1, 7.19

Cotula, L., 'Freezing the Balancing Act? Project Finance, Legal Tools to Manage Regulatory Risk, and Sustainable Development', Chapter 6 in S. Leader & D. Ong (eds), *Global Project Finance, Human Rights and Sustainable Development*. Cambridge: Cambridge University Press, 2011

Cotula, L., 'Investment Contracts through a Development Lens', in E. Blanco & J. Razzaque (eds), *Natural Resources and the Green Economy: Re-defining the Challenges for People, States and Corporations*. Leiden: Martinus Nijhoff Publisher, 2012

DufeyA. & Kazimova, R., 'Baku–Tbilisi–Ceyhan Project: Implications of Project Finance', Chapter 12 in S. Leader & D. Ong (eds), *Global Project Finance, Human Rights and Sustainable Development*. Cambridge: Cambridge University Press, 2011

Sheppard, A. & Crockett, A., 'Are Stabilisation Clauses a Threat to Sustainable Development?' Chapter 14 in M. C. C. Segger, A. Newcombe& M. W. Gehring (eds), *Sustainable Development in International Investment Law*. The Hague: Kluwer, 2010

Articles, seminars/conference and research papers

Al-Faruque, A., 'The Rationale and Instrumentalities for Stability in Long-Term State Contracts: The Context for Petroleum Contracts', *The Journal of World Investment & Trade* Vol. 7, No. 1 (2006) 85

Al-Faruque, A., 'Typologies, Efficacy and Political Economy of Stabilisation Clauses: A Critical Appraisal', *OGEL, Journal of Oil and Gas Energy Law Intelligence*, Vol. 4, No. 5 (2007) 33

Al-Faruque, A., 'Validity and Efficacy of Stabilisation Clauses: Legal Protection vs. Functional Value', *Journal of International Arbitration*, Vol. 23, No. 4 (2006) 319

Al-Qurashi, Z.A., 'International Oil and Gas Arbitration', *OGEL, Journal of Oil, Gas and Energy Law Intelligence*, Vol. 3 (2005) 181–182

Asante, S. K. B., 'Stability of Contractual Relations in the Transnational Investment Process', *International and Comparative Law Quarterly*, Vol. 28 (1979) 401

Berger, K. B., 'Renegotiation and Adaptation of International Investment Contracts: The Role of the Contract Drafters and Arbitrators', *Vanderbilt Journal of Transnational Law*, Vol. 36 (2003) 1361

Bernardini, P. 'Stabilization and Adaptation in Oil and Gas Investments', *Journal of World Energy Law and Business*, Vol. 1, No. 1 (2008) 100

Bishop, R. D., 'International Arbitration of Petroleum Disputes: The Development of Lex Petrolea', *Yearbook of Commercial Arbitration*, Vol. 23 (1998) 1159

Clinch, D. & Watson, J., 'Stabilisation Clauses – Issues and Trends', Herbert Smith Freehills LLP 2010, available at <www.lexology.com/library/detail.aspx?g=c5976193-1acd-4082-b9e7-87c0414b5328>

Coale, M. T. B., 'Stabilization Clauses in International Petroleum Transactions', *Denver Journal of International Law and Policy*, Vol. 30 (2002) 223

Cotula, L., 'Regulatory Takings, Stabilization Clauses and Sustainable Development', Session 2.2: The Policy Framework for Investment: The Social and Environmental Dimensions, OECD Global Forum on International Investment, 27–28 March (2008) 5, available at <www.oecd.org/investment/globalforum/40311122.pdf>

Crawford, J. & Johnson, W. 'Arbitrating with Foreign States and Their Instrumentalities', *International Finance Law Review*, Vol. 5 (1986) 11

Curtis, C. T., 'The Legal Security of Economic Development Agreements', *Harvard International Law Journal*, Vol. 29 (1998) 347

Delaume, G., 'Comparative Analysis as a Basis of Law in State Contracts: The Myth of the Lex Mercatoria', *Tulsa Law Review*, Vol. 63 (1989) 575

Dickstein, M. E., 'Revitalizing the International Law Governing Concession Agreements', *International Tax and Business Lawyer*, Vol. 6 (1988) 54

El-Kosheri, A. & Riad, T., 'The Law Governing a New Generation of Petroleum Contracts', *ICSID Review*, Vol. 1 (1986) 259

Emeka, J. N. N., 'Anchoring Stabilization Clauses in International Petroleum Contracts', *International Law*, Vol. 42 (2008) 1317

Garcia-Amador, F.V., 'State Responsibility in Case of Stabilization Clauses', *Journal of Transnational Law and Policy*, Vol. 2, No. 23 (1993) 23

Greenwood, C., 'State Contracts in International Law: The Libyan Oil Arbitrations', *British Year Book of International Law*, Vol. 63 (1982) 53

Hildyards, N. & Muttitt, G., 'Turbo Charging Investor Sovereignty: Investment Agreements and Corporate Colonialism' (2004) 47, available at <www.thecornerhouse.org.uk/sites/thecornerhouse.org.uk/files/HGAPSA.pdf>

Higgins, R., 'Legal Preconditions for Foreign Investment', IBA-SERL Seminar Proceeding, Mathew Bender, New York (1986) 233

Jiminez de Arechaga, E., 'State Responsibility of Nationalisation of Foreign Owned Property', *N.Y.U. Journal of International Law and Policy* (1978) 179

Manirruzzaman, A. F. M., 'National Laws Providing Stability of International Investment Contracts: A Comparative Perspective', *Journal of World Investment and Trade*, Vol. 1, No. 2 (2007) 7

Manirruzzaman, A.F.M., 'State Contracts with Aliens: The Question of Unilateral Change by the State in Contemporary International Law', *Journal of International Arbitration* , Vol. 9, No. 4 (1992) 141

Manirruzzaman, A.F.M., 'The Pursuit of Stability in International Energy Investment Contracts: A Critical Appraisal of Emerging Trends', *Journal of World Energy & Business*, Vol. 1, No. 2 (2008) 121

Manirruzzaman, A.F.M., 'International Energy Contracts and Cross-Border Pipeline Projects: Stabilisation, Renegotiation and Economic Balancing in Changed Circumstances', *Oil, Gas & Energy Law Intelligence (OGEL)*, Vol. 4, No. 4 (2006) 1

von Mehren, R. B. & Kourides, P. N., 'International Arbitrations between States and Foreign Private Parties: The Libyan Nationalization Cases', *American Journal of International Law*, Vol. 75, No. 3 (1981) 476

Nwete, B.O.N., 'To What Extent Can Stabilisation Clauses Mitigate the Investor's Risks in a Production Sharing Contract?' *Oil, Gas & Energy Law Intelligence (OGEL)*, Vol. 3 (2005) 56

Nwokolo, A. D. 'Is There a Legal and Functional Value for the Stabilisation Clause in International Petroleum Agreements?' available at <https://uod.app.box.com/s/pwunkrworh8aidrlhu17f56knlt3h6p1>

Paasivirta, E., 'Internationalization and Stabilization of Contracts versus State Sovereignty', *British Year Book of International Law*, Vol. 60 (1989) 315

Pate, T. J., 'Evaluating Stabilization Clauses in Venezuela's Strategic Association Agreements for Heavy-Crude Extraction in the Orinoco Belt: The Return of a Forgotten Contractual Risk Reduction Mechanism for the Petroleum Industry', *University of Miami Inter-American Law Review*, Vol. 40, No. 2 (2009) 351

Redfern, A., 'The Arbitration between the Government of Kuwait and AMINOIL', *British Year Book of International Law*, Vol. 58 (1985) 100

Sornarajah, M., 'The Myth of International Contract Law?', *Journal of World Trade Law*, Vol. 15 (1981) 187

Suratgar, D., 'Considerations affecting Choice of Law Clauses in Contracts Between Governments and Foreign Nationals', *Indian Journal of International Law*, Vol. 2 (1962), 273

United States Agency for International Development (USAID), 'Multilateral Development Bank Assistance Proposals: Likely to Have Adverse Impacts on the Environment, Natural Resources, Public Health and Indigenous Peoples, September 2002–October 2004', available at <https://ecd.usaid.gov/repository/mdb/2004O.pdf>

Waelde, T. W. & Ndi, G., 'Stabilizing International Investment Commitments: International Law versus Contract Interpretation', *Texas International Law Journal*, Vol. 31, No. 2 (1996) 260

Wehberg, H., 'Pacta Sunt Servanda', *American Journal of International Law*, Vol. 53 (1959), 775

White, R. C. A., 'Expropriation of the Libyan Oil Concessions – Two Conflicting International Arbitrations', *International and Comparative Law Quarterly*, Vol. 30, No. 1 (1981) 11

Witten, E.A., 'Arbitration of Venezuelan Oil Contracts: A Losing Strategy?' *Texas Journal of Oil, Gas and Energy Law*, Vol. 4 (2009) 67, available at <http://tjogel.org/archive/Vol4No1/witten.pdf>

Wolff, M., 'Some Observations on the Autonomy of Contracting Parties in Conflict of Laws', *Transactions of the Grotius Society*, Vol. 35 (1949) 143

Reports

BTC Human Rights Undertaking, 22 September 2003, Section 2(a), available at <http://subsites.bp.com/caspian/Human%20Rights%20Undertaking.pdf>

Cameron, P. D., 'Stabilisation in Investment Contracts and Changes of Rules in Host Countries: Tools for Oil & Gas Investors', AIPN, Final Report, 5 July 2006

Joint Statement on the Baku–Tbilisi–Ceyhan Pipeline Project, 16 May 2003, available at <http://subsites.bp.com/caspian/Joint%20Statement.pdf>

Shemberg, A., 'Stabilisation Clause and Human Rights: A Research Project Conducted for IFC and the United Nations Special Representative to the Secretary General on Business and Human Rights', IFC/SRSG Research Paper, 11 May 2009

4 Lenders, risk insurers and rating agencies

Introduction

Project finance is the provision of economic funds for a project arranged in such a way that financial lenders count merely on the assets and cash flow of the project for interest and loan repayment.[1] Project finance has been one of the most popular funding models for the oil and gas industry for decades. There are a number of equity investors involved in project financing including sponsors, commercial banks and other financial lending institutions. Although project finance is the most common financing model in large-scale oil and gas projects, it is not suitable for all investment scenarios. More fragile business environments, unpredictable government behaviour and other political risk phenomena can render the financing of an international energy project challenging.

Project finance defined

There is not, in fact, one universally accepted definition of project finance among either scholars or practitioners. It is possible that the reason for this lies in the dynamic and continuously changing nature of project finance. According to Nevitt and Fabozzi, the term 'project finance' refers to a method of

> financing of a particular economic unit in which a lender is satisfied to look initially to the cash flows and earnings of that economic unit as the source of funds from which a loan will be repaid and to the assets of the economic unit as collateral for the loan.[2]

What is referred to as the economic unit in this definition is a legally and financially free business corporation. In addition, the definition also indicates that the

1 A. C. Inkpen & M. H. Moffett, *The Global Oil and Gas Industry: Management, Strategy, and Finance* (Tulsa, OK: PennWell Corporation, 2011) 286.
2 P. K. Nevitt & F. J. Fabozzi, *Project Financing*, 7th edn (London: Euromoney Institutional Investor, 2000) 1.

repayment of the loan is principally dependent on the cash flow generated by the economic unit.[3] Another definition of project finance is provided by Esty, according to whom it 'involves the creation of a legal and economically independent project company financed with non-recourse debt (and equity from one or more corporate sponsors) for the purpose of financing a single purpose, capital asset usually with a limited life'.[4] Merna and Owen define project finance as follows:

> Each project is supported by its own financial package and secured solely on that project facility. Projects are viewed as being their own discrete entities and legally separated from their founding sponsors. As each project exists in its own right, SPV's [special purpose vehicles] are formulated. Banks lend to SPV's on a non or limited recourse basis, which means that loans are fully dependent on the revenue streams generated by the SPV and that the assets of the SPV are used as collateral. Hence although there may be a number of sponsors forming the SPV, the lenders have no claim to any of the assets other than the project itself.[5]

The following subsection provides a description of the stakeholders in project finance scenarios.

Who are the main stakeholders in project finance?

Generally speaking, there is no one unique project finance model that is applicable to all industries.[6] In other words, as project financing has a complex structure, not all projects follow the same financing method.[7] When the classic model of project finance is considered, the following participants are involved in oil and gas pipeline projects: a parent company or a group of companies in a consortium (project sponsors), special purpose vehicle (SPV), host government, financial institutions (multilateral, regional development banks, bilateral and commercial banks).

Project company: A project company is a core legal entity that can own, develop, construct, operate and maintain a single project. The project company is generally regarded as SPV. In other words, the SPV is 'a legally and economically

3 A. Merna, Y. Chu & F. F. Al-Thani, *Project Finance in Construction: A Structured Guide to Assessment* (Oxford: Wiley Blackwell, 2010) 11.

4 B. C. Esty, *Modern Project Finance* (USA: John Wiley & Sons, 2004) cited in Merna, Chu & Al-Thani (n. 3 above) 12.

5 A. Merna & G. Owen, *Understanding the Private Finance Initiative: The New Dynamics of Project Finance* (Hong Kong: Asia Law and Practice, 1998), cited in T. Merna & F. F. Al-Thani, *Corporate Risk Management*, 2nd edn (Chichester: John Wiley & Sons, 2008) 111.

6 J. Dewar, *International Project Finance: Law and Practice* (Oxford: Oxford University Press, 2011) 22.

7 Ibid.

independent project company financed with non-limited recourse debt for the purpose of financing a single purpose, capital asset usually with a limited life'.[8] A sponsor company sets up an SPV for the sole purpose of achieving the limited goals of construction and operation of a particular pipeline, dam, hydroelectric, etc. project in a host country. Therefore, it is subject to the laws of that country 'unless appropriate "commissions" can be paid so that key government officials can grant "exceptions" to the project'.[9] Furthermore, the role of the SPV is dependent on the organisation of the sponsor companies in question.

If the project involves more than one sponsor, a state corporate entity, partnership construction trust or a contractual joint venture may be formed. According to Smith and Walter, the existence of more than one sponsor may be necessitated by the following factors:[10]

- The oil or gas resource is jointly owned.
- The government of the country where the project is located mandates a joint venture with local interests.
- The size of the project is so massive that it yields greater economies of scale than several smaller units.
- The capabilities of the sponsors are complementary.
- The project obviously exceeds the technical, human or financial resources of a single company.
- There is a clear need for risk sharing.

The main purpose of the SPV is to maximise project income levels.[11] In addition to its main objective, some scholars have drawn attention the role and why setting up a SPV is necessary. According to Norton,

> [S]etting up a SPV is to afford reassurance (or 'ring-fencing') to investors, enabling cash flows to be de-linked from the credit of the originator/seller. The SPV will receive foreign earnings paid into an account in its name rather than that of the originator; after interest payments have been made to investors the balance will be 'passed through' to the originator.[12]

Paoli also describes the role of an SPV in the following terms:

8 Merna, Chu & Al-Thani (n. 3 above) 14.
9 A. Fight, *Introduction to Project Finance* (Oxford: Elsevier, 2008) 12.
10 R. C. Smith & I. Walter, *Global Banking* (New York: Oxford University Press, 1997) 61.
11 S. Leader & D. Ong, *Global Project Finance, Human Rights and Sustainable Development* (Cambridge: Cambridge University Press, 2011) 115.
12 S. D. Norton, 'Securitisation in the Extractive Industries: Stakeholder Sensitivities, Environmental Protection and the Cost of Capital', *Greener Management International*, No. 53 (November 2007) 62.

> [T]he reason for forming a SPV is that it can in certain limited circumstances enable the originator to '*pierce the sovereign ceiling*', meaning that it is able to raise capital at lower cost than can the government of the country where it exists.[13]

All in all, SPVs are basically 'robot firms that...have no employees, make no substantive economic decisions, have no physical location, and cannot go bankrupt'.[14]

Generally speaking, collateralisation refers to a property or other assets that a borrower offers a financial institution to protect a loan. If the borrower cannot make the payment of the assured loan, then the lender can seize the collateral to recover its injuries. Norton emphasises that the SPV established by the project sponsors is a shell corporation and emphasises the necessity of SPV collateralisation. According to the author:

> The originator may sometimes retain the first loss tranche under the securitisation, having the same economic effect as collateralisation, but without constituting a guarantee within the strict legal sense. Collateralisation may be required to compensate for risks accruing to the issue. Without such collateralisation the greater the level of perceived risk, the lower the rating assigned to the issue by the bond rating agencies, Standard & Poor's and Moody's, Fitch and DBRS and the higher the rate of interest that must be paid by the originator.[15]

Sponsor company: The project sponsor is the entity that takes an active role in managing the project. As the owner of the SPV, the project sponsor can be a parent company, group of companies (consortium) or a subsidiary of another company that initiates a project.[16] The project sponsor supplies management, operational and technical knowledge and experience to a particular project. The project sponsor may be required to provide some guarantees to cover certain liabilities or undertake the risks of the project.[17] Furthermore, no project can be maintained without the presence of a project company.

Host governments: A host government is the government of the state in which an investment project is executed. There is no doubt that the role played by a host government is significant in project financing. For example, the political

13 B. De Paoli, 'Costs of Sovereign Default', *Bank of England Quarterly Bulletin*, Vol. 46, No. 3 (2006) 297–308, cited in Norton (n. 12 above).

14 G. B. Gorton & N. S. Souleles, 'Special Purpose Vehicles and Securitization', Chapter 12 in M. Carey and R. M. Stulz (eds), *The Risks of Financial Institutions*, National Bureau of Economic Research Conference Report (Chicago: University of Chicago Press, 2007) 550.

15 Norton (n. 12 above) 63.

16 A. Slivker, 'What Is Project Finance and How Does It Work?', University of Iowa Centre for International Finance and Development (April 2011) 5, available at <http://ebook.law.uiowa.edu/ebook/uicifd-ebook/what-project-finance-and-how-does-it-work-0>

17 Fight (n. 9 above).

motivation and sustained political support of a host government are indispensable to project financing. In order to demonstrate this willingness, host governments enter into agreement with sponsors, 'providing guarantees and the security of project facilities as well as financial and other assurance'.[18] The host government's role and lenders' assessment criteria will be discussed in detail in the section devoted to the assessment of project risk in host countries.

Financial institutions: There are numerous financial institutions that have some involvement in project finance transactions. Furthermore, there is an even greater variety of capital support structures that a financial organisation can provide for a project. Most projects around the world, particularly in developing states, are financed through some combination of multilateral banks, export credit agencies and other financial agencies (bilateral agencies or commercial banks). These organisations were set up to supply financing for governmental and private sector transactions in developing states where the political risks are high and often serve to inhibit financial institutions from providing loans. Yet, in spite of the importance of direct funding provided by official agencies, their most crucial role is that their capability in diminishing the political risks for private sector lenders and thereby to attract them to contribute to financing projects in developing countries.[19]

The main financial institutions in project financing

Multilateral development banks (MDBs)

MDBs are international institutions established by international agreement between multiple countries whose aim is to promote investment development among all its member nations by providing loans and grants.[20] These development goals concentrate on, primarily, the economic and social benefits to be had through investment as well as supplementary issues such as the protection of the environment and sustainability.[21] Project loans include large infrastructure projects, such as pipeline construction in energy investment projects, highways, power plants, port facilities as well as social projects. Multilateral banks operate both globally and regionally. The World Bank Group is the principal globally active, multilateral body that provides loans and grants to

18 T. Sorell, 'Project Financing in Developing Countries, New Corporate Social Responsibility, Human Rights, and Multinationals', *Essex Human Rights Review*, Vol. 5, No. 1 (2008) 2.

19 B. Sheppard, 'The Role of Multilateral Banks and ECAs', Chapter 6 in R. Morrison (ed.), *The Principles of Project Finance* (Farnham: Gower Publishing, 2012) 81.

20 For instance, Article 1 (section 1) of the Agreement Establishing the Inter-American Development Bank stated that 'the purpose of the Bank shall be to contribute to the acceleration of the process of economic and social development of the regional developing member countries, individually and collectively'. Available at <www.oas.org/dil/treaties_C-15_Agreement_Establishing_the_Inter-American_Development_Bank.htm>

21 Dewar (n. 6 above) 218.

private sector financing through its affiliate International Finance Corporation (IFC) and political risk insurance through the Multilateral Investment Guarantee Agency (MIGA).

For the most part, other multilateral development agencies are more often regional in scope. Examples of these include: European Investment Bank (EIB), European Bank for Reconstruction and Development (EBRD), the African Development Bank (AfDB), the Inter-American Development Bank and the Asian Development Bank (ADB). MDBs are also providers of policy-based loans. Traditionally, this type of loan is granted by the International Monetary Fund (IMF) and which requires typically developing countries who wish to borrow to implement specified economic and financial policies.

The purpose of this international organisation is 'to foster global monetary cooperation, secure financial stability, facilitate international trade, promote high employment, sustain economic growth and reduce poverty around the world'.[22] Despite the fact the organisation states as one of its key aims the creation of a permanently strong economic environment, the IMF does not involve itself directly in the financing of investment projects. In the interests of economy, the following section examines only briefly the players in global finance actors under the World Bank Group.

World Bank Group

The World Bank Group encompasses the following institutions: the International Development Association (IDA), the International Financial Corporation (IFC), the Multilateral Guarantee Agency (MIGA) and the International Centre for Settlement of Investment Disputes (ICSID). The International Bank for Reconstruction and Development (IBRD) and the World Bank are used interchangeably in literature, but are more widely known as the World Bank, which was set up on 27 December 1945. Notably, since its establishment, the World Bank has pursued this objective in several ways.[23] The main objectives of the World Bank are:

- To assist in the development of member countries by facilitating the investment of capital for productive purposes;
- To promote private foreign investment by means of guarantees or participation in loans and other investments made by private investors;
- To promote the long-range balanced growth of international trade and the maintenance of equilibrium in balance of payments by encouraging international investment for the development of the productive resources of

22 See the website of International Monetary Fund (IFM), available at <www.imf.org/external/about.htm>

23 I. F. I. Shihata, 'The Settlement of Disputes Regarding Foreign Investment: The Role of the World Bank, with Particular Reference to ICSID and MIGA', American University Journal of International Law and Policy, Vol. 1, No. 97 (1986) 1.

members, thereby assisting in raising productivity, the standard of living and conditions of labour in their territories;

- To conduct its operations with due regard to the effect of international investment on business conditions in the territories of members and, in the immediate post-war years, to assist in bringing about a smooth transition from a wartime to a peacetime economy.[24]

With this outline of the main purposes and objectives of the World Bank in mind, it is significant to examine examples of the Bank's specific role in oil- and gas-related projects. The World Bank requires a governmental guarantee of repayment of its loans.[25] For this reason, the Bank's financial assistance is not directly extended to the private financing of a project. Therefore, its loans are provided to host governments. It should be noted, however, that the Bank's involvement in an oil and gas project encourages private sector involvement in large-scale oil and gas projects.[26] For instance, the World Bank's involvement could provide extra security to other lenders or international investors who participate the project. The World Bank's guarantees cover risks arising from non-performance of contractual obligations or *force majeure*.[27] Furthermore, the Bank can extend guarantees against political risks, such as expropriation, nationalisation, foreign currency transfer, etc.[28]

International Development Agency (IDA)

The IDA was established in 1960. It aims to reduce poverty by providing subsidised credits (loan) and grants, technical assistance, and policy advice to less developed countries.[29] The organisation has 173 member states which contribute financially every three years.[30] IDA membership is available only to countries who

24 Article (1) of Agreement of the International Bank for Reconstruction and Development, 22 July 1944 available at <http://web.worldbank.org>

25 S. Sinclair, 'World Bank Guarantees for Oil and Gas Projects', in The World Bank, *Natural Gas: Private Sector Participation and Market Development* (Washington, DC: The World Bank, 1999) 87.

26 H. Razavi, 'Oil and Gas Financing by the World Bank', *Energy Policy*, Vol. 23, No. 11 (1995) 1001.

27 H. Razavi, *Financing Energy Projects in Emerging Economies* (Tulsa, OK: PennWell Books, 1996) 35–36 (hereinafter Razavi, *Financing Energy Projects*). The term *force majeure*, meaning 'superior force', has developed into an international doctrine. In project financing, transaction documents ought to contain clauses which specify the events that excuse performance and the legal consequences of each event. These events are common in *force majeure* clauses and refer to specific risks – for instance, war, strikes, lockout, expropriation, requisition, confiscation or nationalisation, changes in law, etc. Cited in Nevitt & Fabozzi (n. 2 above) 25.

28 Ibid. at 35–6.

29 Low-income countries are states with annual per capita income of $1,006 or less. See World Bank's income group assessment, available at <www.worldbank.org/en/country/mic/overview>

30 IDA website, available at <http://ida.worldbank.org/about/what-ida>

are also members of the World Bank. While the IBRD targets middle-income[31] countries and assesses their creditworthiness, the IDA does not consider the creditworthiness of states. Since the IDA does not borrow funds on the credit markets, the organisation does not adopt interest rates on its borrowing charges, whereas the IBRD does.[32] The IDA is regarded as the soft lending window of the World Bank, while IBRD is considered to be the hard lending window.[33]

International Financial Corporation (IFC)

The IFC is a member of the World Bank Group, focused exclusively on the promotion of private sector investment in developing countries. The institution was established in Washington in 1956 and currently has 184 member countries around the world.[34] The objective of the IFC is not merely to support the private projects in which it is involved, but also to attract foreign investment and finance. In contrast to the Word Bank, which supplies capital to host governments, the IFC provides loans to private companies and will not accept repayment from the government of a host state.[35]

Furthermore, the IFC has two different types of loans, A and B. While the former is financed through the IFC's own funds, the latter is financed by external funds. The type B loan offers commercial banks and other financial institutions the opportunity to take part in an investment project financed by the IFC. Unlike the World Bank, which provides guarantees to investors to stimulate the economy of its client country, the IFC does not provide direct protection against political risks to its type B loan syndicate banks.

These loans play a key role in the IFC's effort to mobilize cross-border funding for private sector investment in developing states.[36] The IFC's direct support is significantly improved through its syndication of commercial banks loans. According to Ochieze:

> [A] syndicate of banks should be chosen from as wide a range of countries as possible, to discourage the host government from taking action to expropriate or otherwise interfere with the project and thus jeopardise its economic relations with these countries.[37]

31 According to World Bank's income group assessment, middle-income countries are states with annual per capita income $3,956–$12,235. Available at <www.worldbank.org/en/country/mic/overview>
32 S. L. Hoffman, *The Law and Business of International Project Finance*, 3rd edn (Cambridge: Cambridge University Press, 2008) 260.
33 W. R. Cline & N. P. Sargen, 'Performance Criteria and Multilateral Aid Allocation', *World Development*, Vol. 3, No. 6 (1975) 383–91.
34 For further information, see <www1.ifc.org>
35 Razavi, *Financing Energy Projects* (n. 27 above) 44.
36 International Finance Corporation, Partnering with IFC Syndication: access, cooperation and risk mitigation, available at <www1.ifc.org>
37 C. Ochieze, 'Lender Liability: "To what extent can a lender protect itself?"', CELMP Annual Review, February 2007 available at <www.dundee.ac.uk>

The IFC enjoys special privileges: it is 'exempt from payments from local taxes; its loans have never been rescheduled for political risk; it has access to high-level policymakers and so on'.[38] When it syndicates the loan, the IFC is the lender of record and brings commercial banks under its own 'umbrella'. Hence, the commercial bank loans are treated in the same way as the IFC's loan.[39] Indeed, the IFC takes responsibility for administering the loans and collecting payments from borrowers.[40] IFC also takes the responsibility for appraising the project and coordinating the preparation of the legal and contractual package. With the IFC taking all the lead responsibilities, commercial banks find it more convenient and secure to participate in financing projects in developing countries.[41]

Multinational Investment Guarantee Agency (MIGA)

MIGA is another member institution of the World Bank Group. MIGA has its headquarters in Washington, DC, and operates as an independent international institution with 'full juridical personality'[42] under the umbrella of international law and the domestic laws of its member countries.[43] It was established in 1988 and currently has 179 member states. In June 1988, MIGA defined its Operational Regulations.[44] These serve to set out the main principles 'as to the nature and type of political risk guarantees that MIGA may issue, the eligible investors and investments that may obtain such guarantees, and the basic terms and conditions that must be included in MIGA guarantee contracts'.[45] The objective of the organisation is to promote and encourage private investment in emerging economies. In order to fulfil its mission, the organisation provides investment guarantees against political risks to alien investors and lenders.[46] The political insurance scheme covers five non-commercial areas: (i) currency inconvertibility and transfer restriction; (ii) expropriation; (iii) war and civil disturbances; (iv) breach of contract violation through host government's intervention; and (v) non-honouring of state financial obligations.

38 Razavi, *Financing Energy Projects* (n. 27 above) 44.
39 M. H. Bouchet, E. Clark & B. Groslambert, *Country Risk Assessment: Guide to Global Investment Strategy* (Chichester: John Wiley & Sons, 2003) 203.
40 Razavi, *Financing Energy Projects* (n. 27 above) 44.
41 Ibid.
42 MIGA Convention, Article 1. Convention Multilateral Investment Guarantee Agency, opened for signature 11 October 1985, 24 I.L.M. 1985 (entered into force 12 April 1988).
43 J. W. Salacuse, *The Three Laws of International Investment: National, Contractual, and International Frameworks for Foreign Capital* (Oxford: Oxford University Press, 2013) 266.
44 Operational Regulations of the Multilateral Guarantee Investment Agency, 22 June 1988 (As amended by the Board of Directors 2012) 1227, available at < www.miga.org/documents/Operations-Regulations.pdf>
45 Salacuse, (n. 43 above) 266.
46 MIGA's website: <www.miga.org/investmentguarantees/index.cfm>

Export credit agencies (ECAs)

Nowadays, almost every industrialised state has at least one official export credit agency. However, many developed countries around the world boast two agencies: one for finance and one for guarantees and insurance.[47] ECAs and investment insurance agencies (IIAs) are both referred to as ECAs; they provide government-backed loans guarantees and insurance to support corporations seeking business opportunities in less developed states and emerging markets. ECAs typically supply short-term trade financing, medium-term financing for capital goods, and insurance or guarantees against political risk for export transactions and long-term investments.[48] Such insurance or guarantees may cover either or both commercial and political risk. For instance, if the SPV, established in the host state, imports installations or equipment that are indispensable to construct and run the project, most ECAs are willing to provide political risk coverage, total coverage or direct loans to exporting companies operating in their home country.[49] It should be noted that all major ECAs as well as MIGAs and other private insurers are members of the Berne Union (International Union of Credit and Investment Insurers). The main role and purpose of the Berne Union is to 'work to facilitate cross-border trade by helping exporters mitigate risks through promoting internationally acceptable principles of export credit financing, strengthen the global financial structure, and facilitate foreign investments'.[50]

Bilateral agencies

Bilateral agencies are the third type of official agencies that play an active part in project finance transactions. Most bilateral institutions were established to promote international economic development through loans, guarantees, equity investments and, in some cases, political risk insurance. According to Sheppard, bilateral agencies are a more heterogeneous group than MDBs or ECAs because they cannot be restricted to a single category.[51] For instance, the US finance development institution known as the Overseas Private Investment Corporation (OPIC) is broadly known for its political risk insurance programme which offers cover against certain political risks, including inconvertibility, expropriation and political violence. In addition to its political insurance programme, the organisation also provides project finance on a limited recourse basis for private investment projects through direct loans and loan guarantees.[52]

47 E. D. Gianturco, *Export Credit Agencies: The Unsung Giants of International Trade and Finance* (Westport, CT: Quorum Books, 2001) 63.

48 Sheppard (n. 19 above) 82.

49 S. Gatti, *Project Finance in Theory and Practice: Designing, Structuring and Financing Private and Public Projects*, 2nd edn (Waltham, MA: Academic Press, 2012) 206.

50 J. K. Jackson, 'The Berne Union: An Overview', Congressional Research Service Report (April 2013) 2, available at <www.fas.org/sgp/crs/row/RS22319.pdf>

51 Sheppard (n. 19 above) 82.

52 Hoffman (n. 32 above) 298.

Commercial banks

Commercial banks are also among the most significant players in project finance transactions. A loan may be granted through the domestic commercial bank of the country where the project is to be undertaken or through international commercial banks. Obtaining a grant from a domestic bank may be advantageous for project sponsors because of the bank's knowledge of local law and 'customs as well as the ability to offer loans in the local currency'.[53] It should, however, be noted that some developing countries' domestic bank markets may not be sufficiently developed to provide the capital required for a long-term investment project.[54] Furthermore, the attractiveness of commercial banks for investors in project finance is perhaps the flexible terms they offer to investors on the repayment of loan. A loan granted by an international commercial bank usually has a specific period within which it is repayable in accordance with a pre-arranged reimbursement schedule.

Notably, this specific-term loan includes flexibility 'as to when repayments will begin, when the loan will be repaid, in equal or variable payments over time and the frequency of interest payments in order to align the project's projected revenue streams and operating costs with the borrower's repayment obligations'.[55] In the energy sector, the participation of international commercial banks consists in their provision of syndicated loans. As mentioned above, the IFC and some MDBs have a sizeable remit in putting together syndicated loans for developing countries. According to Razavi, the IFC's participation offers international commercial banks convenience and reassurance as follows: the IFC (i) handles all the technical and legal matters including risk mitigation measures; (ii) ensures that a default on repayment to any of the participating banks will be viewed as a default on the entire syndicated loan and therefore a default on repayment of the IFC loan; and (iii) is responsible for administration of the syndicated loan and all matters related to the disbursement and repayment of the loans.[56]

The role of lenders in inclusion of stabilisation clauses

As touched upon in the Introduction, the political and social stability of a host state is undoubtedly the most significant concern for investors and lenders. No matter within which jurisdiction the project is located, the laws and regulations of the host country have the potential to affect every aspect of the project company's activities.[57] While legal issues are one of the potential problem areas that lenders will take into account, there are other significant factors to take into consideration

53 D. Nordstrom, S. Dickens, M. Brown & K. Stirling, 'Multisource Project Financing', Chapter 4 in R. Morrison (ed.), *The Principles of Project Finance* (Farnham: Gower Publishing, 2012) 40.

54 Ibid.

55 Ibid.

56 Razavi, *Financing Energy Projects* (n. 27 above) 98.

57 Dewar (n. 6 above) 7.

which may be technical or environmental in nature. The following section explores these non-commercial considerations.

Host government policy: There is no doubt that, in the interests of the sustainability of the project, the lender will wish to have made a thorough assessment of the following: the interest/or intention of the host country regarding the project, the host state's investment policy and the long-term viability of host government policy. Host government policy must be deemed to be in harmony with the interests of project sustainability, and the host state will be expected to clearly state its intentions in a way that is not easily open to misinterpretation or misunderstanding. Most importantly of all, host state policy must be stable, and supported by immutable sources of law. From the lender's perspective, this requirement is easily comprehensible, as naturally a lender will wish to have clear agreement on in exactly what circumstance 'the project company will bear the risk of the host country government changing policy and interfering with the success of the project'.[58]

Permitting: Operation of an investment project necessitates the authorisation of a wide range of permits and consents to the project company. Such permits and approvals need to be in place in order for the project sponsor to develop, construct, start up and operate the project. In the absence of these permits and approvals, 'the project would be unfinanceable because it would exist in a state of uncertainty, subject to potential unacceptable changes'.[59] The project finance lender will monitor whether the permit is issued and the consents have been given or will be given in the ordinary course without undue expense, delay or conditionally.[60]

Nationalisation and expropriation: As discussed previously, sovereign power allows the right to expropriate or nationalise private property of an alien investor registered or located in its boundaries as long as the eminent domain pays timely compensation to investors in accordance with all necessary requirements under international law. Implementation of specific legislation creates a secure investment environment and trusted guarantees. Lenders wish to be reassured that if direct or indirect expropriation or nationalisation does occur, a substantial sum will be offered in compensation to the project company.

Change in law: It is a fact that the repayment of loans granted for a specific project may span decades. During this repayment period, a project may be exposed to risks in the form of changes in law, as a result of government change or a change in political regime. According to Delmon:

> [O]ne of the most significant risks posed by a change in law is the modification of performance requirements, including output and environmental requirements during the concession period, increasing the cost of output and

58 J. Delmon, *Private Sector Investment in Infrastructure: Project Finance, PPP Projects and Risks*, 2nd edn (Alphen aan den Rijn: Wolters Kluwer, 2009) 136.
59 Hoffman (n. 32 above) 375.
60 Dewar (n. 6 above) 10.

> potentially having a negative impact on productivity. Such changes may have a substantial impact on the profitability of the project.[61]

As this kind of change may pose a threat to the economic health of the project, most host states, particularly developing countries, agree to freeze the application of laws to the project company through stabilisation clauses. If any changes are made by the government in violation of such stabilisation clause, compensation must be paid to the investor.

Environmental and social considerations: Environmental and social issues are the other significant concerns that lenders take into account before investing capital in a specific project, for the simple reason that these can also have a direct impact on the loan repayment. This means that if the environmental and social risk of a project is high, lenders may not leap at the prospect of financing the project. Consequently, environmental and social risk assessments are required by lenders for almost all energy investment projects. The question of what lenders require of a project company for projects that are deemed to be exposed to high environmental or social risk is answered by Dewar. According to the author, project finance lenders will generally

> require as a minimum, the project company to undertake to comply with all environmental and social laws and regulations binding it. The lenders will also likely require the development of, and compliance with, an agreed environmental and social risk management plan. This is both to insulate the project company, and the lenders, from legal risk but also to preserve the lenders' reputation as responsible parties.[62]

Political risk insurance providers

Traditionally, the risk that international investors faced over the course of the project was divided into the following two categories by business analysts: commercial risk and political risk. Commercial risk includes more regular economic activity such as 'fluctuations in commodity price, the failure of a new technology to perform as expected, or the advent of a new competing product that makes the investor's product obsolete'.[63] Political risk cover provides for political risk that emerges due to a host country's adverse action or inaction. The concept of political risk includes, for instance, currency convertibility and transfer restriction, expropriation, civil unrest, war and terrorism, breach of contract and non-honouring of sovereign financial obligations.

Accordingly, political risk insurance is a contractual agreement between an investor and an insurer to compensate the investor's financial loss by reason of the host country's adverse action or inaction, such as expropriation or war and terrorism. Political risk insurance, which emerged in the aftermath of the Second

61 Delmon (n. 58 above) 136.
62 Dewar (n. 6 above) 13.
63 Salacuse (n. 43. above) 245.

World War, was developed primarily by governments and governmental agencies in capital-exporting countries to motivate their entrepreneurs to invest in foreign countries around the world. Most of the OECD member states as well as non-member countries of this organisation have national agencies that supply their domestic firms with export credit and political risk insurance. The national political risk insurance providers comprise of national (ECAs) and investment insurance entities which focus on cross-border investment. The next section addresses political risk insurance through government agencies.

National political risk Insurance providers

Several capital-exporting countries have formed government corporations that have in turn become global providers of political risk insurance. OPIC, founded in 1971, is a prime example. This organisation's primary goal was to stimulate US investment into developing countries, through the provision of political risk insurance and project finance.[64] According to OPIC's 2017 annual report, investment across 80 new projects was committed in 2016 in low- and middle-income countries, located in a variety of different regions around the world.[65] It is expected that these projects would create over 10,000 job opportunities and support $4.5 billion worth of procurement of goods and services.[66] OPIC provides the following services to these projects: project finance in the form of direct loans and loan guarantees; insurance against a broad range of political risks, such as war, coups, expropriation (including creeping expropriation), nationalisation, revolution, currency inconvertibility and political violence and terrorism.[67]

Several other developed countries also have their own export credit agencies with similar insurance programmes and also actively promote investment abroad. These include Japan's Bank for International Cooperation, Germany's Hermes Kreditversicherung AG, France's Compagnie Française d'Assurance pour le Commerce Extérieur, and Export Development Corporation of Canada. In parallel to these export credit agencies, MIGA also provides insurance to international investors. However, what differentiates MIGA from these national export credit agencies is that MIGA is an internationally based investment insurance company.

Private political risk insurance

Political risk insurance is also provided through private insurance companies. The largest private political risk insurer in the US is the American International Group

64 A. Van de Putte, D. F. Gates & K. Holder, 'Political Risk Insurance as an Instrument to Reduce Oil and Gas Investment Risk and Manage Investment Returns', *Journal of World Energy Law and Business*, Vol. 5, No. 4 (2012) 291.

65 Overseas Private Investment Corporation, 'Annual Report on Development Impact: Fiscal Year 2016', (2017) 5, available at <www.opic.gov/sites/default/files/files/FY16_Annual_Development_Report_Final.pdf>

66 Ibid.

67 See the official website of the OPIC, available at <www.opic.gov>

(AIG). Other significant political risk insurers in the private market include: Lloyd's of London, Aon, Sovereign Risk Insurance Ltd, Zurich Emerging Market Solutions, and Export Insurance Company. These organisations provide political risk insurance coverage against currency inconvertibility and transfer restriction; confiscation, expropriation, nationalisation; political violence; default on obligations such as loans, arbitral claims and contracts. Over recent years, the insurance market has grown rapidly due to a mushrooming of the number of private insurers offering political risk coverage. The entrance of these private insurers into the market has created an environment of considerable competitive intensity, with national insurance providers and private corporations vying to offer coverage for the most attractive investment projects.

Risk premium calculation

The concept of risk premium calculation is a 'function that takes as an argument a risk and returns the premium that should be charged for it'.[68] In the current political risk insurance market, every risk insurance provider applies a different methodology to quantify the risk premium to be applied. The question is which method they use and how they calculate risk premium. It goes without saying that political risk is dynamic and a complex issue. For this reason it is difficult apply the same principles and weighting to every type of political risk. According to Rolfini and Paciotti:

> [Some political risk insurance providers] simply use the OECD categories to apply a fixed premium rate depending on the risk category. Some other political risk insurers have a flat premium rate, relying on the existence of a BIT agreement and not reflecting the actual level of risk faced by the guarantee holder.[69]

Technically, political risk insurers establish a scoring system and categorise every country in terms of political risk and allocate a premium rate to every risk group.[70] In the calculation of the risk premium, a cap and floor are assigned in terms of basis points for each scoring.[71] It should be noted that 'within every premium range the final rate can be increased or decreased according to variables such as: a) type of investment b) size of the investment c) tenor of the investment d) exposure and level of portfolio concentration in the host country'.[72]

68 A. Tsanakas & E. Desli, 'Measurement and Pricing of Risk in Insurance Markets', *Risk Analysis*, Vol. 25, No. 6 (2005) 1654.

69 R. Rolfini & S. Paciotti, 'Political Risk Insurance: A Technical Approach', SACE Working Paper No. 14 (November 2010) 21, available at <www.globalexport.it/GestDb/Pub/Upload/Pub911.pdf>

70 Ibid.

71 Ibid.

72 Ibid.

The role of political risk insurance providers in the inclusion of stabilisation clauses

To attract foreign investors, most states, particularly developing countries, are willing to accept stabilisation clauses when they enter into a contractual relationship with a project sponsor (investor). Furthermore, there is no hindrance inherent in such a clause to states exercising their sovereignty or protecting public interest by passing new laws and regulations during the course of the project. For this reason, political risk insurance providers will not insure losses incurred by investors as a result of such changes, as these sovereign rights are recognised in international law. Jenney notes that political risk insurers have always been disposed to cover unlawful regulatory takings of a host state, but categorically exclude legitimate takings.[73] In some cases, particularly in the context of expropriation claims, 'it may be necessary to make use of contractual dispute resolution mechanisms to benefit from insurance protection due to the requirement that covered investors take all reasonable measures to prevent expropriation action'.[74] According to Hoffman, political risk insurers may provide cover against the risk that stabilisation clauses are rejected or revoked, via arbitral award default coverage.[75]

Similarly, Jenney suggests that political risk insurers

> could provide arbitral award default coverage of contractual stabilisation clauses. For political risk insurers, international arbitration also serves to sort out the political actions of the host government from its legitimate contractual claims. Arbitral panels can sort out fact-specific questions with respect to regulation, including in connection with investment agreements containing stabilisation clauses protecting against the effects of regulatory changes.[76]

It should be noted that arbitral award default coverage of stabilisation clauses is designed to protect the insured assets of an agreement with inbuilt international arbitration mechanisms.[77] If the arbitral court's decision favours the investor, the failure of the contracting state to make the awarded payments will trigger the insurance cover concerned.[78] In other words, a political risk insurer who pays an expropriation claim must in turn lodge a corresponding claim against the host government to recover its debt.[79]

73 F. E. Jenney, 'A Sword in a Stone: Problems (and a Few Proposed Solutions) Regarding Political Risk Insurance Coverage of Regulatory Takings', in T. H. Moran, G. T. West & K. Martin, *Political Risk Management: Needs of the Present Challenges for the Future* (Washington, DC: The World Bank Group, 2008) 178–9.
74 Dewar (n. 6 above) 97.
75 Hoffman (n. 32 above) 70.
76 Jenney (n. 73 above) 113.
77 R. Kazimova, 'Insurance as a Risk Management Tool: A Mitigating or Aggravating Factor?' Chapter 9 in Leader and Ong (n. 11 above) 259.
78 Ibid. at 260.
79 Jenney (n. 73 above) 182.

This means that if the contract contains stabilisation clauses and the government forges ahead with a change of law and neglects to pay compensation, political risk insurers may foot the bill initially, but will make sure that the government ultimately pays for its unlawful actions.[80] By seeking reimbursement, political risk insurers simply aim to balance their books, but some attention should be given to what compels host governments to compensate them. An examination of the legal standing of public or private insurance companies in reimbursement claims and the extent of insurers influence on arbitration panels will contribute to a better understanding of this.

Subrogation rights: The doctrine of subrogation means that 'when one has been compelled to pay a debt which should have been paid by another, he is entitled to a cession of all the remedies which the creditor possessed against that other'.[81] This right derives from the indemnity doctrine and refers to the right of an insurer, who has paid the loss, to pursue the wrongdoer on behalf of the insured party.[82] While the existence of this entitlement establishes the legal grounds on which insurers may seek reparation for the capital that they have paid to investors as a result of their loss, the question remains: if the host government makes changes in law in the name of public interest, will the government still be obliged to pay compensate the insurer?

Kazimova expands upon this problem:

> What started as a good intention, though, turned out not to be so good, as what insurers, being shielded by subrogation rights, effectively did was introduce incentives for themselves to compensate easily for losses of investors even when host governments initiate changes in law for a public purpose.[83]

Foreign investors who are concerned about political risk in a host country can purchase insurance through public and private organisations. It is insurance agencies in the public sector that wield the most power over host governments via their influence in investment insurance decisions at arbitral tribunals.[84]

The decision in the investment arbitration case *Enron Corporation and Ponderosa Assets v Argentina*[85] illustrates this point. In *Enron*, the investor relied on a prior claims determination made by OPIC establishing that an expropriation had occurred.[86] Nevertheless, the *Enron* arbitral tribunal rejected

80 Kazimova (n. 77 above) 260.
81 H. N. Sheldon, *Law of Subrogation* (Washington, DC: Beard Books, 2000) 10.
82 Kazimova (n. 77 above) 260.
83 Ibid. at 261.
84 M. Kantor, M. D. Nolan & K. P. Sauvant, *Reports of Overseas Private Investment Corporation Determinations*, Vol. 1 (Oxford: Oxford University Press, 2011) xxiii.
85 *Enron Corporation and Ponderosa v Argentina*, Award, ICSID Case No. ARB/01/3 (2007); see also *Generation Ukraine, Inc. v Ukraine*, Award, ICSID Case No. ARB/00/9 (2003).
86 *Enron Corporation and Ponderosa v Argentina*, Award, at 235; see also Kantor, Nolan & Sauvant (n. 84 above) xxiii.

the OPIC determination as influential authority on the question of whether an expropriation had taken place, noting that the OPIC determination 'responds to a different kind of procedure and context that cannot influence or be taken into account in this arbitration'.[87] While the investment tribunal declined the investor's claim in this case, the Enron tribunal, however, decided that Argentina had violated its treaty obligations to supply Enron fair and equitable treatment.[88]

ECAs support their own nationals by providing finance and political risk insurance when they invest in a foreign country. The major issue is that whenever the host state takes forward administrative measures, the claim is conveyed by the investor to a dispute settlement process before a determination is made about whether the actions of the host government breach stabilisation clauses or not. Claims submitted by investors are invariably accepted by political risk insurers and compensation is paid to them. Admittedly, in an environment where such bias exists, objectivity about the rightfulness of a claim is difficult to achieve.

Credit rating agencies

Several credit rating agencies, including Standard & Poor's (S&P), Moody's and Fitch, play a significant role in financial markets. They analyse and evaluate the default risk of lending to corporate and sovereign borrowers.[89] Conducting assessments of debt ratings is traditionally within the scope of the rating agencies.

> Credit ratings are carried out for debt issues and take into account the borrower's default risk, the nature of the debt obligation, the protection that the issue affords of the debt obligation, the projection that the issue affords, and its relative position in bankruptcy.[90]

Furthermore, ratings are also available for project-specific financing. Rating for a specific project financing is relatively new but is a rapidly growing area.[91] Project ratings are provided by the rating agencies with the aim of assessing and expressing as a value the level of certainty with which the project finance lenders can expect to obtain timely reimbursement of principle and payment of interest, in accordance with the project terms.[92] This type of rating mainly concentrates on the capability of the financing entity, whether a developer or SPV, to make timely

87 Ibid. at 247.
88 Ibid. at 268.
89 M. Elkhoury, 'Credit Rating Agencies and Their Potential Impact on Developing Countries', United Nations Conference on Trade and Development, Discussion Paper No. 186 (January 2008) 1.
90 Razavi, *Financing Energy Projects* (n. 27 above) 104–5.
91 Ibid.
92 S. Thompson, 'Credit Rating and project Finance Default: An Important Risk Management Instrument', *Public Infrastructure Bulletin*, Vol. 1, No. 8 (2012) 2, available at <http://epublications.bond.edu.au/pib/vol1/iss8/10>

repayment of principle and interest to bondholders.[93] Previously, rating agencies delivered their own verdict on the debt rating for a specific project; in doing so they took into consideration the following factors.

(a) Sovereign risk analysis: In sovereign risk analysis, the main consideration is usually the stability of the foreign currency of the state where the project will be executed. The government of a host state can pose a number of risks to an international project. For instance, 'it could restrict the project's ability to meet its debt obligations by way of currency restrictions; it could interfere with project operations; and, in extreme cases, even nationalise the project'.[94]

(b) Currency risk analysis: In this type of analysis, agencies concentrate on the potential for currency depreciation, as this is particularly vital in a project that cannot adjust revenues to offset exchange rate changes.[95]

(c) Political risk analysis: The laws and regulations of the country where the project will be undertaken are also investigated as part of the credit rating process.[96] A stable legal system is a powerful bargaining chip in proving to project creditors that a host country is willing and able to provide a stable and secure environment for a project.

(d) Legal (contract) risk analysis: The legal structure of the project itself is a key area of focus for a rating agency during the assessment process. According to Thompson, 'structural features that are often assessed in this regard include, but are not limited to: the choice of law of the contract documents, and thus legal jurisdiction, documentation risk and international credit arrangements'.[97]

As mentioned above, credit sovereign rating is an activity owned by rating agencies. The main users of country sovereign risk rating are international investors and, more precisely, financial institutions. Broadly speaking, they consider: 'the overall economy of a country, which includes the balance of payments, foreign debt, foreign investment, public and private investment, and foreign currency reserve, development of financial markets and capital market transparency, political stability'.[98] During the determination process, rating agencies apply both qualitative and quantitative methods to understand the economic and political dynamics of the country[99] – for instance, whether the state has a high, low or middle income and how stable the political institutions in that country are, on the whole, when all of the political and economic components of the assessment are taken into consideration. Consequently, it can be said that sovereign credit rating assists investors, particularly foreign institutional investors and those proposing foreign

93 Ibid.
94 'Standard & Poor's Rating Direct: Updated Project Finance Summary Debt Rating Criteria', September (2007) 14, available at <www.maalot.co.il/publications/MT20120529105458.pdf>
95 Ibid.
96 Ibid.
97 Thompson (n. 92 above) 2.
98 T. Siddaiah, *Financial Services* (New Delhi: Pearson, 2011) 258.
99 M. Frenkel & A. Karmann, *Sovereign Risk and Financial Crises* (Heidelberg: Springer, 2004) 91.

direct investment, in gaining a comprehensive oversight as well as specific insights into the financial, legal and political structure and wellbeing of the country to which it is contemplating committing its investment. Perhaps even more crucially, it can aid an investor to foresee, mitigate or avoid risks inherent in the financial, legal and political makeup of the potential recipient of its investment and the project proposed.

In sovereign credit rating, two types of risk are assessed by the agencies: *country risk* and *sovereign risk*. While country risk is a risk triggered by actions in a specific country, which are to some extent within the control of the government concerned, sovereign risk is the risk of providing a loan specifically to the government of a particular state.[100] It is worth noting that the two risks often have strong correlations and therefore they may be referenced interchangeably.[101] Sovereign rating is an opportunity for many developing states to attract foreign investors to their countries and to demonstrate attractive qualities such as the transparency of their financial system and how accountable their political institutions are the country is accountable. Therefore, the notes provided by these agencies (S&P, Moody's, Fitch, etc.) have a direct influence on the flow of foreign investment to these countries.

The role of credit rating providers in the inclusion of stabilisation clauses

Taking the information provided above into account, it can generally be stated that credit rating agencies' assessments are available for large corporations (companies) or for a specific project financing. The ratings are also available for countries to demonstrate their ability and keenness to service their debts. The notifications made by the rating agencies play a persuasive and influential role in the decision of lenders to provide funds to the project and also play a definitive role in the terms and conditions of the investment contract. However, that does not mean that rating agencies have the ability to provide guarantees to lenders that a host government will always be loyal and adhere to its stabilisation commitments when political and economic or even social circumstances are in flux.

Baku–Tbilisi–Ceyhan pipeline project (II)

The BTC pipeline project is a 1,768 km oil pipeline that unites the Caspian Sea and the Mediterranean. This major pipeline carries oil from Baku in Azerbaijan, via Tbilisi in Georgia, to the port of Ceyhan on the Turkish coast of the Mediterranean. The transferral of oil from Baku, shipped by tankers in Turkey to European consumers is one of the main purposes of this project. The scope of the BTC project can also be seen as part of a broader international attempt to establish alternative oil routes and lessen the reliance on oils from the Middle East and

100 Siddaiah (n. 98 above) 258.
101 Ibid.

Russia.[102] The project transports more than a million barrels of oil per day from the Azeri–Chirag–Gunashli fields in the Caspian Sea. The project is recognised as the largest and most difficult cross-border infrastructure project ever undertaken by the project finance community.[103] This pipeline project demonstrates the unique policies of landlocked energy exporters, the quest for exporters to choose appropriate transit countries, and the nexus of political and economic interests in the establishment of major multiple-state energy export projects.[104] The BTC's crude oil pipelines traverse three sovereign states; this necessitates a complex legal framework and extensive coordination. Nevertheless, the project constitutes the single largest FDI in each of its signatory countries.[105] A breakdown of the stakeholders[106] and their interests in this project is helpful to an understanding of the scale and reach of this project.

British Petroleum (BP): This company is the owner and largest shareholder with a 30.1% interest in the project. The role of the company in the project is to take crude oil from a landlocked area in the Caspian Sea in Central Asia and transfer it to the Mediterranean. As well as having the biggest share in the project, it is fair to say that BP is the most powerful stakeholder in the project.

IFC and other stakeholders: Financing cross-border pipeline projects is not a straightforward undertaking as each participant naturally has different interests and expectations from the transaction. According to Dufey and Kazimova:

> The complexity of risk allocation linked to project finance implies that developing countries rarely have an unlimited ability to accept allocation of risk, so they have secure their positions with credible assets and/or payment guarantees from other parties.[107]

102 B. Shaffer, 'From Pipedream to Pipeline: A Caspian Success Story', *Current History*, Vol. 104, No. 684 (2005) 343–6, available at <www.belfercenter.org/sites/default/files/files/publication/shaffercurrenthistoryoct2005.pdf>

103 J. Watkins, 'BTC – Reaching First Drawdown', BTC features', *Project Finance International*, Vol. 298 (2004) 48; see also Inkpen & Moffett (n. 1 above) 411.

104 B. Shaffer, *Energy Politics* (Philadelphia: University of Pennsylvania Publishing, 2009) 54.

105 D. Blatchford, 'Environmental and Social Aspects of the Baku–Tbilisi–Ceyhan Pipeline', Chapter 7 in S. F. Starr & S. E. Cornell (eds), *Baku–Tbilisi–Ceyhan Pipeline: Oil Window to the West* (Washington, DC: Central Asia-Caucasus Institute & Silk Road Studies Program, 2005) 119, available at <www.silkroadstudies.org>

106 British Petroleum (BP): 30.10; SOCAR: 25.00; Unocal Ltd: 8.90; Statoil: 8.71; TPAO: 6.53; ENI: 5.00; Total: 5.00; Itochu: 3.40; Inpex: 2.50; ConocoPhillips: 2.50; Hess Corporation: 2.36. It should be noted that as a shareholder of the project, Amerada Hess announced on 7 September 2012 that the company sold its stake to ONGC Videsh Ltd (OVL), an Indian state-owned company. For further detail, see Oil and Gas Online Journal, <www.ogj.com/articles/2012/09/hess-to-sell-interests-in-acg-fields-btc-line-to-ongc-for-1-billion.html>

107 A. Dufey & R. Kazimova, 'Baku–Tbilisi–Ceyhan Project: Implications of Project Finance', Chapter 12 in Leader and Ong (n. 11 above) 373.

In cross-boundary projects of this scale, it is necessary to involve multilateral financial institutions such as the IFC and ECAs.[108] Since the advent of the financial crisis, the role played by financial institutions has become even more fundamental.[109] Financing projects without consortium participation, support from financial institutions and support from developed countries (for instance, the US) would be complex to say the least and perhaps even impossible.

In the late 1990s, commercial studies and diplomatic initiatives were set in motion to attempt to uncover the energy transportation challenges and difficulties of the Caspian region.[110] BP and its partners formed a working group to assess export routes for the extracted crude oil from the Azeri–Chirag–Gunashli field under the Caspian Sea. Based on their findings, the working group concluded that carrying Caspian crude oil by pipeline would be the most economically efficient way of transporting oil from the Caspian region to Europe and the United States. Ilham Shaban, an oil analyst, stated that 'the pipeline is of strategic importance not only to Azerbaijan, but to the other new independent states as well. This is a reliable route to world markets.'[111]

An intergovernmental agreement was signed between Azerbaijan, Georgia and Turkey, in Istanbul, in November 1999, to legitimise the international scope of the BTC pipeline project. In October 2000, BP and its BTC partner companies also committed to host government agreements with these three states. In July 2001, the investment bank Lazard Brothers, incorporated in the UK, was selected by BP to advise on the most convenient financing structure for the BTC project. The BP also assigned an American law firm, Sullivan & Cromwell, to deal with the legal side of the financing structure. In August 2002, the BTC sponsor groups signed the required agreements in London to officially form the BTC Company. As the project costs amounted to billions of dollars, the BTC Company approached a wide range of financial institutions to seek capital loans.

In December 2002, BP announced that finding a loan for the project might be delayed by at least six months due to ongoing negotiations with lenders, as a number of concerns had been voiced of both a social and environmental nature, as well as expression of some doubt regarding the validity of the predicted economic returns of the project. In 2003, the BTC project consortium officially approached the IFC and the EBRD with the hope of thereby obtaining the sought-for project loan. The loan in question was approved in the same year after a series of complex talks and negotiations. Financing agreements were finally signed by the IFC, the EBRD and the BTC lender group on 3 February 2004.[112]

108 Hoffman (n. 32 above) 256.

109 Thomson Reuters, 'Back in the Funding Mix: Multilaterals Report 2009', *Project Finance International*, cited in Dufey & Kazimova (n. 107 above) 373.

110 J. Elkind, 'Economic Implications of the Baku–Tbilisi–Ceyhan Pipeline', Chapter 3 in Starr & Cornell (n. above 105) 116.

111 Ilham Shabani, BBC News, 'Caspian Pipeline Dream Becomes Reality', 17 September 2002, available at <http://news.bbc.co.uk/1/hi/world/europe/2263611.stm>

112 For further information, see the official website of BP, available at <www.bp.com/genericarticle.do?categoryId=2012968&contentId=2016340>

The financing package agreed and signed by the parties includes 208 finance documents, with over 17,000 signatures from 78 different parties. In addition, it represents a major milestone in the establishment of financing arrangements for this major cross-boundary pipeline project. The financial providers who supplied loans, export credits and risk insurance to BTC comprise of:[113]

- multilateral lending agencies: the IFC and the EBRD;
- ECAs and political risk insurers from seven different states: the Japan Bank for International Cooperation (JBIC), Nippon Export and Investment Insurance (NEXI-Japan), the Export Import Bank of the United States of America (US Ex-Im), the Export Credit Guarantee Department (ECGD-UK), the Overseas Private Investment Corporation (OPIC-USA), Compagnie Française pour le Commerce Extérieur (COFACE-France), Euler Hermes Kreditversicherung AG (HERMES-Germany) and SACE SpA-Servizi Assicurativi del Commercio Estero (SACE-Italy);
- a syndicate of 15 commercial banks led by ABN AMRO (leading institution) Citibank, Mizuho and Société Générale with Banka Intesa, BNP Paribas, Crédit Agricole Indosuez,[114] Dexia, HypoVereinsbank, ING, KBC, Nateix Banques Populaires, San Paolo IMI, WestLB and Royal Bank of Scotland;
- loans provided by BP, Statoil, Total and ConocoPhillips as senior sponsor lenders.

The BTC major pipeline project was financed according to protocols of project finance structure. As mentioned earlier, the term 'project finance' is used to refer to a non-recourse or limited recourse financing structure, in which debt, equity and credit enhancement are combined for the construction and operation of the refinancing of a particular facility in a capital-intensive industry in which lenders base credit appraisals on the projected revenues from the operations of the facility, rather than the general assets or the credit of the sponsor of the facility, and rely on the assets of the facility, including any revenue-producing contracts and other cash flow generated by the facility, as collateral for the debt.[115] Taking this into consideration, the financing methods applied in the BTC project conform to the limited recourse project finance model. Dufey and Kazimova explain that:

> For sponsor guarantees to fall away, a number of specifications had to be met, one of which was pipeline operations. This relates to evidence that the BTC Co. could operate the pipeline to the planned capacity for a period of

113 Dufey & Kazimova (n. 107 above) 375.

114 Crédit Agricole Indosuez and Crédit Lyonnais merged and created Calyon on 30 April 2004. However, in February 2010 Calyon changed its organisational name to Crédit Agricole Corporate and Investment Bank (Crédit Agricole CIB). For further information, see the organisation's official website:<www.ca-cib.com>

115 S. L. Hoffman, 'A Practical Guide to Transactional Project Finance: Basic Concepts, Risk Identification, and Contractual Considerations', *The Business Lawyer*, Vol. 45, No. 1 (1989) 181.

> time, i.e., that the company could reach peak capacity. This extended further to whether the pipeline was complying with environmental and social standards, and that there were no material breaches of BTC Co. obligations. This was dealt with through environmental and social audits by lenders' consultants, which took place in May and June 2007, and the certification was completed after dealing with various issues that arose from that process in September of the year. Until then the lenders had recourse to the sponsors' assets. Thereafter, the loan became non-recourse.[116]

In BTC's financial arrangement, the financing debt package is $2.589 billion (up to a 12-year term). The debt package consists of US$500 million in A and B loans, provided equally by the IFC and the EBRD; a US$100 million OPIC-covered loan; a US$300 million JBIC overseas investment facility; and US$766 million in ECA-covered facilities. Of ECA guaranteed debt, US$180 million is covered by JBIC; US$120 million by NEXI; US$150 million by US Ex-Im; US $106 million by ECGD; US$90 million by each of COFACE and Hermes and US $30 million guaranteed by SACE.[117]

Azerbaijan

As an oil-producing country with a relatively small economy, the main objective of Azerbaijan was to be in a position to sell its oil reserves to the Western world. Broadly speaking, the overarching significance of the BTC project for Azerbaijan is its potential to 'decrease its dependence on Russia in terms of export routes for oil and gas as well as to build new economic political and security links with Turkey, Azerbaijan's ally, and subsequently with Western Europe'.[118] This view is supported by President Aliyev's words in his opening ceremony speech:

> I do not doubt that the BTC will be of use both to Azerbaijan and our neighbours. This pipeline will, first of all, help solve economic and social problems, but the role of the pipeline in strengthening peace and security in the region is also not small.[119]

Moreover, via this project the country expects to benefit from oil revenues over a 20-year period from the resources of the Azeri–Chirag–Gunesli offshore oilfield.

116 Dufey & Kazimova (n. 107 above) 375–6.
117 For further information about the financial arrangement of BTC, see R. Weston, 'The Project Financing of Cross-Border Pipelines', Presentation to the Energy Charter Workshop, Brussels (17 October 2006), slide no. 19, available at <https://energycharter.org/fileadmin/DocumentsMedia/Events/20061017-WORDITMAFCBP_RWeston.pdf >; Dufey & Kazimova (n. 107 above) 376.
118 S. E. Cornell & F. Ismailzade, 'The Baku–Tbilisi–Ceyhan: Implications for Azerbaijan', Chapter 4 in S Starr & Cornell (n.107 above) 63.
119 M. Tran, 'Caspian Oil Pipeline Opens', Wednesday 25 May 2005, *The Guardian*, available at <www.guardian.co.uk/business/2005/may/25/oilandpetrol.news1>

With SOCAR's 25% stake in BTC Co., the Azerbaijani government bears direct responsibility for ensuring the successive construction and operation of the pipeline; however, since its share in overall project cost responsibilities is 30%, Azerbaijan does not bear the full cost burden of the project alone.[120] The downside of this arrangement is that there is a limit to the extent to which it can exercise sovereign control over the project.[121]

Georgia

Despite being a country bereft of significant mineral resources, its auspicious geographical location rendered Georgia a beneficiary of the economic and political gains to be had from the BTC pipeline project. The government of Georgia adopted the BTC project as a country strategy with the stated goal of elevating the living standards of its people and thereby raising them from widespread poverty, while, from a strategic political perspective, improved relations with the United States and the protection this might afford from the Russian threat was a highly attractive by-product of Georgia's involvement in this project. In the same opening ceremony, echoing the words of Aliyev, President Mikheil Saarkashvili described the BTC project as a 'geopolitical victory' for Caspian Basin countries. He was alluding to the fact that securing independent energy export sources would allow both Georgia and Azerbaijan to defend themselves more effectively against geopolitical pressure previously aggressively asserted by Russia.[122]

Furthermore, Georgia is expected to receive US$62.55 million in transit fees,[123] to reflect its status as a transit country in the BTC project. Aside from this capacity, Georgia is not a BTC Co. contributor, and there is no evidence of Georgian influence in the rest of the financial package prepared for BTC project.[124] Moreover, since the country does not financially subsidise the construction, operation or maintenance of the BTC pipeline project, Georgia has an advantage in terms of bargaining power, since it is the only country that can grant the right of passage of the pipeline through Turkey. Naturally, this endowed the country with a strong bargaining position from which to re-negotiate transit fees on an annual basis to its advantage.

120 E. J. Omonbude, *Cross-border Oil and Gas Pipelines and the Role of the Transit Country: Economics, Challenges and Solutions* (Basingstoke: Palgrave Macmillan, 2013) 73.

121 Ibid.

122 T. Babali, 'Implications of The Baku–Tbilisi–Ceyhan Main Oil Pipeline Project', *Perceptions* (Winter 2005) 46, available at <http://sam.gov.tr/wp-content/uploads/2012/02/TuncayBabali.pdf>

123 V. Papava, 'The Baku–Tbilisi–Ceyhan Pipeline: Implications for Georgia', Chapter 5 in Starr & Cornell (n. 107 above) 87.

124 Omonbude (n. 120 above) 74.

Turkey

Turkey participated in the project through its state-owned oil company, Türkiye Petrolleri Anonim Ortakliği (TPAO). The aforesaid company is an equity participant of BTC Co. While Turkey has the role of transit company in common with Georgia, Turkey, unlike Georgia, bears some of the costs of the project and subsidises the construction, operation and maintenance of the pipeline. The BTC project has also had the added advantage of reducing oil tanker traffic on the Bosphorus, thereby conferring ecological side-benefits to the city of Istanbul and the surrounding area. Turkey placed more emphasis on the strategic importance of its participation in the project than any of the other participants. In fact, the direct economic benefit of the project was not even a topic of discussion during the initial negotiations between the parties.[125]

Equator Principles and the BTC project

The Equator Principles (EPs) are a 'risk management framework, adopted by financial institutions, for determining, assessing and managing environmental and social risk in investment projects and [are] primarily aimed to supply a minimum standard for due diligence to support responsible risk decision making'.[126] In other words, the EPs are simply a 'set of voluntary rules aimed at the development of socially responsible projects that reflect sound environmental management practice'.[127] In 2003, a group of ten large international institutions developed the EPs as a response to criticisms by NGOs regarding the human rights negligence and environmental damage that resulted from international projects during the 1990s. Currently, 93 financial institutions have adopted the EPs to date.[128] The BTC project was the first and best opportunity to test the EPs as the implementation of this major crude oil pipeline project required resolution of sensitive environmental and social matters. According to the EPs' preamble, the projects are categorised as A, B and C (high, medium and low environmental and social risk).[129] At $3.6 billion, the BTC project was the first to be categorised in the 'A' category of the EPs. Nevertheless, the project was criticised by a number of NGOs which found numerous breaches of the EPs. Simply, NGOs believed that although the project was considered to be a high-risk project in terms of both environmental and human rights, the principles were not applied in the BTC and the financial institutions failed in that major project.

125 Z. Baran, 'The Baku–Tbilisi–Ceyhan Pipeline: Implications for Turkey', in Starr & Cornell (n. 107 above) 103.

126 <http://equator-principles.com/about>

127 C. Girardone & S. Snaith, 'Project Finance Investment and Political Risk: An Empirical Investigation', Chapter 8 in Leader & Ong (n. 11 above) 115.

128 For further information, visit the Equator Principles website (n. 126 above).

129 Ibid.

Legal framework of the BTC Agreements

The BTC oil pipeline project is subject to a bespoke legal regime that was established between the BP Company and the three host states, namely Azerbaijan, Georgia and Turkey. Three host government agreements (HGAs) were also annexed to the IGA, one between each host state and the BTC Company. In practice, this meant that versions of the IGA were ratified and adopted in each host state's parliament and consequently became legally binding under international law and controlling domestic law in Azerbaijan, Georgia and Turkey. Another key legal document to become subject to BTC Agreements is the Lump Sum Turnkey Agreement.[130] An LSTA is a contractual agreement in which a fixed price is agreed for the implementation of a project or part of a project.[131] Through this agreement, the risk and responsibilities for the construction of the project are transferred to the constructor. As a state-owned petroleum pipeline company, BOTAS defined the LSTA with the BTC Company, contained in appendix 2 of the Turkish HGA. This agreement effectively transfers the risk and responsibilities for the construction of the project to the constructor. In two signatory states, Azerbaijan and Georgia, BTC Company and BP, as an operator, directly supervise and control all aspects of the pipeline construction. In Turkey, BOTAS, the Turkish state-owned pipeline construction company was the manager of the construction and operation of the pipeline.

Intergovernmental agreements (IGAs)

The overarching objective of the IGA in the context of the BTC pipeline project is 'to give the project's legal and commercial terms the support and framework of international law' to 'ensure principles of freedom of transit of petroleum'.[132] The IGA is a treaty subject to public international law 'through which the host states formally agree to ensure the safety and security of project personnel, facilities, assets, and in transit petroleum'.[133] In practice, the IGA serves as an umbrella legal document for the BTC pipeline project, with the goal of providing a prevailing regime for the pipeline project within each contracting state's domestic law. The following bullet points set out the key terms of the IGA between Azerbaijan, Georgia and Turkey:

130 See <http://subsites.bp.com/caspian/BTC/Eng/agmt5/agmt5.PDF>

131 F. K. Crundwell, *Finance for Engineers: Evaluation and Funding of Capital Projects* (London: Springer, 2008) 14.

132 IGA among the Azerbaijan Republic, Georgia and The Republic of Turkey, available at <www.bp.com/content/dam/bpcountry/en_az/pdf/legalagreements/BTC_eng_agmt4_agmt4.pdf>

133 A. Dufey, 'Project Finance, Sustainable Development and Human Rights, Case Study 1: The Baku–Tbilisi–Ceyhan (BTC) Pipeline', International Institute for Environment and Development, Environmental Economics Programme (April 2009) 15; see also Dufey & Kazimova (n. 107 above) 379.

- A commitment from each signatory state to present the IGA, the HGAs and the other related documents to its national parliament for ratification/or adoption in order to make it effective under its Constitution and render it the prevailing legal regime in its state;[134]
- A general assurance from each host state to support and encourage the pipeline project, including: guaranteeing freedom of petroleum transit, guaranteeing the performance by state entities of certain project contracts[135] and granting exclusive land rights to the project;[136]
- A commitment from each host government to provide security for the pipeline;[137]
- A general commitment from each state to cooperate and coordinate with each other's activities, and work with the project consortium to formulate and establish uniform technical services, health and safety standards and environmental safeguards for the project;[138]
- Confirmation that the only taxes imposed on the project would be those set out in the HGAs and an agreement on how to allocate taxable profits between the project states;[139]
- A statement that the project was not intended to or required to operate in the service of the public interest in each state's territory and agreements in whole or part, as a concession contract or a special administrative contract granting a concession.[140]

The first five bullet points demonstrate that in order to enable 'freedom of transit pipeline', the signatory states assured the consortium that they would restrict their future regulatory developments, expediting the expropriation of land spanned by the pipeline, and that they would indemnify the project consortium against liability for human rights violations, resulting from pipeline security measures. Furthermore, the last bullet point asserts that the BTC mega-project will not be used for the public purpose of the signatory states and that project agreements annexed to the IGA could not be deemed as concession contracts. This last point is of note and somewhat controversial, as if Azerbaijan, Georgia or Turkey decided to expropriate a land for the consortium, the expropriation would need to be justified by public purpose. However, the clause explicitly illustrates that the project is not intended to operate in the service of public interest in the host states. By definition, this would mean that due to the absence of public purpose, any expropriation activity by the countries would technically be illegal.

134 Inter Governmental Agreement (IGA) among the Azerbaijan Republic, Georgia. IGA Article II (1).
135 Ibid., Article II (4)(ii) and (iii).
136 Ibid., Article II (4)(iv).
137 Ibid., Article V (1).
138 Ibid., Article IV.
139 Ibid., Article V.
140 Ibid., Article II (8).

George Goolsby, the head lawyer for the US law firm working on the BTC project, Baker Botts, explained the legal tactics of the consortium members' lawyers as follows: 'the foreign companies want confidence ... Without having to amend local laws, we went above or around them by using a treaty.'[141] In fact, as a result of the strategy described by George Goolsby, if any dispute were to arise between the states in the future, the consortium would automatically be granted the protection of international law. In other words, rather than relying merely on HGAs, the lawyers created a protective regime designed to safeguard the BTC consortium's interests in any circumstance they could foresee.

Host government agreements (HGAs)

HGAs are regarded as private law contracts, as they are signed between a private investor and a host state. In practice, such agreements can provide excessive control to international oil and gas companies over the domestic law of host countries. As mentioned previously, if a host state's regulatory and legislative changes have a negative impact on investor activities and their expected resultant revenues, foreign investors can legitimately claim compensation for the losses and inconveniences incurred. Traditionally, concession agreements are subject to the domestic law of the host country. In contrast:

> [T]he HGAs for the BTC pipeline have been drawn up under (and therefore rest within) the framework of what is in effect an international investment treaty. The companies therefore claim that HGAs automatically assume the status of international public law while simultaneously remaining private contracts.[142]

In this respect, it can be said that treaty status has been apportioned to HGAs in the context of the BTC project and the HGAs' provisions are deemed to prevail over the domestic law of three sovereign states.

Taking the facts above into account, it is evident that any failure on the part of Azerbaijan, Georgia or Turkey to maintain their pre-existing 'economic equilibrium' would render them liable to pay compensation to the project consortium. Such economic equilibrium clauses 'boost the investor's confidence and ensure that the long-term investment will yield the expected results, by shielding the contract from some of the many risks associated with the investment'.[143] In

141 Quoted in D. Eviatar, 'Wild-Cat Lawyering', *American Lawyer*, Vol. 4. November 2002, cited in J. Marriott & M. M. Paluello, *The Oil Road: Journeys from the Caspian Sea to the City of London* (Oxford & New York: Verso, 2012) 144.

142 N. Hildyards & G. Muttitt, 'Turbo-charging Investor Sovereignty: Investment Agreements and Corporate Colonialism' (2006) 46–7, available at <www.thecornerhouse.org.uk/sites/thecornerhouse.org.uk/files/HGAPSA.pdf>

143 B. O. N. Nwete, 'To What Extent Can Stabilisation Clauses Mitigate the Investor's Risks in a Production Sharing Contract?' *Oil, Gas & Energy Law Intelligence* (*OGEL*), Vol. 3 (March 2005) 118.

summary, it can be concluded that a sovereign state is still within its rights to make changes in its law or fiscal regime or to take other host governmental measures, and the insertion of such a clause does not necessarily immunise an international oil company from any such change.[144] However, it 'guarantees the investor compensatory benefit, should such change or act affect the economies or financial premises of the project'.[145] However, stabilisation clauses in the form of economic equilibrium clauses in the HGAs of the BTC project illustrate that the intended cover as well as the related effects of such clauses are much wider than they should be.[146] What this means is that if a host state directly or indirectly jeopardises the economic equilibrium of an investment project, they have to pay compensation to the project consortium as a result of any changes, including the measures aimed to protect human rights and environment.

In light of this fact, it can be asserted that the economic equilibrium stabilisation clause effectively relegates the international treaty obligations designed to protect the environment and human rights to measures only applicable in extreme circumstances. Nevertheless, all three host states accepted contractual terms in which such an economic equilibrium clause in the form of stabilisation clauses will have effect for the next 40 to 60 years with the proviso that this duration can be further extended by the consortium twice, each time for a further ten-year period. It is worth emphasising that BP and the other member oil companies must have dictated to their lawyers the exact terms and conditions of the arrangement they sought to achieve, as successfully obtaining investment loans and insurance from the World Bank Group and the EBRD and the other ECAs depended on them future-proofing the stability of the investment environment.

Conclusions

This chapter has examined the role of lenders, political risk insurance providers and credit rating agencies in project financing regarding the inclusion of stabilisation clauses. As a case study, this chapter gave particular attention to the BTC pipeline project.

The motivation for investors to include stabilisation clauses derives from a multitude of considerations. On contemplating the provision of a loan to a specific project, all the circumstances that may affect or delay the repayment of credit are taken into account. Change in the law, the introduction of new regulations, expropriation or nationalisation, currency volatility, changes in tax regime and all manner of political risks all have the potential to endanger an investment.

In the face of political risks, the inclusion of stabilisation clauses have become a *sine qua non* requirement for investors applying for substantial loans to fund

144 A. S. Reyes, 'Protecting the Freedom of Transit of Petroleum: Transnational Lawyers Making (up) International Law in the Caspian', *Berkeley Journal of International Law*, Vol. 24, No. 3 (2006) 857.

145 Nwete (n. 143 above) 118.

146 Reyes (n. 144 above) 858.

projects of the scale of transnational pipeline projects. The lenders, in turn, require that these risks be managed and mitigated to secure the prospect of repayment. Furthermore, while lenders may appear to be backstage players, not directly involved in the project, it has been revealed that from behind the scenes this party is highly influential and that the requirement for a host state to commit to not introducing new laws that may affect the sustainability and cost of the project often derives from this source.

The critical importance of insurers in an investment project is self-evident, as neither investors nor lenders would ever consider committing to a project without cover to protect the loan from political risk. Furthermore, in order to shield their clients from political risk, insurers provide arbitral award default coverage of stabilisation clauses. This coverage provides insurance cover to the investor in the event that the host state fails to make a compensation payment triggered by the violation of a stabilisation clause incurred by a change in law. It was also found that national insurance agencies hold subrogation rights against host states, enabling pressure from another third party to be applied to the host state. Insurers are free to apply pressure to the host state to make compensation payments to their clients even before an arbitral tribunal's decision is reached. In cases where a host government caves in to this pressure, this may appear to be an admission of guilt and thereby prejudice the arbitrator and, it can be argued, the outcome.

The final external influencer examined was credit rating agencies and their role in the inclusion of stabilisation clauses. Rating agencies assess and evaluate the risk of lending to sovereign countries and international corporations. Ratings are also available for specific project financing. These agencies take into account a number of project-related areas such as sovereign risk analysis, currency risk analysis, political risk analysis and contract risk analysis in the assessment they make.

The BTC pipeline project was chosen as a case study as its scale and complexity provide a wealth of material for analysis. It was found that each signatory state's interests and bargaining positions have their unique points. In the case of Azerbaijan, the project is regarded as critical to territorial integrity and economic improvement. Azerbaijan saw the economic benefits to be gained from involvement in the project as a means to invest in their military might and thereby gain power over the Nagorno-Karabakh region. In the case of Georgia, the BTC project would serve as a catalyst for economic growth and the improvement of living standards in the country. The project was also seen as a strategic means for gaining political protection from their Russian neighbours. Georgia held a strong bargaining position as the only country able to secure pipeline transit in the region should a dispute arise between Armenia and Azerbaijan. Meanwhile, from the perspective of Turkey, the improvement of strategic relations with diplomatic partners in the EU and the US outweighed the economic benefits to be had.

The analysis demonstrated the multifaceted nature of the agreements forged for a complex mega-project of this kind. Through the IGA, the consortium aimed to establish a prevailing legal regime for the pipeline in the national law of Azerbaijan, Georgia and Turkey. Although the main purpose of this was supposed to be to grant the pipeline freedom of transit, unfortunately the signatory states ultimately assigned some of their sovereign rights to the consortium in their territories. The IGA restricted the states' future regulatory activities, accelerated expropriation activities deemed to be without public purpose, and indemnified the consortium against responsibility for human rights violations.

Also discussed were the HGAs annexed to the IGA. It is a well-established principle that HGAs are private law contracts and subject to a host country's domestic law. However, in the BTC project, the lawyers internationalised these agreements, thereby enabling them to prevail over each country's domestic law. This may be taken as evidence that the consortium wished to circumvent the judicial courts and legal systems of Azerbaijan, Georgia and Turkey.

Bibliography

Legislation (national and international) and guides

Inter-Governmental Agreement among the Azerbaijan Republic, Republic of Georgia and Republic of Turkey signed 18 November 1999

MIGA Convention (Multilateral Investment Guarantee Agency), October 1985, 24 I.L.M. 1985

Cases and arbitral awards

Enron Corporation and Ponderosa v Argentina, Award, ICSID Case No. ARB/01/3 (2007)

Internet websites

http://equator-principles.com/about
http://news.bbc.co.uk/1/hi/world/europe/2263611.stm
web.worldbank.org
www.ca-cib.com
www.dundee.ac.uk
www1.ifc.org
www.opic.gov
http://subsites.bp.com/caspian/BTC/Eng/agmt5/agmt5.PDF
www.bp.com/genericarticle.do?categoryId=2012968&contentId=2016340
www.oas.org/dil/treaties_C-15_Agreement_Establishing_the_Inter-American_Development_Bank.htm
www.imf.org/external/about.htm
www.miga.org/documents/Operations-Regulations.pdf
www.ogj.com/articles/2012/09/hess-to-sell-interests-in-acg-fields-btc-line-to-ongc-for-1-billion.html
www.worldbank.org/en/country/mic/overview
http://ida.worldbank.org/about/what-ida
www.bp.com/content/dam/bpcountry/en_az/pdf/legalagreements/BTC_eng_agmt4_agmt4.pdf
www.silkroadstudies.org

Books and monographs

Bouchet, M. H., Clark, E. & Groslambert, B., *Country Risk Assessment: Guide to Global Investment Strategy*, Chichester: John Wiley & Sons, 2003

Crundwell, F. K., *Finance for Engineers: Evaluation and Funding of Capital Projects.* London: Springer, 2008

Delmon, J., *Private Sector Investment in Infrastructure: Project Finance, PPP Projects and Risks*, 2nd edn. Alphen aan den Rijn: Wolters Kluwer, 2009

Dewar, J., *International Project Finance: Law and Practice.* Oxford: Oxford University Press, 2011

Ebel, R. & Menon, R., *Energy and Conflict in Central Asia and the Caucasus.* Boston: Rowman & Littlefield Publishers, 2000

Esty, B. C., *Modern Project Finance.* USA: John Wiley & Sons, 2004

Fight, A., *Introduction to Project Finance.* Oxford: Elsevier, 2008

Frenkel, M. & Karmann, A., *Sovereign Risk and Financial Crises.* Heidelberg: Springer, 2004

Gatti, S., *Project Finance in Theory and Practice: Designing, Structuring and Financing Private and Public Projects*, 2nd edn. Waltham, MA: Academic Press, 2012

Gianturco, E. D., *Export Credit Agencies: The Unsung Giants of International Trade and Finance.* Westport, CT: Quorum Books, 2001

Hoffman, S. L., *The Law and Business of International Project Finance*, 3rd edn. Cambridge: Cambridge University Press, 2008

Inkpen, A. C. & Moffett, M. H., *The Global Oil and Gas Industry: Management, Strategy, and Finance.* Tulsa, OK: PennWell Corporation, 2011

Kantor, M., Nolan, M. D. & Sauvant, K. P., *Reports of Overseas Private Investment Corporation Determinations*, Vol. 1. Oxford: Oxford University Press, 2011

Leader, S. & Ong, D., *Global Project Finance, Human Rights and Sustainable Development.* Cambridge: Cambridge University Press, 2011

Marriott, J. & Paluello, M. M., *The Oil Road: Journeys From The Caspian Sea to the City of London.* Oxford & New York: Verso, 2012

Merna, A. & Owen, G., *Understanding the Private Finance Initiative: The New Dynamics of Project Finance.* Hong Kong: Asia Law and Practice, 1998

Merna, A., Chu, Y. & Al-Thani, F. F., *Project Finance in Construction: A Structured Guide to Assessment.* Oxford: Wiley Blackwell, 2010

Merna, T. & Al-Thani, F. F., *Corporate Risk Management*, 2nd edn. Chichester: John Wiley & Sons, 2008

Nevitt, P. K. & Fabozzi, F. J., *Project Financing*, 7th edn. London: Euromoney Institutional Investor, 2000

Omonbude, E. J., *Cross-border Oil and Gas Pipelines and the Role of the Transit Country: Economics, Challenges and Solutions.* Basingstoke: Palgrave Macmillan, 2013

Razavi, H., *Financing Energy Projects in Emerging Economies.* Tulsa, OK: PennWell Books, 1996

Salacuse, J. W., *The Three Laws of International Investment: National, Contractual, and International Frameworks for Foreign Capital.* Oxford: Oxford University Press, 2013

Shaffer, B., Energy Politics, Philadelphia: University of Pennsylvania Publishing, 2009

Sheldon, H. N., *Law of Subrogation*, Washington, DC: Beard Books, 2000

Siddaiah, T., *Financial Services.* New Delhi: Pearson, 2011

Smith, R. C. & Walter, I., *Global Banking.* New York: Oxford University Press, 1997

Chapters in books

Baran, Z., 'The Baku–Tbilisi–Ceyhan Pipeline: Implications for Georgia', Chapter 6 in S. F. Starr & S. E. Cornell (eds), *Baku–Tbilisi–Ceyhan Pipeline: Oil Window to the West*, Washington, DC: Central Asia-Caucasus Institute & Silk Road Studies Program, 2005

Blatchford, D., 'Environmental and Social Aspects of the Baku–Tbilisi–Ceyhan Pipeline', Chapter 7 in S. F. Starr & S. E. Cornell (eds), *Baku–Tbilisi–Ceyhan Pipeline: Oil Window to the West*, Washington, DC: Central Asia-Caucasus Institute & Silk Road Studies Program, 2005

S. E. Cornell& Ismailzade, F., 'The Baku–Tbilisi–Ceyhan: Implications for Azerbaijan', Chapter 4 in S. F. Starr & S. E. Cornell (eds), *Baku–Tbilisi–Ceyhan Pipeline: Oil Window to the West*, Washington, DC: Central Asia-Caucasus Institute & Silk Road Studies Program, 2005

Dufey, A. & Kazimova, R., 'Baku–Tbilisi–Ceyhan Project: Implications of Project Finance', Chapter 12 in S. Leader and D. Ong (eds), *Global Project Finance, Human Rights and Sustainable Development*. Cambridge: Cambridge University Press, 2011

Elkind, J., 'Economic Implications of the Baku–Tbilisi–Ceyhan Pipeline', Chapter 3 in S. F. Starr & S. E. Cornell (eds), *Baku–Tbilisi–Ceyhan Pipeline: Oil Window to the West*, Washington, DC: Central Asia-Caucasus Institute & Silk Road Studies Program, 2005

Girardone, C. &Snaith, S., 'Project Finance Investment and Political Risk: An Empirical Investigation', Chapter 8 in S. Leader& D. Ong (eds), *Global Project Finance, Human Rights and Sustainable Development*. Cambridge: Cambridge University Press, 2011

Gorton, G.B. & Souleles, N.S., 'Special Purpose Vehicles and Securitization', Chapter 12 in M. Carey & R. M. Stulz (eds), The Risks of Financial Institutions, National Bureau of Economic Research Conference Report. Chicago: University of Chicago Press, 2007

Jenney, F.E., 'A Sword in a Stone: Problems (and a Few Proposed Solutions) Regarding Political Risk Insurance Coverage of Regulatory Takings' in T. H. Moran, G. T. West & K. Martin (eds), *Political Risk Management: Needs of the Present Challenges for the Future*. Washington, DC: The World Bank Group, 2008

Kazimova, R., 'Insurance as a Risk Management Tool: A Mitigating or Aggravating Factor?', Chapter 9 in S. Leader & D. Ong (eds), *Global Project Finance, Human Rights and Sustainable Development*. Cambridge: Cambridge University Press, 2011

Nordstrom, D., Dickens, S., Brown, M. & Stirling, K., 'Multisource Project Financing', Chapter 4 in R. Morrison (ed.) *The Principles of Project Finance*. Farnham: Gower Publishing, 2012

Papava, V. 'The Baku–Tbilisi–Ceyhan Pipeline: Implications for Georgia', Chapter 5 in S. F. Starr & S. E. Cornell (eds), *Baku–Tbilisi–Ceyhan Pipeline: Oil Window to the West*, Washington, DC: Central Asia-Caucasus Institute & Silk Road Studies Program, 2005

Sheppard, B., 'The Role of Multilateral Banks and ECAs', Chapter 6 in R. Morrison (ed.) *The Principles of Project Finance*. Farnham: Gower Publishing, 2012

Sinclair, S., 'World Bank Guarantees for Oil and Gas Projects', in The World Bank, *Natural Gas: Private Sector Participation and Market Development*. Washington, DC: World Bank Publications, 1999

Articles, seminars/conference and research papers

Babali, T., '*Implications of The Baku–Tbilisi–Ceyhan Main Oil Pipeline Project*', *Perceptions* (Winter 2005 2005) 46, available at <http://sam.gov.tr/wp-content/uploads/2012/02/TuncayBabali.pdf>

Balat, M. &Ersoy, G., 'Baku–Tbilisi–Ceyhan Oil Pipeline (BTC) Project and Turkey: Investments, Future Developments and Environmental Impacts', *Energy Exploration and Exploitation*, Vol. 23, No 1 (2005) 33, available at <http://journals.sagepub.com/doi/pdf/10.1260/0144-5987.23.1.31>

Cline, W. R. & Sargen, N. P., 'Performance Criteria and Multilateral Aid Allocation', *World Development*, Vol. 3, No. 6 (1975) 383–391

De Paoli, B., 'Costs of Sovereign Default', *Bank of England Quarterly Bulletin*, Vol. 46, No. 3 (2006) 297–308

Dufey, A., 'Project Finance, Sustainable Development and Human Rights, Case Study 1: The Baku-Tbilisi-Ceyhan (BTC) Pipeline', International Institute for Environment and Development, Environmental Economics Programme (April 2009) 15

Elkhoury, M., 'Credit Rating Agencies and Their Potential Impact on Developing Countries, United Nations Conference on Trade and Development', Discussion Paper No. 186 (January 2008) 1

Hoffman, S. L., 'A Practical Guide to Transactional Project Finance: Basic Concepts, Risk Identification, and Contractual Considerations', *The Business Lawyer*, Vol. 45, No. 1 (1989) 181

Hildyards, N. & Muttitt, G., 'Turbo-charging Investor Sovereignty: Investment Agreements and Corporate Colonialism', available at <www.thecornerhouse.org.uk/sites/thecornerhouse.org.uk/files/HGAPSA.pdf>

Norton, S. D., 'Securitisation in the Extractive Industries: Stakeholder Sensitivities, Environmental Protection and the Cost of Capital', *Greener Management International*, No. 53 (November 2007) 62

Nwete, B.O.N., 'To What Extent Can Stabilisation Clauses Mitigate the Investor's Risks in a Production Sharing Contract?' *Oil, Gas & Energy Law Intelligence (OGEL)*, Vol. 3 (March 2005) 118

Ochieze, C., 'Lender Liability: "To what extent can a lender protect itself?"', CELMP Annual Review, February 2007, available at <www.dundee.ac.uk>

Razavi, H., 'Oil and Gas Financing by the World Bank', *Energy Policy*, Vol. 23, No. 11 (1995) 1001

Reyes, A.S., 'Protecting the Freedom of Transit of Petroleum: Transnational Lawyers Making (up) International Law in the Caspian', *Berkeley Journal of International Law*, Vol. 24, No. 3, (2006) 817

Rolfini, R. & Paciotti, S., 'Political Risk Insurance: A Technical Approach', SACE Working Paper No. 14 (November 2010) 21, available at <www.globalexport.it/GestDb/Pub/Upload/Pub911.pdf>

Shihata, I. F. I., 'The Settlement of Disputes Regarding Foreign Investment: The Role of the World Bank, with Particular Reference to ICSID and MIGA', *American University Journal of International Law and Policy*, Vol. 1, No. 97 (1986) 1

Shaffer, B., 'From Pipedream to Pipeline: A Caspian Success Story', *Current History*, Vol. 104, No. 684 (2005) 343,available at <www.belfercenter.org/sites/default/files/files/publication/shaffercurrenthistoryoct2005.pdf>

Slivker, A., 'What Is Project Finance and How Does It Work?' University of Iowa Centre for International Finance and Development (2011) 5, available at <http://ebook.law.uiowa.edu/ebook/uicifd-ebook/what-project-finance-and-how-does-it-work-0>

Sorell, T., 'Project Financing in Developing Countries, New Corporate Social Responsibility, Human Rights, and Multinationals', *Essex Human Rights Review*, Vol. 5, No 1 (2008) 2

Standard &Poor's Rating Direct, 'Updated Project Finance Summary Debt Rating Criteria' September (2007) 14, available at <www.maalot.co.il/publications/MT20120529105458.pdf>

TsanakasA. & DesliE., 'Measurement and Pricing of Risk in Insurance Markets', *Risk Analysis*, Vol. 25, No. 6 (2005) 1654

Thompson, S., 'Credit Rating and Project Finance Default: An Important Risk Management Instrument', *Public Infrastructure Bulletin*, Vol. 1, No. 8 (2012) 2, available at <http://epublications.bond.edu.au/pib/vol1/iss8/10>

Tran, M., 'Caspian Oil Pipeline Opens', Wednesday 25 May 2005, *The Guardian*, available at <www.guardian.co.uk/business/2005/may/25/oilandpetrol.news1>

Van de Putte, A., Gates, D. F. & Holder, K., 'Political Risk Insurance as an Instrument to Reduce Oil and Gas Investment Risk and Manage Investment Returns', *Journal of World Energy Law and Business*, Vol. 5, No. 4 (2012) 291

Waters, C. P. M., 'Who Should Regulate the Baku–Tbilisi–Ceyhan Pipeline?' *Georgetown International Law Review*, Vol. 16 (2004) 404

Watkins, J., 'BTC – Reaching First Drawdown', BTC features, *Project Finance International*, Vol. 298 (2004) 48

Weston, R., 'The Project Financing of Cross-Border Pipelines', Presentation to the Energy Charter Workshop Brussels (17 October 2006), slide no. 19, available at <https://energycharter.org/fileadmin/DocumentsMedia/Events/20061017-WORDITMAFCBP_RWeston.pdf >

Reports

Jackson, J. K., 'The Berne Union: An Overview', Congressional Research Service Report (April 2013), available at <www.fas.org/sgp/crs/row/RS22319.pdf>

Overseas Private Investment Corporation, 'Annual Report on Development Impact: Fiscal Year 2016' (2017), available at <www.opic.gov/sites/default/files/files/FY16_Annual_Development_Report_Final.pdf>

Thomson Reuters, 'Back in the Funding Mix: Multilaterals Report 2009', *Project Finance International* (2009)

5 Political systems and laws on foreign investment in Azerbaijan and Turkey

Introduction

The attraction of foreign capital through foreign investment is a major undertaking for a host state. In the petroleum sector, cheap labour, large oil and gas reserves and a welcoming investment environment are all considered fundamental criteria by alien investors. In addition, foreign investors will also seek legal, fiscal and constitutional guarantees that their property and contractual rights are well protected over the course of their investment activities. The governments of Azerbaijan and Turkey have both secured political stability and established an appealing investment environment via adjustments to their domestic law, as well as signing up to bilateral and multilateral international investment treaties over the past decade.

Turkey has liberalised its previously restrictive foreign investment policy to give encouragement to international investors. In fact, Turkey went as far as to adopt a new law pertaining to foreign direct investment (FDI) in 2003. The implementation of this new legislation sought to address the need to have a well-established FDI law amenable to alien investors that would be more compatible with global requirements, as well as reflecting the changing role of Turkey in the Caspian and Middle East region.

Since the establishment of the Republic of Azerbaijan, its legal authorities have been active in passing various laws with regard to FDI, most significantly the Law on the Protection of Investments (1992), the Law on Investment Activity (1995), the Law on the Privatisation of State Property (2000), and the Law on International Arbitration (2000). These laws have provided foreign investors with currency convertibility, guarantees regarding the stability of the legal framework, the right to repatriate funds and free access to international arbitration.

As previously mentioned, both countries, along with Georgia, are signatory parties of the BTC agreements. The rigid legal framework of the agreements, as explored in the previous chapter, is often to the detriment of the host country. While it is reasonable to expect that these countries need to legislate and regulate in the interests of safeguarding foreign investment in order to attract it in the first place, why they went as far as to give consent to potentially debilitating stabilisation clauses in their HGAs in the BTC agreement is still in question.

Azerbaijan

Azerbaijan (officially, the Republic of Azerbaijan) is the largest country in the Caucasus region. Lying at the crossroads of Eastern Europe and Western Asia, the country enjoys a unique geographical location, which benefits its world economic and cultural links. Azerbaijan is bordered by the Caspian Sea to the east, by Iran to the south, by Armenia to the west, and Georgia and Russia to the north. The Azeri autonomous republic of Naxcivan forms an enclave within the Republic of Armenia; located to the west, it borders Turkey. The total surface area of Azerbaijan is 86,600 km^2;, which is slightly bigger than Austria or Portugal. Baku is the capital and Azerbaijan's largest city, as well as being the largest city in the Caspian region. Baku is situated on the southern shore of the Absheron Peninsula, which projects into the Caspian Sea. As well as its strategic location, the country is notable for its rich oil reserves and was classified as an upper-middle income country by the World Bank in 2017.[1]

Since the fall of the Soviet Union, most former soviet states have been anxious to become a part of the global economy while still maintaining their new status as sovereign states. Among the CIS countries, Azerbaijan's performance was the most significant in terms of attracting FDI into its country, particularly in the oil sector. As referenced in this chapter's introduction, a series of laws regarding the protection of foreign investment have been put in place in Azerbaijan. For instance, the Law on the Protection of Investments (1992) includes significant safeguards for private investors. In the same vein are the Investment Activity Law (1995), the Privatisation Law, the second Privatisation Program and the Law on International Arbitration (2000). These are sufficient examples to demonstrate the extent of Azerbaijan's ambition in securing alien investors. In addition to these incentives, a number of bilateral investment and other treaties were signed to create a more favourable investment climate and provide further guarantees to private investors.

The Law on the Protection of Foreign Investments (15 January 1992)

Definition

The Azerbaijani Law on the Protection of Investment, Article 2 defines foreign investors as:

> The following persons and entities might be foreign investors in the Azerbaijan Republic: a) foreign legal entities b) foreign citizens, stateless citizens and

1 The official website of the World Bank, available at <http://data.worldbank.org/country/azerbaijan>

citizens of the Azerbaijan Republic permanently living abroad, if they have been registered as participants of economic activity in the country of their citizenship or permanent residency c) foreign states d) international organizations.[2]

The Law on the Protection of Investment in the first place defines foreign investors, in which category it includes (1) foreign entities, (2) governments, (3) international organisations and (4) individuals permanently residing outside Azerbaijan. The legal condition as stated in the article is that alien investors can undertake their investment activities uninhibited by Azerbaijani law.

Legal protection of foreign investors

Article 5 provides for national treatment or non-discrimination of foreign investors. In other words, the 'not less favoured' regime automatically applies to private investors within the territory of the Republic of Azerbaijan, unless otherwise stipulated by an applicable international law, and unless otherwise provided by Azerbaijani foreign investment law, by default foreign investors who enjoy the same rights as domestic investors, and upon whom may additionally be bestowed preferential rights that might not be ceded to domestic investors.[3]

Stability of legislation

Article 10 of Azerbaijani Law on the Protection of Foreign Investment regulates guarantees against changes in legislation. In the context of this article, the law provides for protection against adverse changes in the law for the ten-year period subsequent to the investment.[4] In other words, if a law adopted by the Azerbaijani parliament adversely affects an investor's investment, the application of that change is subject to a ten-year moratorium. Notably, the moratorium has the force of law, and therefore it is enforceable and has a binding effect over all Azerbaijani state bodies. Article 10 also clearly states the reach of such guarantees with changes in legislation in the area of national security, defence, public health, environmental protection, as well as legislation affecting credits and finances, falling outside the scope of the moratorium.[5] This article clearly states that stabilisation clauses are available under the foreign direct investment law of Azerbaijan.

Repatriation of profits and convertibility

Under article 14 of the legislation, private investors are entitled to repatriate profits in convertible currency after the payment of applicable taxes and other

2 Article 2, Law of the Azerbaijan Republic on the Protection of Foreign Investments (1992).
3 Ibid. at Article 5.
4 Ibid. at Article 10.
5 Ibid.

charges that are due.[6] This article makes it clear that Azerbaijan is keenly aware of and willing to legally recognise one of the most crucial interests of private investors, with perhaps its only condition being the payment of taxes. Nevertheless, the repatriation of profits can entail a long bureaucratic procedure. Despite the fact that by law foreign entities/companies are free to transfer their capital out of Azerbaijan, in practice there are some constraints made by the National Bank of Azerbaijan, mostly related to the transfer of money to offshore accounts.[7]

Expropriation/nationalisation

Article 11 of the legislation regulates the advent of expropriation/nationalisation in Azerbaijan. This article clearly states that in normal conditions foreign investments will not be subject to expropriation or nationalisation in Azerbaijan. However, the article also stresses that expropriation may take place if deemed in the interests of public purpose by the Supreme Council of Azerbaijan. Confiscation is also possible according to this article; however, this type of taking must be executed only in circumstances of natural disaster, epidemic and other extraordinary situations by decision of the cabinet of Ministers. In both expropriation and confiscation cases, private investors have the right to receive prompt, adequate and effective compensation. It should be noted that no expropriation or nationalisation cases have emerged in Azerbaijan thus far against foreign investors.

Settlement of disputes

Article 42 of the legislation regulates the settlement of disputes between foreign investors, foreign institutions and state organs of Azerbaijan. According to this provision:

> Disputes or disagreements arising between foreign investors and enterprises with foreign investments and state bodies of the Azerbaijan Republic, enterprises, public organizations and other legal entities of the Azerbaijan Republic, disputes and disagreements between participants of the enterprise with foreign investments and such enterprise itself are to be settled in Law Courts of the Azerbaijan Republic or, on agreement between the Parties, in the Court of Arbitration, including those abroad.[8]

According to this article, a dispute between a foreign company undertaking its activities in the territory of Azerbaijan and a local entity may be settled in

6 Ibid. at Article 15.

7 United Nations, *Foreign Direct Investments in Central Asian and Caucasian Economies: Policies and Issues, Papers and Proceedings Presented at the Regional Round Table on Foreign Direct Investment for Central Asia*, Dushanbe, 3 and 4 April 2003 (New York: United Nations Publications, 2003) 75.

8 Law of the Azerbaijan Republic on the Protection of Foreign Investments (n. 2 above) Article 42.

accordance with the arbitration method by national or international courts as long as both parties can incorporate this in their agreement. The law also provides for disputes between private investors and state authorities or legal bodies with regard to the amount of damages that may be decided upon by an international arbitral tribunal, if parties have given consent to arbitration. It is clear that a mechanism for the settlement of disputes exists in law; however, 'effective means of protecting and enforcing property and contractual rights are by no means assured'.[9] In addition to this, it is worth mentioning that Azerbaijan has been a party to the Convention on the Recognition and Enforcement of Foreign Awards since 1999. On becoming a party to this treaty, the government adopted the Law on International Arbitration (2000) and the Law on the Civil Procedure Code (2000).

There is some doubt as to whether these laws are actually the major steps they might at first appear, in terms of the guarantees they offer to foreign investors. The Law on International Arbitration provides recognition and enforcement of foreign arbitral awards in Azerbaijan; however, in practice the enforcement of foreign arbitral awards in Azerbaijan is not a well-oiled process because local courts have had little opportunity to gain experience with commercial arbitration cases in general.[10] Although, the FDI law provides for the possibility of application to local arbitration in international commercial issues, in reality Azerbaijani courts are not perceived to be the best venue to resolve disputes by foreign investors. The reason for this is perhaps the transparency or reliability issue.[11] What this means is that there is no evidence that government officials officially intervene in the economic court system, but in practice economic courts are weak, judges are inexperienced and corruption is widespread, with the result that judges' decisions are often inconsistent.[12]

Concession agreements

Technically speaking, there is no law on concession or institutional legal framework for concession in place in the Azerbaijani legal system. The Law on the Protection of Foreign Investment and the Civil Code refers to concession agreements; however, the laws do not actually define the concession concept itself. Under Article 40 of the Foreign Investment Law of Azerbaijan, concession rights are granted by the Cabinet of Ministers of the Republic of Azerbaijan and approved by the Supreme Council;[13] however, there is no definition of the term 'concession', and the rights granted for concession are limited to natural resources only, while the article applies merely to private investors.

9 Global Investment Centre, *Azerbaijan: Mineral, Mining Sector Investment and Business Guide: Strategic Information and Regulations Vol. 1* (Washington, DC: International Business Publications: 2012) 37.
10 Ibid.
11 Ibid.
12 Ibid.
13 Law of the Azerbaijan Republic on the Protection of Foreign Investment (n. 2 above) Article 40 (1).

In the interests of increasing its attractiveness to foreign investors, Azerbaijan would be well advised to add to this article a definition of 'concession', and the scope of the concession ought to be explicitly extended beyond the scope of natural resources. Indeed, in the long run it is essential that the government of Azerbaijan implements a proper concession law if they wish to continue to attract foreign investors into the country, not only from the oil industry but from any sector. Despite the fact that these laws provide a considerable amount of protection to foreign investors, broader guarantees have also been provided by the Azerbaijani government, establishing a separate legal framework through Production Sharing Agreements (PSAs) for alien investors in the oil industry.

Legal status of PSAs in the Azerbaijani legal system

In order to accelerate the flow of foreign investment, President Heydar Aliyev created a new PSA model with the oil industry in mind. Since 1994, Azerbaijan has concluded a total of 32 PSAs: internationally recognised mechanisms that include stabilisation and arbitration provisions as a means of providing a secure investment environment to oil companies. Moreover, as opposed to standard tax and royalty PSAs in Azerbaijan, this is 'a physical mechanism for rendering to the Azerbaijani states its share of profits while allowing foreign energy companies to recoup their investments'.[14]

The question as to why Azerbaijan adopted this model was raised by the former president of the State Oil Company of Azerbaijan (SOCAR). According to Sabit Bagirov, the main reason why Azerbaijan preferred PSAs was that, as a newly founded state, especially one without its own financial capital, it was unable to apply other types of contract model that would be beneficial to it as a country.[15] More importantly, immediately following its establishment the country suffered from a low credit rating and was consequently unable to obtain long-term loans from foreign credit institutions to fund its oil and gas projects.[16] Furthermore, as mentioned in the analysis of host government agreements, various different PSA models have been adopted by petroleum-producing countries around the world.

What distinguishes Azerbaijani PSAs from the other types is that when SOCAR officials and foreign company representatives reach a mutual agreement on a PSA, the approval of the president is subsequently required. On obtaining this approval, the contract is then sent to the Azerbaijani parliament for ratification. Once parliament has ratified the contracts, it is then returned to the president for final confirmation. After the signature of the president and declaration to the public, the contract is accepted as having the force of law and prevails over existing or future laws or decrees whose provisions diverge from or are inconsistent with this

14 D. I. Hoffman, 'Azerbaijan: The Politicization of Oil', Chapter 4 in R. Ebel & R. Menon (eds), *Energy and Conflict in Central Asia and the Caucasus* (Lanham, MD: Rowman & Littlefield Publishers, 2000) 58.

15 A. Ciaretta & S. Nasirovm, 'Development trends in the Azerbaijan Oil and Gas Sector: Achievements and Challenges', *Elsevier Energy Policy*, Vol. 40 (2012) 15.

16 Ibid.

contract. In other words, while some petroleum-producing countries regard PSAs as a type of pure contract, in Azerbaijan all PSAs have the power of law and have a higher legal status than other existing laws in the Azerbaijani legal system.

It should be noted that the legal framework for the regulation of oil and gas agreements is based on the Subsoil Act[17] and the Energy Act.[18] As these laws are in effect a collection of uncoordinated laws that furnish a general framework for energy resource legislation in Azerbaijan, in many cases their provisions are inconsistent with each other. In fact, there is no particular wording to state whether or not the general Energy Act takes precedence over the Subsoil Act.

In Azerbaijan, a different tax regime is applicable to PSAs. If a contractor has entered into a PSA in the oil and gas industry in Azerbaijan, such an agreement will stipulate the tax protocols relevant to that particular investment. The tax regime for PSAs in Azerbaijan is called the Oil Consortia; it applies to the contractor and all the other project participants of a PSA. Currently, all of the PSAs to which Azerbaijan is party supply a grand total of profit tax of around 20% or 32%, depending on the party's negotiations when the contract was signed.[19] The PSAs also offer protection against future increases in the profit tax rate. The investors are exempted from all the other taxes to which foreign investors are ordinarily subject to outside the oil sector. All evidence suggests that the Azerbaijani PSA model grants investors stability, with full protection guaranteed through the stabilisation clause and the other relevant contractual clauses.

The legal status of international agreements under the Azerbaijani legal system

Article 148 (I) of the Azerbaijani Constitution regulates normative legal acts in the legislative system. According to the said article, the legislative system consists of '1) the Constitution; 2) acts accepted by referendum; 3) laws; 4) orders; 5) decrees of the Cabinet of Ministers of the Azerbaijan Republic and 6) normative acts of central executive power bodies'.[20] In the second section of Article 148 (II) 'international treaties, wherein the Azerbaijan Republic is one of the parties, constitute an integral part of the legislative system of the Azerbaijan Republic'.[21] This article is far from determining the legal status of international law in the Azerbaijani domestic legal system.

The article only goes as far as to assert the importance of international treaties in the national legal system in a general way. However, it should not be assumed that the Constitution disregards this matter. Several of its articles attempt to clarify this. For instance, Article 151 of the Constitution states:

17 Law No. 439-IQ on Subsoil Act dated 13 February 1998.
18 Law No. 541-IQ on Energy Act dated 24 November 1998.
19 Deloitte, 'Taxation and Investment in Azerbaijan' (2018) 21, available at <www2.deloitte.com/content/dam/Deloitte/az/Documents/tax/aze/TaxBrochures2016/Taxation%20and%20investment%20in%20Azerbaijan%202018_new.pdf>
20 The Constitution of Azerbaijan Republic 12 November 1995 and came into force 27 November 1995, Article 148 (I).
21 Ibid., Article 148 (II).

> [W]henever there is disagreement between normative legal acts in the legislative system of the Azerbaijan Republic (except the Constitution of the Azerbaijan Republic and acts accepted by means of a referendum) and interstate treaties wherein the Azerbaijan Republic is one of the parties, provisions of international treaties shall apply.[22]

Political system of Azerbaijan

Political regime

There is a very little consensus on exactly what form of political regime exists in Azerbaijan. Many assessments have been made in an attempt to reach a conclusion in this matter, resulting only in a long list of proposed definitions which include 'neo-patrimonial dictatorship, sultanistic, authoritarian, semi-authoritarian, sultanistic semi-authoritarian, hybrid, and partially democratic'.[23] Despite the lack of unanimity among scholars on the most accurate description of the political regime, it is widely acknowledged that Azerbaijan belongs to the category of presidential republic, due to the existence of state institutions and general elections for the presidency and for the parliament (both elected for five-year terms), which are, in a broad sense, defining features of a democracy. Although these formal institutions have remained continuously in place over a period of 22 years, Azerbaijan still exhibits many characteristics that correspond with the traditional definition of authoritarianism.[24]

According to Linz, authoritarian regimes are:

> political systems with limited, not responsible, political pluralism; without elaborate and guiding ideology, but with distinctive mentalities; without extensive or intensive political mobilisation, except at some points in their development; and in which a leader or occasionally a small group exercises power within formally ill-defined, but actually quite predictable limits.[25]

Moreover, a report recently published by Freedom House asserts that Azerbaijan lies in the non-free category due to its insufficient performance in the areas of civil liberties and political rights.[26]

22 Ibid., Article 151. It is worth explaining that the definition of an interstate treaty is a treaty between two states or an agreement between a state and an international organisation.

23 O. Bayulgen, *Foreign Investment and Political Regimes: The Oil Sector in Azerbaijan, Russia and Norway* (Cambridge: Cambridge University Press, 2010) 97.

24 A. Filetti, 'Why So Much Stability? An Overview of the Azerbaijani Political System', *Turkish Policy Quarterly*, Vol. 11, No. 3 (2012) 157.

25 J. J. Linz, 'An Authoritarian Regime: The Case of Spain', in E. Allardt & Y. Littunen, *Cleavages, Ideologies and Party System* (Helsinki: Westermarck Society, 1964) 255, cited in Filetti (n. 24 above) 157.

26 See Freedom House Country report on Azerbaijan available at <https://freedomhouse.org/report/freedom-world/2018/azerbaijan>

Inadequate institutional checks and controls and a lack of political competition due to the absence of strong opposition political parties in Milli Majlis (parliament) are two of the key factors behind Linz's definition. The following subsection will examine these factors and their nexus with the necessity for Azerbaijan to agree to stabilisation clauses in the contracts it signs and to provide robust stability in its laws.

Dependency of the judiciary on the executive

Article 99 of the Azerbaijani Constitution states that executive power in Azerbaijan belongs solely to the president.[27] The main duties of the president are specified by Article 109. For instance, the president appoints the prime minister and the cabinet, issues decrees, announces referendums and signs off laws previously passed from the Azerbaijani parliament. The president has the ability to dissolve Milli Majlis and call parliamentary elections. Notwithstanding the fact that the Azerbaijani 1995 iteration of the Constitution provided for a 'system of government based on a nominal division of powers between a strong presidency, a legislature with the power to approve the budget and impeach the president, and a judiciary with limited independence, in reality these state institutions bolster rather than moderate the power of the executive'.[28]

Article 109 of the Constitution indicates that the president submits proposals to the parliament of Azerbaijan regarding the appointment of the judges of the Constitutional Court, the Supreme Court and the Court of Appeal as well as for the judges of other courts in the Azerbaijan Republic. In addition, the president has the power to appoint prosecutors, pending the consent of Milli Majlis. It is apparent that 'the legislative realities are such that judges effectively operate under direct control of the presidential administration'.[29] It can logically be concluded that it is highly probable that the criteria for appointment to the position of judge or prosecutor may depend heavily on being part of the president's inner circle, demonstrating loyalty to this figure and sharing his politics.[30]

Dependency of Milli Majlis on the executive

Technically, Articles 95 and 96 of the Constitution of Azerbaijan provide that Milli Majlis works independently as a legislative branch from the executive authorities. However, in reality the powers of the parliament and the scope of its functions are vastly overshadowed by the scope of presidential powers.[31] Over the past

27 Article 99, Constitution of the Republic of Azerbaijan.

28 O. Bayulgen (n. 23 above) 98; see also Article 119 of the Constitution of the Republic of Azerbaijan (n. 20 above).

29 S. Bagirov, 'Azerbaijan's Oil Revenues: Ways of Reducing the Risk of Ineffective Use', unpublished research paper (January 2007) 55–56.

30 Ibid.

31 R. Badalov & N. Mehdi, 'The Political Institutions of Azerbaijan: A Dichotomy Between Text and Reality', in A. Arakelian (ed.), *Constitutional/Political Reform*

almost two decades, all the elections held in Azerbaijan have been reported to involve serious irregularities and even cases of fraud. The last presidential election was held in Azerbaijan on 11 April 2018. Although President Ilham Aliyev won a fourth term as president, the country has met with severe criticism and its elections have been branded as unfair, non-democratic and not free.[32] Milli Majlis should consist of 125 members using a mixed majority–proportional electoral system that stipulates that parliamentary elections be held every five years.[33] It should be noted that constitutional modifications ratified in 2002 removed the proportional representation of 25 seats in the parliament; all 125 seats are now selected via the majoritarian system.[34]

As a result, parliament becomes more dependent on and therefore obedient to the executive. In other words, whenever the executive organ introduces new laws, Milli Majlis is forced to adopt and pass these laws quickly. This fact can be directly linked to the speedy acceptance of PSAs, which include stabilisation provisions. As these types of contracts are accepted as law following their ratification, regardless of whether a PSA includes strong stabilisation provisions that favour foreign investors over the state, they have a strong chance of gaining acceptance in parliament. More importantly, as there are limited seats for opposition parties, even if they make a claim about the inconsistency of PSAs with existing law, the claim would probably be rejected or ignored by Constitutional courts. As Constitutional courts are not independent, they would consequently avoid making decisions that might contradict the policy of the executive branch.

Absence of strong opposition political parties

In addition to weak political institutions, the political party system in Azerbaijan is also underdeveloped. Azerbaijan is dominated by a single party. The New Azerbaijani Party is currently the ruling party in the country and has enjoyed unbroken power since 1993. There are around 40 political parties in Azerbaijan; nonetheless, there are only six opposition political parties[35] in the Azerbaijani parliament. 'The majority of political parties are small, and unknown to the public'.[36]

Process in Georgia in Armenia and Azerbaijan: Political Elite and Voices of the People (Tbilisi: International Institute for Democracy and Electoral Assistance/Caucasus Institute for Peace, Democracy and Development, 2005) 145, available at <www.idea.int/sites/default/files/publications/the-constitutional-political-reform-process-in-georgia-armenia-and-azerbaijan.pdf>

32 N. Bagirova, 'Azerbaijan's Aliyev wins fourth term as president', Reuters, 11 April 2018, available at <www.reuters.com/article/us-azerbaijan-election/azerbaijans-aliyev-wins-fourth-term-as-president-idUSKBN1HH3CJ>

33 Ibid.

34 Badalov & Mehdi (n. 31 above) 156.

35 Yeni Azerbaijan Party (New Azerbaijan Party), Azerbaijan Democratic Party, Civil Solidarity Party, Motherland Party, Equality Party, Azerbaijani Popular Front Party.

36 O. Bayulgen (n. 23 above) 101

Weak civil society and interest groups

There are a number of interest groups in Azerbaijan, concentrating on issues such as gender inequality, human rights in the Karabakh war, legal awareness and ecological problems. While civil society organisations are officially allowed to operate, their development in Azerbaijan has been hampered on one hand by their relative newness and inexperience and on the other by their limited or non-existent financial resources. Like political parties of the opposition, they receive little public support and are often regarded with suspicion, mostly due to the fact that they rely heavily on financial aid from international donor associations. Moreover, the influence of civil society organisations on government policies is very limited. For example, although laws officially allow the foundation of trade unions and the right to strike, the vast majority of trade unions remain closely allied with the government, and most major industries are state-owned.

How active is the political regime in promoting FDI and giving consent to stabilisation clauses in investment contracts in Azerbaijan?

Since its establishment as a republic, providing a stable and flexible investment environment for alien investors has always been a touchstone of Azerbaijani oil and gas industry policy. Given the compatibility of their interests, and lack of hindrance in pursuing them, political leaders and private investors in Azerbaijan are effectively in cahoots. An assessment of the Azerbaijani political structure has revealed that there is a distinct lack of robust bodies, political or otherwise, likely to present a case against this policy, let alone be in a strong enough position to veto it. In any case, there is no precedential evidence to suggest that they would win the backing of the Azerbaijani general public. The absence of credible opposition has enabled the elite few in life-long positions of power to make investment decisions and define policy with complete free rein. This has given them carte blanche to provide direct, uninhibited and, to a degree, unregulated access to foreign investors during the decision-making process of oil and gas agreements. In Azerbaijan, the president enjoys unique authority and ultimate power in dictating energy investment policy on behalf of the whole country.

As some form of administrative and operational body was required to run refineries and pipelines and oversee the international consortia that develop them, the State Oil Company of Azerbaijan (SOCAR) was formed in 1992. Apart from being a state-owned oil company, SOCAR initially functioned as a government ministry and SOCAR's president carried the rank of minister, and consequently was in direct contact with the president. It is clear that formal government hierarchy and administrative bodies were bypassed and SOCAR was the sole body tasked with responsibility to maintain investment activities and deal with contract design and negotiations. It is also worth underlining that SOCAR's management board and its president have always been appointed from the select group who have ties of kinship with President Aliyev or are in some way close to his family.

For instance, Ilham Aliyev,[37] appointed vice president of SOCAR in 1994, was the son of the then president, Heydar Aliyev. Natig Aliyev, who was the president of SOCAR during Aliyev's presidency, shares the same name but is not a direct relation of the president. He was nevertheless regarded as one of the loyalist elite in President Aliyev's regime. Crucially, important strategic decisions regarding Azerbaijani hydrocarbon development were made within this inner circle, independent of the usual formal government hierarchy. This method enabled President Heydar Aliyev to avoid any potential political divisions, which may have constituted a threat to his control over energy resources. It is clear that unlike the other Turkic countries which have rich natural resources, but are hampered in their actions by complex bureaucratic procedures, Azerbaijan circumvented such obstacles by ring-fencing decision-making for the energy sector and assigning it to a select group of compliant associates, thereby achieving the outward appearance of stability.

A country that is ruled by one man is more appealing to investors than one run by a democratic regime, because it is in a position to provide contractual flexibility in every respect, which supplies a great number of opportunities to foreign investors. Conversely, it is difficult in modern democracies to gain approval for foreign investment contracts that include stability provisions, because political parties in opposition and complex legal structures do not permit governments to get such agreements through parliament with the same ease.

Turkey

Turkey (officially, the Republic of Turkey) is famously located at the crossroads of the Eastern and Western worlds. The country, in senses beyond the palpable geographical one, creates a bridge between the continents of Europe and Asia. The country has borders with eight different states: Greece to the west; Bulgaria to the northwest; Georgia to the northeast; Armenia, Azerbaijan and Iran to the east; and Iraq and Syria to the southeast. The total area of Turkey is 780,000 km^2 and its capital city is Ankara. The population of Turkey is almost 81 million and its largest city is Istanbul, with a burgeoning population of an estimated 14 million. Turkish is the official language of the country and the largest religious group is Sunni Islam. Unlike Azerbaijan, Turkey is not a petroleum-producing country, nor does it have rich oil and gas reserves. However, the country is nevertheless widely regarded as a political and economic powerhouse as well as an energy hub for Europe due to the pipelines which criss-cross its territory. Turkey is also a significant international producer of agricultural goods, textiles, motor vehicles and construction materials.

While, unlike Azerbaijan, Turkey is not a petroleum-rich country, its role in the transit of oil and its importance for the security of energy supplies to Europe is irrefutable. Although the country acts as an energy hub for the Western world, its transit role in the BTC project did not make a significant contribution to its

37 Ilham Aliyev has been the president of Azerbaijan since 2003.

economy; Turkey's interest in involvement was largely strategic. Taking into account the country's rapid economic growth over the last decade, despite the global economic crisis, it would not be wrong to surmise that Turkey's bargaining position would be likely to alter if new oil and gas projects were executed in the Caucasus. Furthermore, the Republic of Turkey is presently the sixth major economy in Europe and it is estimated by some economists that the country is set to reach fourth position by 2050.[38] The conditions responsible for prompting such impressive economic growth over this challenging decade is possibly having the right liberalisation effect in the FDI sphere, the adoption of new FDI law and sound government institutions. During the examination of Turkey, two divergent laws on FDI will be focused upon. When the BTC agreement was signed, Turkey was using the Law for the Encouragement of Foreign Capital No. 6224, adopted on 18 January 1954. The new Law on FDI No. 4875 was adopted on 17 June 2003, and has granted much-welcomed safeguards to alien investors. For this reason, a legal comparison should be made.

Foreign Direct Investment Law No. 4875 (June 2003)

Definition

Article 2(a) of Turkish FDI Law No. 4875 defines foreign investors as: 'Real persons who possess foreign nationality and Turkish nationals resident abroad and foreign legal entities established under the laws of foreign countries and international institutions, who make foreign, direct investment in Turkey.'[39] The article clearly divides foreign investors into two categories. The first includes real persons who have foreign nationality and Turkish nationals who are residents abroad. The second is foreign legal entities formed under the laws of foreign states and international institutions. The definition of the second category is quite narrow because it does not clearly provide for the legal status of Turkish citizens who are permanently or temporarily resident in Turkey, while simultaneously shareholders of a foreign entity formed under the legal system of a foreign state. Compared with the newer Turkish FDI Law No. 4875, the previous Law for the Encouragement of Foreign Capital No. 6224 did not provide an exact definition of a foreign investor. In the absence of a clear definition, perhaps a private investor would have been regarded as a person who had a foreign nationality or a legal entity formed according to a foreign legal system.

Legal protection of foreign investors

The Freedom of Investment and National Treatment principle is regulated under Article 3(a) of FDI Law 4875. According to Article 3(a), '[f]oreign investors are

38 M. Broad, 'Turkey booms – but where are the Brits?' BBC News, 17 May 2013, available at <www.bbc.co.uk/news/business-22562237>

39 Article 2(a) Foreign Direct Investment Law No. 4875, 17 June 2003.

free to make foreign direct investments in Turkey; and foreign investors shall be subject to equal treatment with domestic investors.'[40] Similar to the new FDI law, the previous legislation stipulated a non-discrimination principle under Article 10. According to Article 10, 'all rights, exemptions, privileges and facilities recognised for domestic capital and enterprises shall be equally applicable to foreign capital and foreign enterprises engaged in comparable fields of business'.[41] It is clear that both articles provide non-discriminatory principles.

Stability of legislation

This subject will be revisited more comprehensively in the comparative analysis of this chapter; however, at this point it is worth noting that, unlike Azerbaijani foreign investment law, neither the new FDI Law nor the old Turkish FDI Law includes any stability provisions.

Expropriation/nationalisation

Regulations regarding expropriation and nationalisation are specified in the sub-paragraph (b) of the Article 3 of FDI Law No. 4875 in Turkey. According to sub-paragraph (b), the private property or assets of alien investors cannot be expropriated and nationalised except for public purpose, the consideration of which is paid in accordance with the due process of law.[42] There is no doubt that the article complies with international law standards; however, some ambiguity in this article is to be found in the absence of a definition of public interest. Notably, although previous foreign investment law did not regulate protection against expropriation or nationalisation per se, the Turkish Constitution of 1982 regulates this principle.[43]

40 Ibid. at Article 3(a).

41 Article 10, Law for the Encouragement of Foreign Capital No. 6224, 18 January 1954 (hereinafter Encouragement of Foreign Capital).

42 Turkish Foreign Direct Investment Law (n. 39 above), Article 3(b).

43 According to Article 46 of the Constitution: 'The State and public corporations shall be entitled, where the public interest requires it, to expropriate privately owned real estate wholly or in part and impose administrative servitude on it, in accordance with the principles and procedures prescribed by law, provided that the actual compensation is paid in advance. The compensation for expropriation and the amount regarding its increase rendered by a final judgement shall be paid in cash and in advance. However, the procedure to be applied for compensation for expropriated land in order to carry out land reform, major energy and irrigation projects, and housing and resettlement schemes and a forestation, and to protect the coasts and to build tourist facilities shall be regulated by law. In the cases where the law may allow payment in instalments, the payment period shall not exceed five years, whence payments shall be made in equal instalments. Compensation for the land expropriated from the small farmer who cultivates his own land shall in all cases be paid in advance. An interest equivalent to the highest interest paid on public claims shall be implemented in the instalments envisaged in the second paragraph.' Article 47 of the Constitution also states: 'Private enterprises performing public services may be nationalized when this is required by the exigencies

For as long as the Law for the Encouragement of Foreign Capital No. 6224 was in place, there was no specific article to regulate expropriation or nationalisation cases or any article to determine the compensation due. During that time, Expropriation Law No. 2942 was applied for expropriation and compensation.[44] The valuation of the property or asset and determination of the compensation still applies the rules stipulated by the Expropriation Law of Turkey. It should be noted that when the BTC project agreements were signed, the absence of specific articles on expropriation/nationalisation in the Law for the Encouragement of Foreign Capital No. 6224 would have been regarded as a major cause of concern by the project consortium. It should be noted that the country has, as of yet, had no cases lodged against it regarding expropriation or the nationalisation of foreign investors' property.

Repatriation of profits and convertibility

Another principle framed within Article 3(c) of the new FDI Law is the transfer of funds. According to this article:

> Foreign investors can freely transfer abroad: net profits, dividends, proceeds from the sale or liquidation of all or any part of an investment, compensation payments, amounts arising from licence, management and similar agreements, and reimbursements and interest payments arising from foreign loans through banks or special financial institutions.[45]

It is apparent that through this principle for transfer of funds, Turkey aimed to create an environment in which business transactions could take place freely and efficiently. Indeed, in practice, it is fair to say that foreign investors do not generally experience difficulty in obtaining foreign exchange, and no foreign exchange restrictions are actively enforced in Turkey. The previous FDI law also provided safeguards for the free transfer of profits, fees and royalties, and repatriation of capital; however, in some respects the old law was more restrictive compared with the new legislation.

Article 4(a) of the old FDI Law No. 6224 regulated the availability of transfer of profits for foreign investors in the following ways:

> Net profits accruing in favour of the owner of the principal capital out of income are calculated in accordance with the tax laws in force, in case of a partial or total liquidation of an enterprise established under the present law, the share accruing in favour of the owners of the principal foreign capital at reasonable prices, the proceeds obtained from the sales, at a reasonable price

of public interest. Nationalization shall be carried out on the basis of real value. The methods and procedures for calculating real value shall be prescribed by law.'

44 Turkish Expropriation Law No. 2942, 8 November 1983.

45 Turkish Foreign Direct Investment Law (n. 39 above), Article 3(c).

> and whether in whole or in part, of the principal foreign capital invested in a business founded or working under the terms of the present law, repayment instalments and interest payments, as they become due and payable in accordance with the respective foreign loan agreements.[46]

In addition, Article 4(b) of the now-defunct FDI Law stated that, if considered necessary, the Ministry of Finance or the Committee may be rendered able to order the examination of the accounting books and tax declarations of an enterprise formed under this legislation, in order to determine the amount available for transfer and to order an inquiry to ascertain whether the sale of capital shares or liquidation sale of assets or credit loans were executed in good faith.[47] Furthermore, Article 4(c) of the old FDI law states: 'Upon applications for the transfer of profit shares, sales proceeds, loan repayment instalments and interest payments of the sorts classified as transferable in paragraph (a) of this Article, the Ministry of Finance will grant permission for the same.'[48] In effect, paragraph (a) of Article 4 states that profits and capital funds could only be transferred abroad in the national currency of the principal foreign capital at the current official exchange rate.

All evidence suggests that the old FDI law was very restrictive in transferring the shares of private investors because the law stipulated very detailed terms regarding transferable profit as well as appointing the Ministry of Finance or the Committee to control whether the amount was available for transfer or not and to check whether a would-be alien investor's operations were executed with good faith or not. Admittedly, it is impossible to find such detailed rules for the repatriation of profit as well as bureaucratic checking authority in modern FDI laws because the expectation of contemporary foreign investors, in the context of a global economy, is to be left unbridled to operate their business and transfer their profits free of these bureaucratic hurdles. In addition, the law provides that profits and capital funds could only be moved abroad in the domestic currency of the principal foreign capital at the current official exchange rate. This rule is not compatible with international investment standards, which allow an alien investor the freedom to repatriate their profit by choosing the currency that most benefits them.

Foreign petroleum companies operating in Turkey met with some obstacles in transferring their profits due to the inadequacies of the Petroleum Law of 1954. This law posed some major issues for foreign investment scenarios and needed to be amended in a number of areas. In June 2013, the Turkish parliament adopted a new Turkish Petroleum Law.[49] With this new law it aimed to remove the barriers with which foreign oil companies had previously struggled and to harmonise Turkish law with EU legislation. The removal of the repatriation of registered capital was one of the major incentives offered by the new law.[50] It should be

46 Encouragement of Foreign Capital (n. 41 above), Article 4(a).
47 Ibid. at Article 4(b).
48 Ibid. at Article 4(c).
49 Turkish Petroleum Law No. 6491, 11 June 2013.
50 Ibid. at Article 14.

noted that as Azerbaijan does not have a formally adopted petroleum law, the FDI law of the country regulates the repatriation of profit.

Settlement of disputes

Article 3(e) of the new FDI Law No. 4875 outlines the procedure for the settlement of disputes. This article grants an alien investor the option to apply either to the authorised national local courts or to international arbitration to settle a dispute. The article clearly states:

> For the settlement of disputes arising from investment agreements subject to private law and investment disputes arising from public service concessions contracts and conditions which are concluded with foreign investors, foreign investors can apply either to the authorized local courts, or to national or international arbitration or other means of dispute settlement, provided that the conditions in the related regulations are fulfilled and the parties agree thereon.[51]

Providing an opportunity to apply to the arbitration process both in local courts and international arbitration institutions is a major step. Unfortunately, however, the local court system is overburdened and the decision-making process is very slow.

In contrast with the new law, its predecessor, the Law for the Encouragement of Foreign Capital No. 6224, did not provide any article that enabled foreign investors to apply to international arbitration to settle their disputes. Nevertheless, it should not be assumed that this impeded the resolution of disputes entirely, as Turkey is a signatory country to some international agreements on arbitration. For instance, the ICSID is one of the multilateral agreements to which Turkey is a party. In addition, the BITs that Turkey entered into also enable foreign investors to use the international arbitration process to settle their investment disputes. Taking all of this into consideration, it is probably fair to say that foreign investors did not face major obstacles if their home country entered into BITs with Turkey. Nonetheless, through Article 3(c), the boundaries of arbitration applications have been widened in the Turkish legal system for the first time and any issues regarding the uncertainty and confidence of private investors addressed. All in all, foreign investors are free to apply to arbitration to settle any disputes arising from concession contracts as well as disputes arising from agreements subject to private law. It should be noted that when the Turkish HGA of the BTC project was signed, there was no opportunity for the consortium to apply to international arbitration, because the legal status of concession contracts was that of administrative contracts that could only be arbitrated in accordance with Turkish law.

51 Turkish Foreign Direct Investment Law (n. 41 above), Article 3(g).

Concession agreements

There is no specific concession law provide for by the Turkish legal system; however, concessions have long been in common use and are referenced in several laws,[52] which, however, do not go as far as to provide a definition of the concept in the context of Turkish law. Until 1999, constitutional amendments and concession agreements between private parties and state entities were subject to the jurisdiction of administrative law in Turkey, and therefore any dispute arising out of the concession contracts between a project company and the relevant administration were resolved by the administrative courts, and not by international arbitration courts. For this reason, international arbitration on concession had always been very problematic and was a hindrance to the raising of necessary finance from international markets required for energy projects.

Prior to constitutional amendments, Article 155 of the Turkish Constitution provided that concession agreements were subject to the review of the High Administrative Court (Danistay) in Turkey. In other words, Danistay was the unique authority and had exclusive power of jurisdiction over concession agreements. This constituted a paradox, as although no definition for concession existed in the Turkish Constitution, it did provide for the appointment of the high administrative court as a unique authority for these types of agreement. The necessity of taking the major step of allowing international arbitration was eventually acknowledged by the Turkish government and several amendments were made to the Turkish Constitution to this end.

In August 1999, Articles 47, 125 and 155 of the Constitution were revised, allowing public entities to enter into private law contracts with private parties for the performance of public services. The following provisions were added to Article 125: 'Concession agreements concerning public services may provide that the disputes arising from such agreements are settled by national or international arbitration.'[53] Moreover, with the amendment of Article 155 of the Constitution, the role of the highest administrative court (Danistay) in reviewing the concession agreements and settling disputes was changed. According to these changes, the administrative court could only give its opinion on the correct resolution. Such opinions would no longer be mandatory or legally binding and should be given within a limited period of time.[54]

Article 47 of the Turkish Constitution was also altered to 'Nationalisation and Privatisation'. Before the constitutional amendment was executed, Article 47 did not provide for privatisation. This amendment inserted the concept of privatisation in that article. Article 47 sets out the principles and procedures by which the privatisation of a state-owned business may occur, and outlines which economic enterprises and other public legal entities are governed by the statute. The said

52 For instance, BOT Law No. 3996, 11 June 2011; Law No. 4501 on International Arbitration Relating to Concessions; International Arbitration Law No. 4686.

53 Article 125 of the Constitution of Republic of Turkey, 7 November 1982, came into force 18 November 1982.

54 Ibid. at 155.

article states that 'which of the investments or services that are carried out by the state, state economic enterprises or other public corporations may be performed by or delegated to real or corporate bodies through private law contracts are prescribed by law'.[55] This means that the requirements and the procedures for privatisation of public investments and services are regulated by statute and the privatisation of such investments and services are governed by private law. Articles 47, 125 and 155, can be interpreted as a concerted effort by the Turkish parliament to remove impediments to accessing foreign investment. The only outstanding piece of legal work that remains is the drafting and implementation of a watertight concession law.

Legal status of international agreements under the Turkish legal system

The 1982 Constitution determines the status of international treaties under Article 90 (5): 'International agreements duly put into effect bear the force of law. No appeal to the Constitutional Court shall be made with regard to these agreements, on the grounds that they are unconstitutional.'[56] In May 2004, the Turkish parliament adopted Law No. 5170, which amends several provisions of the Turkish Constitution. Among other things, perhaps the most noteworthy amendment was to the legal status of international treaties. The new law inserted a new sentence into Article 90:

> In the case of a conflict between international agreements in the area of fundamental rights and freedoms duly put into effect and the domestic laws due to differences in provisions on the same matter, the provisions of international agreements shall prevail.[57]

On the adoption of this new law, the question of the superiority of international treaties on human rights over domestic law was laid to rest. Even if the provisions of an international treaty related to human rights were in conflict with the provisions of domestic law, the international agreement would automatically prevail over domestic law. While this can legitimately be considered an advance in human rights provision in Turkey, this amendment has generated several inconsistencies within the Turkish Constitution because Article 90 itself does not determine the hierarchical status of international treaties (other than human rights).

Therefore, even if any provisions of BITs, IGAs or HGAs are in conflict with provisions made by national law, these agreements will take precedence over national law. International treaties other than human rights should not have superiority over domestic law when they are in conflict with the provisions of domestic law. Evidently, the Turkish Constitutional Court regards international treaties to be at the same level as domestic laws, and in the case of a conflict

55 Turkish Constitution 1982 (n. 53 above), Article 147.
56 Ibid., Article 90 (5), Ratification of International Treaties.
57 Ibid.

between the provisions of an international agreement and a domestic law, the same principles as those applied in determining the superiority between two domestic laws would apply in order to determine which one prevails.[58] These standards are that: the specific provision prevails over the general one; the newer provision has superiority over the older one; and the explicit provision prevails over the implicit one. If such agreements were in conflict with the provisions of the Constitution, what would be the status of these agreements? In such scenarios, it cannot be considered that they have superiority over the Constitution because no law can be in conflict with constitutional provisions or have a higher status than the Constitution.

Political system of Turkey

Political regime

Since its establishment, the political regime of Turkey has hovered between authoritarian regime and democracy. For this reason the definition of Turkey's political regime has always been under debate. The regime combines both democracy and authoritarianism; rather, it is a hybrid regime. According to Marshall and Jaggers:

> Hybrid regimes possess a wide mixture of democratic and authoritarian characteristics. The ruling elites generally keep themselves in power, despite the presence of some institutional features of a democracy. Elections are often not competitive and political liberties may be constrained.[59]

According to the Economist Intelligence Unit's democracy index classification, Turkey is categorised as a hybrid regime.[60]

Turkey has had a parliamentary system in place since 1920. In addition, the country has been a secular state since 1937 and has boasted a multi-party system since 1946. After the adoption of a multi-party system in 1946, most of the governments formed in Turkey have been coalitions of two or three political parties. Indeed, between 1991 and 2002 seven different coalition governments[61] were formed, with the longest duration of a single government being three and a half years, in part due to internal divisions and also because much-needed steps to promote investment in Turkey were not taken. A chaotic investment environment

58 Turkish High Court Decision No. E.1996/55, K.1997/33 dated 27 February 1997.

59 M. G. Marshall and K. Jaggers, 'Polity IV Project: Political Regime Characteristic and Transition, 1800–2013', available at <www.systemicpeace.org/polity/polity4.htm>

60 The Economist Intelligence Unit's Democracy Index 2017, available at <https://infographics.economist.com/2018/DemocracyIndex>

61 It is worth mentioning that during the analysis only the coalition governments which governed the country during the economic downturns (1994, 1999 and 2001) will be examined to understand the economic and political conditions in the country when the BTC agreements were signed.

was a mainstay of the coalition years. The current government, the Justice and Development Party (JDP), elected in 2002, was the first party since 1991 to be formed by a single majority party that succeeded in retaining strong public support.

In 2017, the country held a referendum to vote for constitutional amendments, the outcome of which was in favour of a change of Turkey's parliamentary regime to an executive presidency. Why would Turkey contemplate this transition? Arguably, among the multitude of motivating factors that inform any individual voter's decision, from a legal and political perspective the motivating factors are twofold. First, a parliamentary system limits the president's duties, responsibility and legal power. This was perceived to be a handicap by those in favour of a presidential system because the president's right of veto often resulted in delays to the adoption of new laws. Second, under an executive presidential parliamentary regime the government's lifespan is relatively longer, allowing for more long-term planning and substantive reform. However, others believe that an executive presidency could trigger greater polarisation in society and that transparency and accountability issues may ensue if it is not implemented with the correct checks and controls. It should be noted that under the system endorsed, the elected president becomes not only the head of the executive organ but also the head of state and he/she can also continue to be the leader of his/her own political party.

Some constraints on the executive

The 1982 Constitution explicitly states that the Turkish political regime is based on a parliamentary regime; indeed, the Constitution has introduced a *sui generis* system with regard to the legal power invested in the presidency.[62] It is a combination of a parliamentary presidential and a semi-presidential system, and is not purely a parliamentary system.[63] Moreover, the presence of this dual-headed structure has been problematic, precisely when there has been conflict between the prime minister and the president. When the president and the parliamentary majority have differences of opinion, compromise has proven difficult to achieve and such scenarios have often resulted in deadlock of the political system.[64] The record of the last president, Ahmet Necdet Sezer (2000–2007), is testament to this. Sezer used his right to veto draft law a full 73 times. Naturally, this had an effect on government morale and its external image, and, in practical terms, affected parliament's productivity and delayed the enforceability of new legislation in the Turkish legal system.

62 B. Kuzu, 'Türkiye Icin Ba⊠kanlık Sistemi' (in Turkish) *Liberal Düsünce Dergisi*, C.1, S.2 (1996), cited in R. Turk, 'Feasibility of Presidential System in Turkey', *Turkish Journal of Politics*, Vol. 2, No. 1 (2011) 35.

63 Ibid.

64 P. Uran, 'Turkey's Hasty Constitutional Amendments Devoid of Rational Basis: From a Political Crisis to a Governmental System Change', *Journal of Politics and Law*, Vol. 3, No. 1 (2010) 6.

Unfair and limited competition

The organisation of the electoral system in Turkey is the best explanation for why there have been so many coalition governments with consequent effects on decision-making processes in the country, particularly during the late 1990s. The electoral system has also been criticised for placing political parties representing minority groups in the country at an unfair disadvantage. In Turkey, a 10% threshold has been applied in general elections since the creation of the 1982 Constitution. This threshold is higher than any corresponding rate in Europe, and can be said to constitute a major obstacle to the sustainability of Turkish democracy. Rates in the EU include 8% in Liechtenstein, 5% in Germany, Romania and the Czech Republic, 4% in Austria, Spain and Bulgaria, and 3% in Sweden and Greece. Under such an exacting threshold system, only three or four of the stronger political parties can successfully pass the threshold barrier and thereby exercise their elected powers and have a hand in policy-making. Votes in favour of a multitude of other political parties are rendered effectively void. Until this threshold rate is addressed through constitutional amendments, it will be difficult to talk about a pluralist democracy in Turkey.

Weak coalition government years, economic downturns and lethargic legislative activity

In the years between 1991 and 2002, Turkey was administered by a series of seven different incohesive governments whose ineffectiveness at agreeing legislation had a negative impact on development of the country. The last of these was composed of: *Demokratik Sol Party* (left wing), *Milliyetci Haraket Partisi* (nationalist) and *Anavatan Partisi* (centre right). It is perhaps surprising, when the incompatibility of their political views is taken into account, that these parties consented to set about forming a government and ruling the country. As is commonly the case in countries with less mature democracies, the coalition governments found it very difficult to implement macro-economic discipline and establish an environment of political stability conducive to long-term economic growth.[65] This was yet another repetition of the failure to provide economic stability of a coalition government in Turkey and provoked the third major economic downturn in Turkey in less than a decade.

The first of these economic crises occurred in 1994. With no external factors at play, the crisis was attributable solely to the economic blunders of the coalition government of the *Dogru Yol* (True Path) and *Sosyal Demokrat Halkci* (Social Democratic Populist) parties, in power from 1992 to 1995. The second crisis was deeper and emerged in late 1999, while the last crisis closely followed in 2001. The last two crises were to manifest themselves during the term of the coalition government of *Demokratik Sol Party* (Democratic Left Party), *Milliyetci Haraket*

65 Z. Onis, 'Crises and Transformations in Turkish Politics', *Turkish Policy Quarterly*, Vol. 9, No. 3 (2010) 57.

Partisi (Nationalist Action Party) and *Anavatan Partisi* (Motherland Party). Following the 1999 economic downturn, the coalition government forged a stand-by agreement with the International Monetary Fund (IMF) in exchange for which it was required to initiate radical economic reforms in accordance with the stabilisation programme proposed by the IMF. In line with this programme, the Turkish coalition government started to implement a number of laws designed to remove barriers to international trade, such as international arbitration, changes in the banking system, changes in the tax system, limitations to public sector employment, wage and salary rises, and pledged to accelerate the privatisation programme in Turkey. These reforms must have sufficed to satisfy the IMF of Turkey's commitment to economic responsibility and its desire to modernise because a long-term stand-by agreement was signed between the Republic of Turkey and the IMF in 1999.

In November 1999, the government of Turkey hosted the European Security and Cooperation Organisation (ESCO) in Istanbul and signed the Intergovernmental Agreement of the BTC project along with Azerbaijan and Georgia. The country was accepted as a candidate country to the EU in the same year and was required to implement a series of political reforms. The same coalition government oversaw the inclusion of Turkey in the G20. Policy reforms and an improved relationship with the West gave the sense that things were on the up until 2001, when the country faced a dramatic repetition of economic breakdown. The same coalition government that had seemed to offer so much promise two years earlier had fallen into disarray due to a disagreement between the president and the prime minister. In February 2001, at a meeting of the National Security Council, President Ahmet Necdet Sezer flung the Constitution Book on to his desk and warned Prime Minister Bulent Ecevit that the government should respect the rules and activities of the Constitution. According to some observers, the president was poised to raise allegations of corruption against certain members of the cabinet.[66] This fierce public showdown between president and prime minister served to emphasise the fragility of the country's political cohesion and its economy was to be the next victim of this, as was the coalition government itself, as elections were called early, on 1 November 2002.

Absence of strong opposition political parties

Since 3 November 2002, Turkish politics have been shaped by a single-party regime. Under the JDP, the country has reached a state of economic and political stability and taken its place among the fastest-growing countries in the world,[67] even while it was surrounded by economic and political crisis in neighbouring countries.

66 M. Hic & A. H. Gencer, *Turkish Economy and Politics: From 1923, the Foundation of the Republic until 2002* (Istanbul: Beykent University Press, 2010) 192.

67 The World Bank in Turkey, available at <www.worldbank.org/en/country/turkey/overview>

Weak public interest groups

The transition to democracy in Turkey during the 1990s was directly shaped by the bureaucratic and military elites, rather than public interest groups.[68] More recently, partly as a result of the ongoing EU accession process, civilian organisations have increased in number and activity. However, there is still a long way for them to go before they can enjoy the same levels of influence as their Western European counterparts. For example, according to the Turkish Petroleum Law No. 6491, the Council of Ministers is the only authority able to provide licences to petroleum companies to explore and extract petroleum resources in a specific region. However, in most modern democracies, governments have a duty to first inform public interest groups and invite their assessments of how this will affect the region before granting licences to foreign investors. The local knowledge of such groups and the crucial communication links they can provide by being on the ground, informed and being economically, politically and socially aware can be a huge asset to both government and society if properly harnessed. Effective consultation with such groups is emblematic of a transparent and accountable regime. It is indicative of the distance the Turkish government still needs to travel that although there are hundreds of unions and chambers of commerce in Turkey, their role in shaping government policy is negligible.

How effective is the political regime in promoting FDI and giving consent to stabilisation clauses in Turkish investment contracts?

An analysis of the political regime in Turkey illustrates the significance of political institutions in the attraction of FDI. The ineffective performance of the series of coalition governments in legislative activities, the emergence of three economic crises in less than a decade, the president's excessive power to veto government decisions, the military's disproportionate control of domestic and foreign policy, and the weakness of public interest groups all contributed to the bleak picture of Turkish development in the decade from 1992 to 2002. This situation of political and economic instability accounts for the weak bargaining position Turkey found itself in when it was on the point of signing the BTC agreements. This can be contrasted with the leverage that Turkey enjoys under the current political regime.

Retrospectively, the first decade of the new millennium can be seen as a turning point for Turkey's standing in the international arena. Strengthened political and economic stability, a flexible investment environment, newly adopted laws and an increase in the number of signed BITs with partner states are the key factors to which the country's accession to a roles as a key world player can be attributed. Does that mean that Turkey is likely to agree to stabilisation clauses in its host government agreements in the future? Arguably, it is fair to assert that a single-party regime has improved stability and sustainability in many sectors in Turkey.

68 See T. Cetin, 'The Role of Institutions over Economic Change in Turkey', Chapter 2 in T. Cetin & F. Yilmaz (eds), *Understanding the Process of Economic Change in Turkey: An Institutional Approach* (Turkey: Nova Science Publishers, 2010) 25.

In order to attract foreign investors in the energy sector, the country may agree such clauses in their future agreements.

A comparison of guarantees available under FDI laws and political regimes in Azerbaijan and Turkey

In Turkey, FDI Law No. 4875 has introduced a number of safeguards for alien investors not provided for by the version it replaced. There is still scope for improvement in order to render it truly comprehensive. For instance, Article 2 of the new law defines the foreign investor; however, the article does not explicitly outline the status of those individuals who hold Turkish citizenship and live permanently or temporarily in Turkey, but who are at the same time shareholders in a foreign entity registered abroad. Arguably, perhaps the second paragraph of Article 2 could be interpreted as referring to a Turkish national who is resident abroad or in Turkey; a shareholder of a foreign legal entity formed in accordance with a foreign legal system is also accepted as foreign investor. Similarly, notwithstanding the fact that Article 3 of the new FDI law determines the legal justification (public purpose) for expropriation and nationalisation of a property or an asset, public purpose should be explicitly referenced, or at least relevant examples should have been provided. Although previous FDI law did not regulate protection and nationalisation, no expropriation or nationalisation cases have ever emerged in Turkey.

The new FDI law allows for disputes to be settled in either local or international tribunals. This option has been provided to alien investors; however, considering the backlog of cases in local courts, the vast majority of investors would prefer to settle their disputes in international courts. For this reason, reform in the judicial system is urgently called for. Furthermore, there is no article that regulates concession contracts in the FDI law of Turkey. Indeed, there is no specific concession law in the country. Despite its aspiration to EU membership, it still does not have a proper concession law. Although constitutional law refers to concession agreements, and points out that they are subject to private law, the country urgently requires the implementation of a proper concession law.

The legal status of international treaties under the Turkish legal system is another issue that needs to be addressed. Article 90 of the Turkish Constitution clearly states that international agreements on human rights have a higher status in the legal hierarchy than domestic law. Even where conflict arises between the provisions of domestic laws and international treaties, the latter prevails. However, the article does not clarify the status of international treaties in areas other than human rights and the environment, thereby creating an ambiguity that can be exploited to infer that every international treaty has a higher status and prevails over national law. In terms of legal practice international treaties other than human rights and environment should not prevail over domestic laws. If treaties and domestic law provisions are head to head, the same principles as those that are applied in determining the superiority between two domestic laws should be applied in order to determine which prevails. Consequently, an amendment to

Article 90 of the Constitution is needed to determine the legal status of international agreements other than those regarding human rights.

Unlike Azerbaijan, the political regime in Turkey is of a hybrid nature. However, after the adoption of new political system the country will no longer be governed by the parliamentary regime after the presidential election, held on 24 July 2018. The 10% threshold is an additional stumbling block for Turkish democracy. In order to create a system that gives representation to minorities as well as the overwhelming majority in the context of a country with a number of under-represented minority groups, a constitutional amendment needs to be drafted to limit the current threshold.

Azerbaijan has established an open and liberal investment regime for private investors through its legislation. The 1992 FDI law includes a number of safeguards for alien investors; however, a well-written modern FDI law is urgently required. The equal treatment principle (applicable to domestic and foreign investors), guarantees against expropriation and nationalisation, dispute settlement mechanisms, repatriation of profits and convertibility are all forms of protection provided by current Azerbaijani FDI law. It is worth noting that no expropriation and nationalisation cases have yet been brought in Azerbaijan. Nevertheless, although FDI law regulates the free transfer of profits, some restrictions are imposed by the National Bank of Azerbaijan. Furthermore, unlike Turkey, Azerbaijan provides stability of legislation under its FDI law. Article 10 provides a ten-year stability guarantee for alien investors in the event that the Azerbaijani government makes changes in law. Notably, this rule is not applied to changes related to the tax system.

The existing settlement of dispute mechanisms in Azerbaijan, coupled with Azerbaijani FDI law, enables investors to resolve their disputes either in local courts or international arbitral tribunals. Unlike Turkey, where local courts are simply overwhelmed with cases, the Azerbaijani local court system and mechanisms for dispute resolution are still evolving and the rights of investors may not be handled with the expected impartiality due to institutionalised corruption and the fact that judges often struggle to keep abreast of new legislation, resulting in inconsistent rulings. In relation to these weaknesses in the judiciary system, the enforcement of foreign arbitral awards is also inconsistent, despite the fact that the country is a member of the New York Convention formed in 1958.

In contrast with Turkey, Azerbaijani FDI law does regulate concession contracts, but the extent of this regulation is limited to national resources, and the article that regulates these contracts does not provide a proper definition of the concept of concession contracts. In addition, like Turkey, Azerbaijan does not have a concession law within its legal system.

Considering the dependence of the Azerbaijani economy on the oil sector, it seems paradoxical that it does not have a petroleum law and that oil agreements are executed through PSAs. When these types of agreements are passed by parliament and ratified by the president of the country, they take on the status of laws and prevail over existing domestic law. Conventionally, oil and gas agreements are regulated through the Subsoil Act and the Energy Act. While these laws provide a general framework for the exploitation of energy resources in Azerbaijan, their provisions are inconsistent with each other and do not match or reference the provisions provided under PSAs. Surprisingly, there is no single ruling which determines whether the general Energy Act takes precedence over the Subsoil Act.

The Azerbaijani political structure is based on a presidential parliamentary system. However, due to the fact that the regime is unconstrained and uncompetitive; the Azerbaijani state is widely regarded as authoritarian. Parliament itself is also under the influence of the executive branch.

Whenever new laws or PSAs are introduced by the executive, draft laws pass with suspicious speed through parliament. In Azerbaijan, there are no veto players within the state as the Milli Majlis (parliament) is a symbolic institution and there are no strong opposition political parties. Like their Turkish counterparts, public interest groups in Azerbaijan are weak and do not enjoy a consultative role in decision-making processes.

Conclusions

Through the analysis of this chapter, the guarantees available to private investors under the respective FDI laws and political regimes of Azerbaijan and Turkey were examined. The clear picture that emerges from an examination of the guarantees available to foreign investors under the FDI laws of Azerbaijan and Turkey is that both countries' present laws share the goal of providing a friendly investment environment. Providing a stable legal framework in FDI law and a predictable legislative and regulatory framework in PSAs have been key accomplishments of the Azerbaijani government. However, taking into account the country's commercial potential, Azerbaijani FDI law is arguably an insufficient pull factor for foreign investors outside the oil sector. While, on the one hand, the law on FDI offers assurance to investors regarding non-discriminatory treatment, stability in legislation, protection against risks such as expropriation and nationalisation, dispute settlement mechanisms, repatriation of profits and convertibility, on the other hand, corruption, red tape, an inexperienced and inefficient judiciary, and a poor track record for the enforcement of foreign arbitral awards detract from Azerbaijan's appeal. In addition, the country's heavy dependence on the petroleum sector has the potential to trigger social unrest and ensuing economic instability.

As stated above, Azerbaijan relies heavily on its rich oil resources and provides a number of guarantees through its PSAs. Paradoxically, the country has no petroleum legislation to execute and arrange these contracts. Instead, the contracts are drawn up as a result of negotiation between oil companies and the country's state-owned petroleum company, SOCAR. The intergovernmental agreement is a treaty per se and is an umbrella legal document of the BTC pipeline project that aimed to create a prevailing regime for the pipeline project in each contracting state's domestic law. As mentioned above, in some cases where immediate actions are required, the Constitution of Azerbaijan enables the government to enter into intergovernmental agreement with other states.

The Azerbaijani HGA that was annexed to the IGA in the BTC project has the status of law as it was added to the treaty. The problem here is that the HGA is a concession or commercial contract and should be subject to private law and therefore cannot be regarded as an international treaty. The reason why the BTC Consortium's lawyers applied this method perhaps lies in concerns regarding the weakness of the country's legal system and the fact that international arbitration for this type of agreement was not possible when the HGA was signed. In essence, Azerbaijan consented to a stabilisation clause because this was the will of the authoritarian regime. The regime did not invite comment on this from the parties that would normally be consulted in a more developed and freer regime. The overriding objective of the regime was to secure investment for this project so important to their economic prosperity and political independence, and their determination that this project should go ahead silenced any other concerns. Indeed, the overwhelming will of authoritarianism serves as a guarantee to foreign investors, providing to them the security that the continuation of the project is so clearly in the interests of the regime that it will use all of its might to ensure it goes ahead.

Turkey took a major step in liberalising its economy by adopting new FDI legislation in 2003. The Law on the Encouragement of Foreign Capital that it replaced also recognised the principle of national treatment to alien investors and the free transfer of profits derived from that investment. However, the old law did not provide guarantees against expropriation or nationalisation or a mechanism for settlement of disputes. In the absence of these legal protections, doing business on Turkish territory was perceived to be too high a risk by many investors. This goes some way to explain why Turkey gave consent to a stabilisation clause in the HGA for the BTC agreement.

Article 90 of the Turkish Constitution regards international agreements and their related legal documentation (HGAs) as having prevailing status over domestic law. It has been also emphasised that in the case of a conflict between the provisions of an international agreement and a domestic law, the same principles as those that are applied in determining the superiority between two domestic laws apply in order to determine which one prevails, and that is simply that only those that pertain to human rights can be given superior status.

The legal status of HGAs in the BTC project is another anomaly. These types of contracts are subject to administrative law or private law and not to international law. Notably, in most civil law systems, these types of contracts are subject to administrative law and the awarding authority is the administrative courts. More significantly, when the impact of HGAs and IGAs on Turkey's national sovereignty is considered, these agreements should not have had a prevailing status over domestic law because their provisions contradict the state sovereignty principle provided by the Turkish Constitution. Indeed, the Turkish government and the political parties represented in parliament should have considered this before they approved the BTC agreements, as Article 11 of the Turkish Constitution explicitly forbids state organs, decision makers and veto players from being party to such agreements.

The Intergovernmental Agreement of the BTC project was signed on 18 November 1999. It is revealing that only nine months later constitutional amendments were executed in Turkey to change the status of concession agreements from administrative contracts to private agreements so that they could become subject to international arbitration. It is conceivable that the BTC Consortium perceived the status of concession contracts under the Turkish legal system to be an obstacle, which may have prompted them to lobby privately for the amendment of the Turkish Constitution before a host government agreement was signed between the consortium and Turkey. In order to ensure that access to international arbitration could be gained, and to facilitate the adoption of the concession contract (which clearly did not have public interest as its goal), it was imperative that Turkey amended articles that regulated the status of concession contracts.

There is a long list of other contributing internal factors that facilitated Turkey's acceptance of a stabilisation clause in its host government agreement for the BTC project, including: the ineffective performance of the weak coalition governments in legislative activities; the country's series of economic crises; the military's influential role on the executive branch; and the weakness of public interest groups. In that respect, it can be said that a politically and economically chaotic and unstable environment influenced not only the attraction of foreign capital into the country but also adversely affected the country's bargaining position in the BTC agreement.

Bibliography

Legislation and guides

Build-Operate-Transfer Law No. 3996, 11 June 2011

Foreign Direct Investment Law No. 4875, 17 June 2003

International Arbitration Relating to Concessions Law No. 4501 (Official Gazette, 21 January 2000, No. 23941)

Law for Encouragement of Foreign Capital No. 6224, (Official Gazette, 18 January 1954)

Law No. 439-IQ on Subsoil Act dated 13 February 1998

Law No. 541-IQ on Energy Act dated 24 November 1998

Law of the Azerbaijan Republic about Protection of Foreign Investments (Official Gazette, 15 January 1992, No. 57)

The Constitution of Republic of Turkey, 7 November 1982 and came into force 18 November 1982

Turkish Expropriation Law No. 2942, 8 November 1983

Turkish Petroleum Law No. 6491, 11 June 2013

Cases and arbitral awards

Turkish High Court Decision No. E.1996/55, K.1997/33 dated 27 February 1997

Internet websites

http://data.worldbank.org/country/azerbaijan

www.bbc.co.uk/news/business-22562237

www.worldbank.org/en/country/turkey/overview

https://freedomhouse.org/report/freedom-world/2018/azerbaijan
https://infographics.economist.com/2018/DemocracyIndex
www.nytimes.com/2013/10/11/world/asia/observers-say-azerbaijan-election-marred-by-fraud.html
www.reuters.com/article/us-azerbaijan-election/azerbaijans-aliyev-wins-fourth-term-as-president-idUSKBN1HH3CJ

Books

Bayulgen, O., *Foreign Investment and Political Regimes: The Oil Sector in Azerbaijan, Russia and Norway*. Cambridge: Cambridge University Press, 2010

Cetin, T., 'The Role of Institutions over Economic Change in Turkey', Chapter 2 in T. Cetin & F. Yilmaz (eds), *Understanding the Process of Economic Change in Turkey: An Institutional Approach*. Turkey: Nova Science Publishers, 2010

Ebel, R. & Menon, R., *Energy and Conflict in Central Asia and the Caucasus*. Boston, MA: Rowman & Littlefield Publishers, 2000

Global Investment Centre, *Azerbaijan: Mineral, Mining Sector Investment and Business Guide – Strategic Information and Regulations Vol. 1*. Washington, DC: International Business Publications, 2012

Hic, M. & Gencer, A. H., *Turkish Economy and Politics: From 1923, the Foundation of the Republic until 2002*. Istanbul: Beykent University Press, 2010

United Nations, *Foreign Direct Investments in Central Asian and Caucasian Economies: Policies and Issues, Papers and Proceedings Presented at the Regional Round Table on Foreign Direct Investment for Central Asia, Dushanbe, 3 and 4 April 2003*. New York: United Nations Publications, 2003

Chapters in books

Cetin, T., 'The Role of Institutions over Economic Change in Turkey', Chapter 2 in T. Cetin & F. Yilmaz (eds), *Understanding the Process of Economic Change in Turkey: An Institutional Approach*, Turkey: Nova Science Publishers, 2010

Hoffman, D. I., 'Azerbaijan: The Politicization of Oil', Chapter 4 in R. Ebel & R. Menon (eds), *Energy and Conflict in Central Asia and the Caucasus*. Lanham, MD: Rowman & Littlefield Publishers, 2000

Linz, J. J., 'An Authoritarian Regime: The Case of Spain', in E. Allardt & Y. Littunen (eds), *Cleavages, Ideologies and Party System: Contributions to Comparative Political Sociology*. Helsinki: Westermarck Society, 1964

Articles, seminars/conferences and research papers

Badalov, R. &Mehdi, N., 'The Political Institutions of Azerbaijan: A Dichotomy Between Text and Reality', in A. Arakelian (ed.), *Constitutional/Political Reform* Process in Georgia in Armenia and Azerbaijan: Political Elite and Voices of the People. Tbilisi: International Institute for Democracy and Electoral Assistance/Caucasus Institute for Peace, Democracy and Development, 2005, available at <www.idea.int/sites/default/files/publications/the-constitutional-political-reform-process-in-georgia-armenia-and-azerbaijan.pdf>

Bagirov, S. 'Azerbaijan's Oil Revenues: Ways of Reducing the Risk of Ineffective Use', unpublished research paper (January 2007).

Ciaretta, A. & Nasirovm, S. 'Development Trends in the Azerbaijan Oil and Gas Sector: Achievements and Challenges', *Elsevier Energy Policy*, Vol. 40 (2012) 15

Filetti, A., 'Why So Much Stability? An Overview of the Azerbaijani Political System', *Turkish Policy Quarterly*, Vol. 11, No. 3 (2012) 157

Kuzu, B., 'Türkiye Icin Ba⊠kanlık Sistemi' (in Turkish), *Liberal Düsünce Dergisi*, C.1 (1996) 2

Marshall, M. G. & Jaggers, K. 'Polity IV Project: Political Regime Characteristic and Transitions, 1800–2013', available at <www.systemicpeace.org/polity/polity4.htm>

Onis, Z., 'Crises and Transformations in Turkish Politics', *Turkish Policy Quarterly*, Vol. 9, No. 3 (2010) 57

Uran, P., 'Turkey's Hasty Constitutional Amendments Devoid of Rational Basis: From a Political Crisis to a Governmental System Change', *Journal of Politics and Law*, Vol. 3, No. 1 (2010) 6

Reports

Deloitte, 'Taxation and Investment in Azerbaijan' (2018), available at <www2.deloitte.com/content/dam/Deloitte/az/Documents/tax/aze/TaxBrochures2016/Taxation%20and%20investment%20in%20Azerbaijan%202018_new.pdf>

Part III

Conclusion and recommendations

6 Conclusions and recommendations

The research findings and conclusions

Oil- and gas-related energy projects and the agreements forged to enable them to go ahead are inherently open to political risk. In fact, these projects are more vulnerable and susceptible to risk than perhaps any other sector in the business world. International investors in the petroleum industry have always been advised to equip themselves against a range of phenomena that may endanger their investment.

In cases of indirect expropriation, the project is intervened in or indeed taken over by the host state either with unilateral state actions or with subtle state actions. In these scenarios the state aims to change the terms and condition of the agreements. However, the latter occurs slowly and aims to exclude investors from the project gradually. Imposing a discriminatory tax regime, interference with the management rights of the investor, interference with contractual rights, revocation of licences and denial of permits are all typical examples of indirect expropriation. It has also been found that measures related to environmental or human rights issues have been used by host states as justification for interference in the energy sector. A reliable litmus test to distinguish between non-compensable regulatory state measures (in the area of environment, human rights, health and safety) has not yet been identified by tribunals and consequently remains a significant and unresolved issue in the agenda of international law.

There are various contractual mechanisms included in oil and gas contracts to minimise risk, many specifically targeting indirect expropriation to protect foreign private investors and to have a stabilising effect on the investment environment of the host state. Stabilisation clauses are one of the most frequently applied contractual clauses in international investment agreements, taking their place alongside arbitration clauses and choice-of-law clauses. There is no doubt that stabilisation clauses preserve the fiscal regime over the course of the project and reduce the political risk which may affect the economic return of the investment. Stabilisation clauses are valid under international law.

However, the validity of these clauses under national law is still a conundrum because laws or legal constraints in the constitution of the state may have significant legal implications for the validity and enforcement of a stabilisation clause. For this reason, international energy investors seek to internationalise contracts. Nevertheless, it should not be forgotten that even if the contract between the parties is governed by international law, the law will not offer full assurances of stability for the contract because it is recognised in international law that a sovereign power has the right to intervene in a contract when significant interests are at stake. This should not be taken to mean that stabilisation clauses have no effect in risk management against unlawful expropriation or nationalisation or indirect expropriation. They have a legal value and effect against any state actions that can be deemed illegitimate or unlawful.

The cited international arbitral awards verified that stabilisation clauses are valid and enjoy legal status in international law. The question is whether stabilisation provisions can preclude host states from lawful expropriation or nationalisation. There is no hindrance to states from interfering in an ongoing project by nationalising or expropriating the property of an investor, if the grounds of the intervention are rooted in public interest and as long as adequate compensation is paid.

Sovereign states may fetter legislative activities and promise that the property of foreign private investors will not be nationalised or that unilateral action will not be undertaken during the lifespan of the project agreement. However, host states cannot be required to forgo their sovereign rights in the areas of human rights and environmental concerns because these are the non-assignable and inalienable rights that stem from international treaty obligations. The reasonable solution would seem to be to narrow or limit the scope of the stabilisation clause in the areas of human rights and the environment. Recently adopted, modern BITs seem to have successfully excluded measures relating to these areas and, in some cases, explicitly assert that measures taken in these areas cannot amount to indirect expropriation.

Despite the provisions for host state sovereignty outlined above, in the agreement signed for the BTC project, the Republics of Azerbaijan, Georgia and Turkey effectively abandoned these irrevocable rights by agreeing not to implement any measures in the area of human rights and environment, health and safety during the lifespan of the project agreements. They agreed that the adoption of new laws in the aforementioned areas would constitute a violation of their commitment to stability in the project agreement. These commitments naturally came under fire from NGOs and the companies involved in the project responded by issuing a legal document called the Human Rights Undertaking. This undertaking guarantees that the consortium participating in the BTC project may not require compensation if these states adopt new laws in the area of human rights and the environment or in the interests of health and safety.

Through the Human Rights Undertaking, the BTC Company gave guarantees that it would not apply the compensation clauses in the IGA and HGAs if one of the host states involved in the project legislated in the interests of human rights, environment, health and safety. From that perspective, it might be said that the Human Rights Undertaking represented a breakthrough and was an innovative work, commissioned by the BTC Company as an expression of their sensitivity towards human rights issues. As this action resulted in a restriction of the reach of the stabilisation clause in the BTC agreements, host states were thereby rendered freer to legislate. In addition, the BTC consortium attempted to limit the scope of the stabilisation clause in certain areas by this undertaking. Notwithstanding, it is the case that, to date, none of the signatory states of the project has proposed or passed new laws in the areas of human rights or the environment to test this hypothesis.

This study has argued that internal and external driving forces trigger the inclusion of stabilisation clauses in investment agreements. The findings relating to external factors demonstrate that lenders, political risk insurance providers and credit rating agencies play a significant role in the insertion of stabilisation provisions in investment agreements. In the event of risks, such as change of law, introduction of new regulations, expropriation or nationalisation, the inclusion of stabilisation clauses is held to be an indispensable contractual requirement for investors. The inclusion of stabilisation clauses also improve an investor's chances of securing the substantial loans required to fund major projects, such as transnational oil and gas pipeline projects. Indeed, the financial institutions able to grant such funds demand that risks are managed to secure the prospect of repayment. Moreover, it was found that financial lenders have a 'behind the scenes' but nevertheless highly influential role in deterring host states from introducing new laws that may affect the sustainability and the cost of the project. On their part, it was observed that lenders would never consider funding or committing to a project without political risk insurance cover.

It was established that insurers involved in projects provide arbitral award default coverage of stabilisation provisions as a safety net for their clients in the event that a host state fails to pay compensation triggered by the violation of stabilisation provisions. National insurance institutions can wield subrogation rights against host states to pressurise them to make payment. In practice, this means that insurers may use their third-party rights to compel the host state to reimburse overdue compensation payments in situations where insurers have provided the missing funds to the investor in lieu of the host state's payment. While this third-party right is recognised in law, the not uncommon practice of asserting this right before an arbitral tribunal has passed judgement on whether the state's action actually violated stabilisation provisions is questionable.

The final external factor presented by this study was the role of credit rating agencies in indirectly advocating the insertion of stabilisation clauses. It was observed that the chief role of these organisations in an investment scenario is to evaluate the risk of lending for sovereign countries and multinational organisations. In this evaluation, the legal framework that underpins the investment agreement between host state and foreign investor may also be taken into consideration. It was made evident that the existence of a stabilisation clause in an agreement maximises the chances of that project winning the commitment of lenders who will consult the information made available to them by credit rating agencies.

The study has shown that the reach of the stabilisation clause in the form of economic equilibrium is much broader in the BTC project than is conventionally acceptable. In this context, whenever a host state affects the economic equilibrium of the project as a result of changes in law they have to pay compensation to the consortium, even when those changes are made in the interests of human rights and the environment. This effectively inhibits the host countries in question from honouring their international law obligations and can be characterised, at the very least, as over-zealous protectionism on the part of the investors and other stakeholders. Although the project consortium lawyers were directly responsible for preparing the legal framework for each contract, these legal professionals were merely following the requirements of their clients. The consortium, for its part, sought to satisfy the World Bank Group (particularly the IFC and the MIGA), the EBRD and the other ECAs, in order to receive the project loan and to gain insurance for this major project. It was also found that the diplomatic power of the European Union, the United States, the World Bank and the EBRD were also highly influential on Azerbaijan, Georgia and Turkey during the during the negotiation of the legal agreements.

The author has also assessed the bargaining position held by each state and noted its interests in the BTC project. In the case of Azerbaijan, as the most significant possessor of natural resource, the country's bargaining position was relatively stronger than that of Georgia and Turkey. However, Azerbaijan's ongoing dispute with Armenia over the Nagorno-Karabakh territory was a major drawback from the perspective of investors. Azerbaijani expectations of the BTC project were both financial and territorial, and the two were interwoven. It was hoped by the Azerbaijani authorities that any economic benefit gained from the project could be used to fund military action against Armenia so that the country could win decisive control over the Nagorno-Karabakh region.

The singular strength of Georgia was its unique position, in light of the dispute between Armenia and Azerbaijan, to act as a conduit country for the natural resources. The weaknesses of the country were the ongoing Russian threat, its fragile economy and poor standard of living. For Georgia, the BTC project had both strategic and economic value. In the case of Turkey, the potential enhancement of its strategic partnership with its diplomatic partners in the EU and the US overshadowed any economic benefits to be had. In any case, Turkey's prospects for financial gain from the project were more modest than those stood to be had by Azerbaijan and Georgia.

The political structure and guarantees available to foreign investors in Azerbaijan and Turkey were the internal driving forces that led them to agree to stabilisation clauses in the BTC project. In the case of Azerbaijan, the 1992 law on FDI provided guarantees to foreign private investors regarding non-discriminatory treatment, legislative stability, protections against risks such as expropriation and nationalisation, dispute settlement mechanisms, repatriation of profits and convertibility. However, in practice, investors face major challenges in dispute settlement, particularly in terms of achieving the repatriation of their profits. In addition, FDI law does not define the term 'concession' and those concessions to be had are limited to natural resources. In fact, there is no concession law as such in domestic legislation. In Azerbaijan, endemic corruption, obstructive bureaucracy and the inexperience of judges all contribute to a very low rate of foreign arbitral award enforcement. In the oil sector, guarantees and assurance are given to foreign investors via PSAs. When these agreements are signed by the president, they take on the status of law and enjoy prevailing status over domestic law. Somewhat surprisingly, no existing petroleum legislation was found to regulate these types of contracts.

An analysis of the political structure of Azerbaijan has evidenced that the president of the country holds almost absolute power. The judicial branch is weak and the legislative organ is under the influence of the executive branch. The absence of strong veto players, strong political parties or opinion-leading public interest groups leave the actions of the executive unchecked.

In the case of Turkey, the law on FDI, implemented in 2003, can be seen as a breakthrough. The law provides a number of safeguards to foreign private investors, although, in the interests of exactness, it would be advisable for several minor amendments to be made, particularly regarding the provision of definitions of 'investor' and 'expropriation'. Comparisons between the Law on the Encouragement of Foreign Capital and the new FDI law demonstrate that guarantees against expropriation or nationalisation and the settlement of dispute mechanism were not available under the previous FDI law in Turkey. It can be surmised that when the BTC project agreements were signed, these omissions must have been regarded as an unwanted complication for the consortium. Furthermore, international agreements and host government contracts have a higher status in the legal hierarchy than domestic law. Notably, an HGA is a concession contract and subject to either administrative or private laws. Before the project agreements of the BTC projects were signed, this type of contract would have been subject to national administrative law. The disputes that arose from concession contracts between foreign investors and the relevant administration used to be managed by national courts rather than by international arbitration courts in the past. Proof that this was seen as a major hurdle is provided by the fact that the project consortium lobbied the Turkish authorities to make constitutional changes to the status of concession contracts in order to render them subject to private law. It was also found that there is no law on concession in Turkey.

An analysis of Turkey's political regime has shown that several factors contributed to Turkey's weak bargaining position on signing the BTC agreement. These included: the unsuccessful performance in legislative activities of a series of weak coalition governments; a chaotic investment environment marred by two dramatic economic crises within a short period; the president's strong veto power in government decisions coupled with the military's excessive control over executive domestic and foreign policy, all unchecked by any significant pressure from public interest groups. The 10% threshold imposed by the 1982 Constitution still constitutes a major problem for the country's future. In addition, public interest groups and political opposition parties are still weak and do not play an active role in decision-making.

Recommendations

Recommendations deriving from the findings of the present study are as follows:

With respect to indirect expropriation and stabilisation clauses

(1) Although indirect expropriation is inarguably the most menacing and destructive form of risk, there are means in existence to prevent its occurrence and to mitigate its

effects. The insertion of stabilisation clauses in the investment agreement is generally the most effective way to discourage host states from interfering in the project unlawfully.

(2) A sovereign state should be free to exercise its sovereignty by regulating matters that have a direct effect on the standard of living and safety of its citizens and its territory such as the environment, human rights and health and safety. Stabilisation commitments in investment agreements cannot force a host state to relinquish its international treaty obligations in these areas. For this reason, stabilisation clauses should be fair and flexible. More significantly, the aforementioned areas of jurisdiction should be singled out from the scope of any stabilisation commitment. Referencing the inalienable rights of a host state to legislate freely in these areas independently of any other commitment in the investment agreement would help avoid any ambiguity and would inhibit an investor from lodging indirect expropriation claims on this basis.

(3) Developing countries' economies are mostly fragile and unsteady. Therefore, contract drafters should take this factor into account. Inserting a broad stabilisation clause may lead a host state to breach the terms and conditions of the contract and trigger resource nationalism in that country. Rather than designing a rigid contract, energy investors should attempt to bring flexibility and stability together in one clause. Perhaps the best method is an equilibrium clause.

(4) When international tribunals are evaluating whether a measure taken by a host state amounts to expropriation, it would be advisable for them to apply both sole effect doctrine and police power notion in order to achieve a balanced assessment, as the use of only the former would suggest a bias in favour of alien investors, while the latter takes into consideration the state's right to regulate. Perhaps this combination of doctrines constitutes the fairest approach, removing the uncertainty around the question of distinguishing a non-compensable regulatory measure from indirect expropriation.

(5) Most of the cited cases demonstrate that the inclusion of stabilisation clauses in investment agreements is valid and has legal standing in international law. These decisions can serve as useful future reference for cases examining the validity of stabilisation clauses under international law; however, it would not be appropriate to regard the outcomes of any of these tribunals from a 'one size fits all' perspective as each case should be considered by tribunals, taking into account each stabilisation provision's *sui generis* character.

With respect to Azerbaijan and Turkey

(7) The Azerbaijani government should extend the reach of their BITs by entering into agreements with more states. This measure would increase their chances of attracting international investors into the country. It is recommended that both Azerbaijan and Turkey modify their BIT models as the current iterations do not define the phenomenon of indirect expropriation. Should this omission be addressed, it would provide further reassurance to potential investors that the countries acknowledge their concerns and are committed to transparent dealings.

(8) The definition of a foreign investor in Turkish FDI law should be amended as currently it does not explicitly provide for the situations of those individuals who hold

Turkish citizenship and live permanently or temporarily in Turkey, at the same time having the status of a shareholder of a foreign entity incorporated abroad. It is recommended that the article defining foreign investors should be amended to read: a *Turkish national who is a resident abroad or in Turkey; a stakeholder of a foreign legal entity formed in accordance with a foreign legal system is also accepted as a foreign investor.*

(9) Azerbaijan's FDI is dated and is unspecific and incomprehensive. Turkey's FDI is, arguably, adequate in comparison, but would still benefit from some minor amendments. For instance, both states' FDI laws regulate for expropriation phenomena in stating that a taking can be made only for public purpose. However neither of the states provides a definition of public purpose.

(10) The Azerbaijani government should either establish a specific institution for the training of economic court judges to educate them in the settlement of disputes in international commercial cases and provide practice of the same or draft judges on to a compulsory training programme abroad. The latter would enable native professionals to gather knowledge of how judges deal with commercial cases abroad that can be adapted to suit the needs of Azerbaijan. In the case of Turkey, the government should establish specialised courts designed to deal solely with disputes between domestic entrepreneurs and international investors. This would alleviate the load of overburdened local courts and reduce the waiting times for cases to be dealt with, meaning there would be a greater chance that such cases could be dealt with in a Turkish court, rather than being escalated to international courts.

(11) Governments of both countries should urgently implement a well-drafted concession law. This would establish a legal reasoning for the types of contracts based on concession. Similarly, host government contracts entered into for the BTC project are commercial or concession contracts; they should therefore be subject to private law rather than international law and should be governed by administrative authorities. Both governments should make constitutional modifications to remove the right of international investors to apply to international arbitration for these types of concession agreements.

(12) The Azerbaijani government should urgently implement petroleum and pipeline legislation. If a new specific petroleum law is implemented, there may be an argument for its reach not extending to previously signed PSAs but future agreements should definitely be provided for. It is of great importance, from the perspective of Azerbaijan's international reputation and in terms of properly exercising its rightful powers, that the government limit the activities of SOCAR in defining PSAs. In this respect, new petroleum laws should explicitly restrict SOCAR's powers.

(13) The legislative organ in Turkey should immediately add a paragraph to Article 90 of the Turkish Constitution to emphasise the legal status of international treaties other than those concerning human rights. An amendment to Article 90 should provide an equal hierarchical position for both international and domestic laws. In the case of conflict between the provisions of national and international treaties, perhaps the best method is to follow the same principles as those that are applied in determining the superiority between two domestic laws in order to determine which one prevails.

(14) Azerbaijani legislative bodies should implement a new petroleum law to run the country's PSAs. The legislative organ should also restructure the existing laws of the Subsoil Act and Energy Act because these laws are uncoordinated and provisions are mostly inconsistent with each other. In terms of hierarchy, the Energy Act should have superiority over the Subsoil Act. Nevertheless, there is no particular wording to state whether the general Energy Act has priority over the Subsoil Act or not. Lawmakers should not underestimate this defect and ought to create a clear hierarchal distinction between these two laws. In the case of Turkey, the recently adopted petroleum law seems to promote FDI flow into the country, as it is more flexible than any previous legislation in place. On the other hand, new petroleum legislation does not go far enough in safeguarding the country's national interests because it gives little consideration to the rights of indigenous people and the protection of the environment. Perhaps the best method is to involve NGOs, and to engage in public consultation in informing any decisions that may affect indigenous people and the environment where the petroleum activities are in operation.

(15) Both Azerbaijan and Turkey should prepare a reform package, which invites and encourages public interest groups to participate in decision-making processes. Perhaps the most important step that can be taken is to make funds available to these organisations to enable them to raise their profile and attract membership to ensure they are truly representative of the civilian population. In order to execute these reforms, both governments should collaborate with the EU.

(16) With the exception of Azerbaijan, which does not have a threshold restriction under its constitution, constitutional amendments should be made, particularly by Turkey, to reduce the threshold from 10% to at least 5% or remove this completely. A survey of the average threshold restriction in modern democracies would guide the Turkish government towards a more reasonable limit.

In conclusion, indirect expropriation cannot be entirely eradicated; however, the risk of it can be mitigated somewhat through the insertion of stabilisation clauses. The stabilisation technique used against indirect expropriation seems to have been applied for many years by energy investors because such risk emerges not only for economic reasons but also in political and legal issues. Generally, it is difficult to ascertain whether the driving forces discussed in this work are the same as those that influence every host state to accept stabilisation clauses in each oil and gas project. However, selected countries in the BTC project have successfully proved the influence of these key factors.

The author hopes that the research has successfully addressed the questions posed and that the analysis provided stimulates further studies into other related issues, which have not been discussed. Further research into stabilisation clauses might look further afield, to petroleum-producing countries from other regions to better understand how internal and external factors conspire to promote the inclusion of stability in their investment contracts. Additionally, further research into stabilisation may also focus on landlocked oil- and gas-importing Turkic countries in the Caucasus region and may introduce the question of how their geographic disadvantages affect their bargaining position in contract negotiation with Western oil companies.

Index

For Product Safety Concerns and Information please contact our EU representative GPSR@taylorandfrancis.com
Taylor & Francis Verlag GmbH, Kaufingerstraße 24, 80331 München, Germany

www.ingramcontent.com/pod-product-compliance
Ingram Content Group UK Ltd.
Pitfield, Milton Keynes, MK11 3LW, UK
UKHW011012180926
475701UK00004B/689
* 9 7 8 1 0 3 2 2 4 1 7 2 2 *